CROWNING THE
KANSAS CITY ROYALS

REMEMBERING THE 1985 WORLD SERIES CHAMPS

JEFFREY SPIVAK

www.SportsPublishingLLC.com

ISBN: 1-58261-826-7

Publishers: Peter L. Bannon and Joseph J. Bannon Sr.
Senior managing editor: Susan M. Moyer
Acquisitions editor: Bob Snodgrass
Developmental editor: Doug Hoepker
Art director: K. Jeffrey Higgerson
Dust jacket design: Dustin Hubbart
Project manager: Greg Hickman
Imaging: Heidi Norsen and Kenneth J. O' Brien
Photo editor: Erin Linden-Levy
Vice president of sales and marketing: Kevin King
Media and promotions managers: Jonathan Patterson (regional), Randy
Fouts (national), Maurey Williamson (print)

Printed in the United States of America

Sports Publishing L.L.C.
804 North Neil Street
Champaign, IL 61820

Phone: 1-877-424-2665
Fax: 217-363-2073
Web site: www.SportsPublishingLLC.com

For my wife—
Through her all my dreams come true.

CONTENTS

PART TWO: 1985 IN MEMORIES AND LORE

ACKNOWLEDGMENTS

There are many, many people who do not appear in the book who helped me with this project, both in researching the World Series and in making connections with former players. I am indebted to, in no particular order, fellow baseball authors Rob Rains, Glenn Dickey, George Castle, Mike Shannon, Dan Levitt, David Siroty, George Cantor and Bob Vanderberg; team officials around baseball like Tom Hart, Ann Wilhelm, Dan Farrell, Brad Hainje, Jay Alves, Larry Babcock, Mark Gorris, Joe Grigoli and Denny Matthews; others who helped in my searches and requests like Dan Perez, Chris Vleisides, Bob Forsch, Bobby Landrum, Ryan Lindell, Dave Jackson, Dan Crivello, Jason Guarente, Carroll Rogers, Rick Nathanson, Dick Kaegel, Loren Foxx, Bob Willson, Alana Hess and Chaundra Tracy; those associated with the Society for American Baseball Research like Rich Gibson, John Zajc, Bill James, Pete Palmer, Jerry Modene and Mike Webber; plus many local Kansas Citians who played roles in bringing the concept of this book to fruition, like Kevin Gray, Steve Parkey, Nate Sutton, Mick Langtry, Scooter Martin, Bill Dalton, along with 810 WHB's Kevin Keitzman and Todd Leabo.

I would especially like to express my gratitude to Sports Publishing for taking on this project, particularly Bob Snodgrass and Doug Hoepker, plus a few people in the Royals organization who made my life easier, like Fred White, Dave Witty and especially Chris Stathos. And, of course, this book would not have happened without the love, support and understanding of my family. I'd like to thank my children, Meghan, David and Mick, who didn't bug their dad too much for hogging the computer, and my wife, Ann, who took care of more bedtimes than I care to admit.

Part One

THE
WORLD SERIES

CHAPTER 1

KANSAS CITY'S BASEBALL MISFORTUNES

I n baseball, some cities are cursed. Some are perpetually heartbroken. Some wile away the years in despair.

Until 1985, the defining characteristic of Kansas City as a major-league baseball town was: just plain unlucky. Scanning the city's history of big-league baseball is akin to reading the Book of Job. The calamities are endless.

In 1954, Kansas City got what it sorely craved—a big-league baseball team. Roy Roberts, then editor of *The Kansas City Star* newspaper, opined in a front-page editorial after the American League approved the transfer of the Philadelphia Athletics to Kansas City: "This is one of those genuinely great days in the history of a city. ...Literally overnight the community sees itself in the big time of cities." And look what it got—a team that not only stunk, it stunk in historic proportions.

The Kansas City A's were the only franchise never to have a winning season during the 20th Century, unless you count one-year stays like the 1969 Seattle Pilots.

The A's posted 13 straight losing seasons in Kansas City. The Brooklyn Dodgers, "Da Bums" who suffered what seemed like centuries of frustration before becoming a powerhouse in the 1940s, never had 13 straight losing seasons. The early New York Mets, those hapless lovable losers, never had 13 straight losing seasons. The original Washington Senators, representing the city known for being "First in War, First in Peace and Last in the American League," never exposed their fans to 13 straight losing seasons. The Cleveland Indians, in their long and largely dismal history, never suffered through 13 straight losing seasons.

A streak of that magnitude is so monumentally ill-fated that one of the only franchises to ever record 13 straight losing seasons was the Boston Red Sox. That streak began the year after they sold Babe Ruth to the Yankees.

The Kansas City A's were so bad partly because whenever they had anyone good, they eventually traded that player to the Yankees. In the five years after owner Arnold Johnson brought the club to Kansas City, the team made 16 deals with the Yankees. He probably had orders from his bosses—Johnson was president of a vending machine company called Automatic Canteen and Yankees' co-owner Dan Topping was on its board of directors.

So, Art Ditmar led the A's with 12 wins in each of their first two seasons; the next year he was shipped to the Yankees. Harry "Suitcase" Simpson drove in 105 runs for the A's in 1956; the next year, he was shipped to the Yankees. Bob Cerv had the best offensive season ever of any Kansas City Athletic, with 38 homers in 1958, then became the first and only A's player to have back-to-back 20-homer seasons. And the next year, he was shipped to the Yankees. Roger Maris hit 19 and 16 homers for the A's by the age of 24, and the next year, he was shipped to the Yankees. Ralph Terry, Clete Boyer, Bobby Shantz, Hector Lopez—all good young players and all shipped to the Yankees.

"The Yankees were the only team in history that had their own farm club in the same league," an old baseball man once quipped. Occasionally, the A's received a few pretty good players in return. But, none ever bloomed like the talent that went to the Yankees, and the A's never improved as a ball club. Kansas City already had an extreme inferiority complex toward rival cities, and this pinstripe pipeline rubbed the city in a raw spot.

❈ ❈ ❈ ❈ ❈ ❈

Johnson died by the end of the decade. His replacement, crazy Charlie O. Finley, outbid an under-financed Kansas City group after being spurned in attempts to buy two other major-league teams.

In his first few years as owner, the distinguishing characteristic of Finley's franchise was its absolute failure to develop young players. Time after time, the team put an up-and-coming player in the lineup, watched him perform well at first, but invariably falter. Dick Howser hit .280 with 29 doubles and 37 stolen bases as a rookie shortstop in 1961, got hurt and wasn't given another chance. Ed Charles had been kicking around the minor leagues, finally got his chance, hit .288 with 17 homeruns and 20 stolen bases as a rookie in 1962 and never did as well again. Manny Jimenez hit .301 as a 23-year-old rookie in '62, but Charlie Finley told him to hit homers, which he couldn't do. So, Jimenez watched his playing time decrease over the next three seasons—Finley made sure of that, because in those first years the manager had to get approval for his lineups from

Finley. Joe Gordon even got fired as manager after a lineup card with the notation, "Approved by C.O.F." was made public.

Meanwhile, the franchise under Finley developed a circus-like atmosphere. He had his mule grazing in the outfield. He had a mechanical rabbit delivering balls to the home-plate umpire. He inaugurated the era of colorful uniforms. He put on cutesy promotions like cow-milking contests and pregame rodeos. His special promotional "days" at the ballpark knew no boundaries—one time he presented an umpire with a seeing-eye dog.

All the while, Finley drove the city nuts by continually threatening to move the team. One time it was Dallas, another time Louisville. He talked about moving to Phoenix, he talked about moving to Seattle. He talked about moving to cities that didn't even have a ballpark.

Finally, after several years of on-the-job training at Kansas City's expense, the man picked up some baseball insights. He aggressively signed amateur pitchers like Blue Moon Odom, Catfish Hunter and Rollie Fingers. He drafted players like Reggie Jackson, Sal Bando and Vida Blue.

Of course for Kansas City, those players didn't start helping the team until Finley moved it out of town. And, of course for Kansas City, only after the team left town did it start winning championships.

❀ ❀ ❀ ❀ ❀ ❀ ❀

By the grace of power politics, Kansas City landed another American League franchise. On the day that major-league owners allowed Finley to move to Oakland, a K.C. delegation led by Sen. Stuart Symington threatened to hold up the move in court and hold congressional hearings to strip baseball of its cherished anti-trust exemption. By the next morning, Kansas City had been awarded an expansion team for 1969. It became the Royals. And unlike the A's under Finley, this new franchise was run with competence and class.

Owner Ewing Kauffman thought he could outsmart and outproduce his competition, just as he had as a pharmaceutical salesman. He applied business practices to the sport. He organized a group of ticket salesmen, the Lancers, to call on corporations. He created a training academy to teach fundamentals to gifted athletes who simply lacked baseball experience. The academy used stopwatches on the field. It developed exercises to improve a ballplayer's eyesight—like jumping up and down on a trampoline while reading words backwards. The baseball establishment laughed, but the academy produced more than a dozen major leaguers.

As for real baseball, the Royals' first general manager made a string of great trades, acquiring players who actually developed and improved, like Lou Piniella, Amos Otis, Cookie Rojas, Freddie Patek, John Mayberry and Hal McRae. The Royals steadily improved, too. In their third year, they had a winning season. Then they won division crowns and made the playoffs, the first of the four 1969 expansion teams to do so.

Finally, after almost a quarter-century of big league baseball, Kansas City really had something to cheer about. Then look what happened—they had to play the hated Yankees, which had gone in the dumps soon after Kansas City stopped trading with them, only to reemerge and spoil Kansas City's dreams.

That first playoff series in 1976 went down to the ninth inning of the deciding game. In the top of the inning, the Royals had a couple of runners on when the Yankees tried to make a force play on Al Cowens at second base. Cowens beat the throw but was called out—the Royals would have had the bases loaded with George Brett up. Then in the bottom on the ninth, closer Mark Littell, who had given up only one homer all year, served up a game-winning blast to Chris Chambliss.

The next year's playoffs again paired the Royals and Yankees. Again it went down to the ninth inning of the deciding game. The Royals were up 3-2 starting the ninth, and manager Whitey Herzog bypassed his relievers this time and brought in the team's best pitcher—starter Dennis Leonard—to close out the game. But the first batter hit a blooper to center, the next batter walked, Leonard was yanked, and a couple more pitchers couldn't stop the Yankees from scoring and going on to win.

In 1978, it was the Royals and Yankees once more. In one game, Brett hit three homers—a heroic performance under pressure—and the Royals still lost that game. They dropped the series, too.

The team couldn't get the breaks to get them over the top. Their fans got the feeling that Heartbreak was a letter bomb delivered every fall.

But the franchise regrouped. In 1980, the Royals finally got past the hated Yankees and into the World Series. They were over the hump. They were favored to win it all. And then, the unthinkable occurred—their star player got a case of hemorrhoids. Talk about freakishly ill-fated.

The hard luck didn't end there. On offense, the major leagues' best-hitting team that year suddenly started swinging fishing poles with men on base, batting .080 with runners in scoring position in the last five games. On defense, even little tactical moves backfired. In the ninth inning of the fifth game, with the Royals ahead by a run, third baseman Brett played in close against Mike Schmidt because Schmidt had tried bunting for hits a couple of times in previous games. Schmidt rocked a single just off Brett's glove. If Brett had been playing back, he might have made the play. Later in the inning, first baseman Willie Aikens, who was usually benched late in games for a defensive replacement, was still in there and allowed a grounder to scoot by him.

While the Royals couldn't catch a break, the Phillies did. In the ninth inning of the last game, the Phils were up 4-1, but the Royals had the bases loaded with one out and a gassed Tug McGraw was on the mound throwing batting practice strikes. Frank White swung and popped the ball up by the first-base dugout. First baseman Pete Rose and catcher Bob Boone converged. It was the first baseman's ball, but Boone couldn't locate Rose out of the corner of his eye,

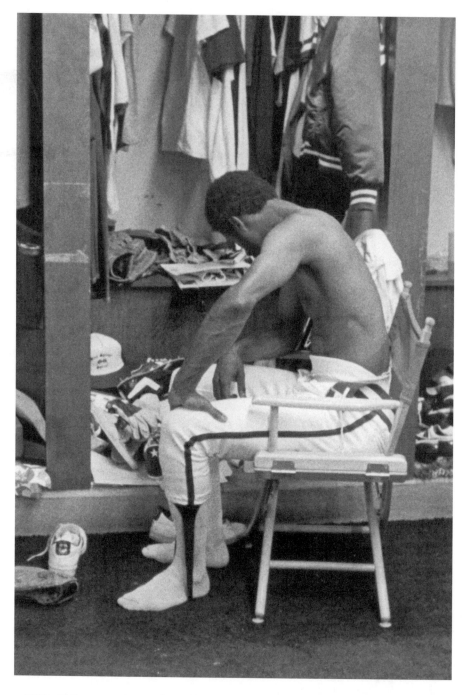

Willie Wilson sits dejectedly in front of his locker after the Royals lost the 1980 World Series. Wilson struck out 12 times in the series and was made a scapegoat. *Courtesy of the Kansas City Royals*

so he took it. The ball descended and curled back toward the field. Boone wondered about the runner on third tagging up. He turned his head an instant too soon. The ball bounced out of his mitt. And Rose, standing a few feet to the side, bent forward and snatched the ball before it hit the ground. The rally, for all intents and purposes, was snuffed.

October wasn't just playoff time for the Royals—it was a padded cell with the door slammed shut.

There would be no more playoff baseball in Kansas City for several years. The franchise, proud of its pristine image, of doing things the proper way, was the first one in baseball muddied by a drug scandal. Four of its players became the first active big-leaguers to serve prison time for drug convictions. The stigma followed the team. A fan's sign at Comiskey Park read: "Hey, Royals players! Don't snort the foul lines." General manager John Schuerholz summed up the conventional wisdom about the Royals during that period: "People looked at us and thought we might never recover from the tailspin."

❊ ❊ ❊ ❊ ❊ ❊ ❊

But recover they did. They retooled the pitching staff. They reaped the benefits of another round of great trades. And they got back in the playoffs in 1984, only to tie a playoff record for futility: the number of league championship series' lost—four.

As usual, though, the Royals persevered. They got over that hump in 1985. They made it back to the World Series, after overcoming a seven-and-a-half game deficit at the All-Star break, winning their division in the last week of the season, then overcoming a 3-1 deficit in games against a seemingly superior Toronto team to win the pennant. And what was their reward? Facing the St. Louis Cardinals, a team upon which the baseball Gods always seemed to smile, a team with more pennants than anyone else in the National League, a team that almost always won when it played in a World Series, a team with a long, revered tradition on its side.

Heck, it was a franchise that had impacted the historical development of the game itself.

With beer: 19th Century owner and saloon-keeper Christian Frederick "Chris" Von der Ahe wanted to sell beer at the ballpark, but was rebuffed. So he bought the team and served beer in the stands, ushering "a turning point in the history of sport," according to Al Spink, founder of *The Sporting News*.

With defensive positioning: 19th Century St. Louis player Charles Comiskey was the initial first baseman to play off the bag with no runner on base, and he helped originate the strategy of pitchers covering first base on ground balls hit that way.

With player development: Branch Rickey, tired of having to buy established minor leaguers, conceived the minor-league "farm" system of teams under the big-league team's umbrella, and put it into practice with the Cardinals.

There was simply no competing with the Cardinals' tradition. St. Louis represented "the real America's team," in the words of esteemed baseball writer Peter Gammons of *The Boston Globe*. Kansas City was not worthy. Kansas City could not compare.

The Cardinals had a tradition of developing Hall of Fame-caliber players just about every decade—Rogers Hornsby in the '20s, Dizzy Dean in the '30s, Stan Musial in the '40s, Bob Gibson in the '60s and Ozzie Smith in the '80s. In 1985 alone, two more Cards joined the Hall—Lou Brock and Enos Slaughter.

The Cardinals had a tradition of playing the "Cardinal Way," a style—of stolen bases and dirty uniforms, taking the extra base and making the hard slide—passed down by Slaughter and Brock and personified in 1985 by Willie McGee, Vince Coleman, Ozzie Smith and even Tommy Herr. First baseman Keith Hernandez once put it this way: "I was taught the Cardinal Way to play. It was so ingrained in you the pride it was to be a Cardinal."

The Cardinals had a tradition of producing great moments in the World Series. In 1926, a hungover Grover Cleveland Alexander came out of the bullpen during Game 7, just one day after a complete-game victory, walked to the mound through a foggy mist and struck out the Yankees' Tony Lazzeri with the bases loaded. In 1931, a brash rookie named Pepper Martin manufactured runs almost single handedly while batting .500 for the series as the Cardinals upended the heavily favored A's. In 1934, the wacky Dizzy Dean entered Game 4 as a pinch runner and got beaned in the forehead while trying to break up a double play, then lost Game 5, but came back to throw a shutout in Game 7. In 1946, with Game 7 tied in the eighth inning, Enos Slaughter took off from first on a looping single to left-center, and surprised the Red Sox by never slowing down— eventually scoring the winning run on what came to be called his "mad dash." In 1967, the fierce Bob Gibson cemented his legend with three dominating wins, including a three-hitter while smacking a homer himself in Game 7. And in 1982, the first successful "Whiteyball" team built on speed and defense clawed back from two runs down late in Game 7 to win, giving the Cardinals a remarkable 7-1 record in seventh games.

In '85, the Cards had added to their post season mystique in the playoffs against the favored Dodgers. In the ninth inning of one game, Ozzie Smith swatted a game-winning homer left-handed, the first time he had hit one from the left side of the plate in more than 3,000 career at-bats. In the ninth inning of another game, first baseman Jack Clark hit another game-winning homer, this time to win the pennant.

All this tradition, all the stars, all these post season dramatics ... after a while for Cardinals partisans, it went to their heads. They thought they were invincible. They thought they were God's gift to baseball. They thought they were better than anybody else.

This attitude, really an overbearing haughtiness, was paraded out in public before the start of the '85 World Series. St. Louis's newspapers and fans went out of their way to belittle Kansas City's baseball acumen. They mocked Kansas City for such indiscretions as not having a fight song like the Cards' "The Heat Is On," not having a mascot like the Cards' Fredbird, and not having enough overly devoted fanatics.

In the hours after the Cardinals won their pennant, St. Louisans streamed to their stadium to begin waiting in line for World Series tickets, eventually producing a line six blocks long the next day. Meanwhile, in the hours after the Royals won their pennant, one Kansas Citian arrived at the stadium around midnight only to be chased away by a security guard. By the next afternoon, only a couple hundred people were in line. The *St. Louis Post-Dispatch* noted this in a story with the headline: "Kansas City Fans: Either Laid Back or Hiding Out."

It was typical St. Louis. All bluster and blather. The St. Louis papers had missed the reception the Royals received after winning the pennant, when fans stood on the bridges over Interstate 29 and cheered the team on its police escort from the airport. And the St. Louis papers conveniently overlooked the fact that the Cardinals had drawn below the average league attendance in five of the previous 10 years, which included a World Series championship. The Royals, meanwhile, had never drawn below the average league attendance after moving into spacious Royals Stadium. Basically, Cardinals fans were bandwagon climbers. Still, that didn't stop one St. Louis newspaper writer from prattling on about St. Louis' supposedly superior fans and eventually declaring, "the suspicion lingers that the Royals fans are not laid back, but afraid."

It was as if St. Louisans thought this World Series would be no contest because it would be decided by which team had the longer history and which team appeared in more books and which team's fans produced the better headlines.

But, as they say in sports, that was all on paper.

CHAPTER 2

THE MATCHUP

R oyals stadium was decked out. The 12-year-old stadium already was one of the most beautiful in baseball, an amphitheater-like setting with an open vista in the outfield and fountains that rose and cascaded beyond the outfield walls. It was not a cookie-cutter, claustrophobic cylinder like so many of its peers built during the stadium-building boom of the '60s and '70s. Baseball aficionado Bob Wood would soon look at everything from seating to hotdogs for a guide to America's top ballparks, and he would rank Royals Stadium at the top, tied with Dodger Stadium. On this night, October 19, it looked even more majestic, with the World Series insignia on the green artificial turf behind home plate, the red, white and blue bunting hanging from the lower-deck railings and the Royals and Cardinals logos on the grass beyond the left-field wall.

It was a cool autumn night for baseball, 62 degrees, as teams began the World Series ritual of lining up along the base lines for introductions. "For the National League-champion St. Louis Cardinals ...," the public address announcer began.

Leading off was centerfielder Willie McGee, a stick figure of a man, all arms and legs, and the N.L. batting champion. Next was Ozzie Smith, the waif-like 150-pound shortstop folks called "the Wizard," with a short-cropped beard. Second baseman Tommy Herr, who came into his own that year, more than doubling his career best in RBIs with 110, batted third. Burly first baseman Jack

Clark, the team's only real home run threat, hit cleanup. Tito Landrum was hot on a beefcake poster then popular in St. Louis and also hot at the plate since replacing rookie leftfielder Vince Coleman, the victim of a freak injury during the playoffs when a mechanical infield tarp rolled over his leg. Rightfielder Cesar Cedeno, a long-faded star who had sparked the team with a .434 average since a late-August trade, batted sixth. Cherubic-looking third baseman Terry Pendleton, in his first full year, was known then more for his fielding than his hitting. Darrell Porter, the catcher with the Buddy Holly glasses, had hit under .200 in the first half of the season before coming around. And starting pitcher John Tudor, a fiercely intense lefty, was toeing the rubber. He had come into his own that season in anchoring a staff that was the first in the N.L. to boast three 18-game winners since the World Series-winning Cardinals of 1964.

This seemed to be a team of destiny. They weren't predicted to win prior to the season's start. They had lost their All-Star closer, Bruce Sutter, to free agency. But those low expectations became a rallying point, and several players had career years. Everything seemed to click, and the '85 Cardinals won more games than any other team in the majors. Then they won the pennant with game-winning home runs in the final two games. In private moments, several Cardinals veterans like Tommy Herr believed: "It was a better team than the one that won the 1982 World Series."

Next, it was the Royals' turn to jog out in their white uniforms with the blue "Royals" script across the chest, blue undershirts, double blue stripes around the sleeves, blue stripe down the leg and even blue shoes.

Leading off was Lonnie Smith, the leftfielder with the turn-of-the-century-like long sideburns who came in a trade that season from, ironically, St. Louis. He was about to become the first player in World Series history to play against the team with which he started the season. Hitting second was Willie Wilson, Kansas City's own rail-thin centerfielder who had a sub-par year marred by late-season injuries. Third baseman George Brett, coming off one of his best years with 30 homers and a .335 batting average, hit third. He was followed by Frank White, who after setting a career-high in homers became the first second baseman to hit cleanup since Jackie Robinson. Catcher Jim Sundberg, a long-suffering veteran of losing teams who was appearing in his first World Series, hit fifth. Darryl Motley, a short, husky young man with a chipper demeanor who was nonetheless frustrated with his season and frustrated with being platooned in right field, was given the start in the sixth slot. Steve Balboni, a first baseman built like a football offensive lineman who set a Royals team record with 36 home runs in 1985 was next. Shortstop Buddy Biancalana, a wafer-thin bundle of nerves who had batted below the embarrassing Mendoza .200 line, was hitting eighth. And Danny Jackson, another fiercely intense lefty, was taking the mound for the Royals. Jackson was part of a rotation in which all five members posted double-digit win totals. He was starting because staff ace Bret Saberhagen had started Game 7 of the playoffs and been hurt. Jackson was hitting for the

The media horde gathered around the batting cage before the start of the 1985 World Series. George Toma and the Royals' grounds crew dressed up Royals Stadium for the affair; hence the World Series logo behind home plate was roped off to avoid unnecessary foot traffic. *Courtesy of the Kansas City Royals*

first time in the major leagues because the World Series at that time didn't use the designated hitter.

No one had expected the Royals to be here, either. They had played just .500 ball for the first half of the season. Then they went on winning streaks, which were soon followed by unexplainable skids against bad teams. Fortunately, one of their streaks coincided with a showdown series with the California Angels for the division title. And another streak occurred in the last half of the playoffs. So when the Royals ended up winning the pennant, it was considered a fluke. But here they were.

This was the first time these two franchises had ever met when the games counted. Kansas City-St. Louis wasn't a sports rivalry like New York-Boston in baseball, in which fans loathed each other, or Pittsburgh-Cleveland in football, in which fans acted like Hatfields and McCoys. Not only was there no history between the Cardinals and Royals, there was no animosity between the players.

The two teams had several ties to each other. They trained close to each other on the western edge of Florida, the Royals in Fort Myers, the Cardinals in

St. Petersburg, so they played every spring and were familiar with each other. The franchises' minor-league AAA affiliates, the Omaha Royals and Louisville Redbirds, played in the American Association together. Plus, several players had switched from the Cardinals to the Royals or vice versa. On the Royals, Lonnie Smith, reserve catcher Jamie Quirk and reserve outfielder Dane Iorg had all played for the Cardinals within the last two seasons. On the Cardinals, Darrell Porter and reserve outfielder Steve Braun had played with the Royals veterans on their teams of the late '70s, and Whitey Herzog had managed those teams. Iorg even lived in Porter's house when he was first traded to Kansas City.

So as the two teams were transitioning off and on the field for practice on the Friday before Game 1, several players made a point of seeking out old friends. Cardinals relief pitcher Todd Worrell approached his former best friend from the Cardinals organization, Iorg. "Take it easy on me," Worrell kidded him. Some of Lonnie Smith's former teammates—Ozzie Smith, Willie McGee and a couple of others—met him in the hallway outside the two clubhouses and presented him with a painting of all of them sitting on the Cardinals bench together. Later on, before another series game in Kansas City, Quirk would grill out burgers in his backyard with Cardinals pitcher Bob Forsch, his old roommate. And before the last series game, Quirk and George Brett would attend part of a Chiefs game in the adjoining stadium with Whitey Herzog. "It wasn't a vengeance type of series," Quirk remembered.

Jack Clark saw some of this and it made him sick. This was his first World Series, unlike most of the other starters on both teams. He wanted bitterness. He wanted hatred. He wanted a fierce rivalry. What he saw was a feel-good, happy-family feeling. *We weren't like this when we played the Mets or the Dodgers,* he thought before Game 1. Later, reflecting back, he recalled: "The juice didn't seem like it was there to me." He wanted to call a team meeting and yell out, "Get your head out of your ---." But that was the manager's job. So Clark held his tongue.

❅ ❅ ❅ ❅ ❅ ❅

The only animosity between the two franchises was off the field. The owners of the Cardinals and Royals were polar opposites—a showy, beer-guzzling, old-money owner vs. a stoic, philanthropist-minded, new-money owner. And no single person spanned and signified those differences more than Whitey Herzog.

Herzog had taken over the Royals in 1975 and immediately became the golden boy. The Royals were languishing with a losing record, and—bang, bang—with decisions like moving Brett to third in the order and making White a starter, Herzog made them winners. They dethroned Charlie Finley's hated Oakland A's from top of the division in 1976. Herzog won Manager of the Year, and the team went on to dominate division play for two more years.

But in the playoffs each year, Herzog's Royals lost to the Yankees. Those Yankees were typically the better team, with deeper pitching and off-season upgrades like Reggie Jackson and Goose Gossage. Yet Herzog always had wild excuses ready. It was always something.

In 1976, Herzog felt the Royals lost because an injury forced him to replace Al Cowens in right field with Hal McRae, who Herzog claimed was "six inches" shorter. The series-winning homer, depending on the story Herzog was telling, either went off McRae's glove or cleared his glove by "six inches"—never mind that McRae really was three inches shorter and the homer landed well beyond the fence.

In 1977, with a 102-win club, Herzog felt the Royals lost because in Game 4, John Mayberry, who "had been out real late the night before with his brothers," ended up missing a pop foul, bobbling a double-play throw and twice striking out feebly. Never mind that Larry Gura got rocked in that game, or that with the Royals leading in the ninth inning of the final game, Herzog brought in Dennis Leonard as the closer just two nights after he had thrown a complete game, a move that even the Yankees questioned after they won the game and the series.

Then, in 1978, Herzog felt the Royals lost because the team hadn't signed any free agents to help get them over the hump. "We've gotta do something … in spite of what the top echelon says," Herzog said about his own bosses. "We've gotta get off our rears."

When the Royals played poorly in 1979, Herzog was fired, and the media made him the victim. Owner Ewing Kauffman and general manager Joe Burke had never liked his outspokenness. They were too sensitive about his public criticisms of the club. And Kauffman's wife, Muriel, resented all the attention Herzog had been given. Herzog encouraged this thinking, telling stories over and over, in movie cowboy Gene Autry's twang, about how Autry, the Angels owner, had encountered Muriel at the 1979 All-Star game.

"How's Mr. K?" Autry inquired.

"He's fine," Muriel replied.

"And how's my good friend, Whitey?" Autry asked.

"Who gives a ----," came the reply.

Herzog landed in St. Louis. He hooked up with an owner, Gussie Busch, who drank beer with Whitey and "was the first guy who realized what I had to offer and how to use it to the utmost," Herzog wrote in his autobiography. Busch let Whitey manage and make player moves. Herzog made daring trades and built the team the way he wanted, mostly all speed and hustle, with a solid closer this time, and in two years won a World Series, which was still eluding K.C.

Still, when things turned sour, Herzog had his excuses ready—like blaming the poor 1983 season partly on the drug use of some of his players, even though some of his players later admitted to using drugs during the pennant-winning year, too. Nevertheless, Herzog was revered all over again and respected as one of baseball's best minds. Players voted him the game's top manager in 1983, and fellow managers followed suit in 1985.

So, even though the Royals and Cardinals players got along and several were friends, there was some lingering bad blood between the Royals and Herzog. He felt the team had wronged him in firing him for finishing in second place. "I never really got along with Ewing Kauffman," Herzog wrote in his autobiography, "and his wife, Muriel, hated my guts." The sentiment, however, was mutual. "In all the years I'd worked there, they'd never once invited Mary Lou (Herzog's wife) upstairs to sit in their warm, enclosed boxes. ...(It was) like we weren't good enough for them."

On the eve of the World Series, then, the media peppered Herzog with questions about a revenge factor. He diplomatically sidestepped the questions. But everyone knew Herzog approached it as a grudge match.

"If you know Herzog, you know he hasn't forgotten the way he was treated by Ewing and Marion Kauffman," sports columnist Kevin Horrigan wrote in the *St. Louis Post-Dispatch* before the series. "So you've got to believe that despite what he says for the record, Herzog would like nothing more than to deny the Kauffmans the world championship they've never won." And Cardinals television announcer Jay Randolph discerned: "It was doubly important to him because of that. It would be something of a vindication."

❋ ❋ ❋ ❋ ❋ ❋

Before the series began, the overwhelming expectation was that Herzog would get his wish. The odds and the predictions all favored St. Louis—by a wide margin. Las Vegas made the Cardinals two to one favorites. Eighty-six percent of sportswriters predicted they would win in fewer than seven games. Thomas Boswell of *The Washington Post*, after noting the past couple World Series' had been swift and lopsided, added: "St. Louis is going to win easily in another five-game semi-bore." *The Kansas City Star's* own Joe McGuff thought: "Picking the Cardinals in four games will be fashionable. The thought here is that it will be the Cardinals in six."

Even Hollywood got into the spirit. A television promo for the popular series, *Moonlighting*, ended with actor Bruce Willis getting in a quick "Cards in five" as the camera faded out.

The basis for the predictions was summed up by the *Post's* Boswell: "Everything the Royals do, the Cardinals do better. *Much* better." The Royals won 91 games, but the Cards won more, 101. The Royals scored 687 runs, the second worst in their league, while the Cards scored 747, tops in their league. Royals pitchers had a 3.49 staff ERA, but the Cards' was superior, at 3.29. The Royals had one all-star that year (Brett), while the Cards had five. The Royals stole 128 bases, but the Cards stole way more—314, the fourth most in the history of the game. As Sonny Reizner, sports book director at the Castaways Hotel & Casino in Vegas then, put it: "Nobody is sure whether the Royals can stop the speed of the Cardinals."

Some new baseball analysts, however, were scoffing at the conventional wisdom. They looked at traditional baseball stats and cried "foul." These analysts—dubbed "sabermetricians" as an expanded acronym of the Society for American Baseball Research—dug deeper to find more meaning in the stats and to develop new ways of measuring the game. And these analysts looked at the matchup of the 1985 World Series through a magnifying glass and saw things the sportswriters didn't.

For one thing, it didn't make much sense to compare team ERAs—the Cards had a built-in advantage because they got to pitch against the other team's pitcher in the N.L. A truer measure of dominance was the spread between team ERA and the league ERA, and the Royals' spread was twice as large as the Cardinals'.

For another thing, the Cards had built up their record and their stats by feasting on their league's worst teams. They were 36 games over .500 against four bad teams, and just four games over .500 against the rest of the N.L. Meanwhile, the Royals were just about the opposite—about .500 against .500-or-less teams, but in the second half they went 23-9 against teams that finished the season with winning records. This meant the Royals were at their best against the best.

Then there was the whole issue of speed.

Whitey Herzog considered it the most valuable commodity in baseball. It was the one asset that could be used for both offense and defense. Artificial turf now covered one-third of all big-league fields, and this put a premium on fast outfielders who could cut off balls scooting through the infields and rolling toward the outfield walls. "Speed in the outfield has changed the game of baseball probably more than any factor in the last 20 years, other than the rise of the relief pitching corps," All-Star first baseman and one-time Cardinal Keith Hernandez opined in his own book about baseball. For offenses, speed could be used for stealing bases and taking extra bases on hits. Ozzie Smith summed up the offensive mindset: "Good pitching may stop good hitting, but does it stop good running? We always have ways to score." The Cards believed that with a runner on, the constant threat of a stolen base forced pitchers to pitch more carefully, which resulted in more walks, and forced pitchers to come in with more fastballs, which hitters preferred to hit. The '85 Cardinals, Herzog once said, were "the perfect team" for this way of operating.

In baseball, the stolen base had been on a general upswing since the early 1970s, and the mid-'80s were producing record league totals. This approach to offense was even in vogue among non-turf teams. New York Yankees owner George Steinbrenner at one point declared that the era of the home run was over; he switched to a slashing, speed-based team. The Chicago Cubs finished 20 games under .500 in 1983 after stealing 40 fewer bases than any other N.L. team, then hired a manager who believed in the running game and acquired speedy leadoff hitter Bobby Dernier. He stole 45 bases in 1984, the team stole 154 and the Cubs went to the playoffs for the first time in four decades.

Nevertheless, the upstart sabermetrician analysts were coming to believe that stolen bases were vastly overrated. Through complicated mathematical computations, they discovered the running game didn't actually lead to a team scoring more runs, in the long run. The outs and thwarted rallies that resulted from caught stealings more than cancelled out the extra bases from successful steals. Bill James, a bearded former night watchman who was the Babe Ruth of sabermetricians, compared the '85 Cardinals to other teams in the past that had put just as many men on base during a season. The other teams usually scored more runs. "This is because power is a much more effective way of increasing the percentage of runners who score than is speed," James wrote in his best-selling annual, the *Bill James Baseball Abstract.*

That was especially true in the World Series, where runs were harder to come by because teams faced better pitching. Historically in the fall, the "big bang" strategy of baseball proved more successful. During the past decade, in roughly three-fourths of World Series games, the winning team scored as many or more runs in one inning as the losing teams scored the entire game. That was typically done with the help of home runs and extra-base hits.

And power was the one part of offense in which the Royals excelled over the Cardinals. The Royals didn't hit for as high an average as the Cardinals, or get as many base hits, or draw as many walks. But the Royals clouted more doubles and almost twice as many homers. Kansas City was a team that often scratched for runs in close ballgames, but they could break games open with extra-base hits.

Over the course of the 1985 World Series, it would become apparent the upstarts knew more about what they were talking about than the traditional experts.

CHAPTER 3

GAMES 1 AND 2:

"ROYALS STADIUM STILL IN A STATE OF SHOCK"

Danny Jackson went into his windup and delivered a called strike. Next pitch, strike two. Then, strike three. Willie McGee was out and a thunderous roar erupted from the sold-out crowd of 41,650. A couple of ground outs later, and the Cardinals were set down 1-2-3. But the Royals followed the same pattern against John Tudor in the bottom half of the first.

The next inning, Jackson stayed ahead of each hitter again. And again, the Cards went in order. For the Royals, Jim Sundberg walked with one out. Darryl Motley singled. With two on, the organ started the "charge" cheer as Steve Balboni stepped to the plate.

The veterans on the Royals had been through a World Series before, but not newer guys like Balboni. The hoopla was all new to him—the media always present in the clubhouse, the baseballs to be signed, the tickets he needed to round up for his new in-laws in St. Louis. On top of that, he was in the midst of one of his worst power droughts, nary an extra-base hit over his last 10 games. And he was coming off a poor series against Toronto, in which he was just three for 25.

Dick Howser decided not to bat him cleanup in the World Series. During the season, Balboni could talk out a slump with Hal McRae at the next locker, or with hitting coach Lee May. But now everything was different. Everyone was busy with the hoopla. He couldn't even take extra swings outside the cage in batting practice because of the media swarm. Balboni was trying not to press, which is what he felt he did against Toronto. So he was not thinking about hitting a home run—only about hitting the ball hard and contributing in some way.

Balboni stood in the box at six foot three, knees slightly bent, his mammoth 36-inch, 36-ounce bat back and held up. He looked "like a condominium standing at home plate," an opposing pitcher once said. Balboni leaned out for a pitch and punched a single to left for the Royals' first run of the game and the Series. The crowd came to its feet screaming. One fan waved a stuffed Cardinal bird with a noose around its neck. During the 1985 season, scoring first in the American League gave that team a two-to-one chance of winning the game.

Buddy Biancalana was up next with runners on the corners. He was the worst-hitting shortstop for a World Series team since 1968, and back then that team (the Tigers) decided to start an outfielder at short instead. Through a quirk of fate, Biancalana's hitting had become the butt of jokes. During Pete Rose's run for the all-time hit record that season, late-night television host David Letterman adopted Biancalana as a representative of a marginal player with no chance for the record himself. Letterman introduced a hand-made hit counter showing Biancalana several thousand hits short of Rose or Ty Cobb. Biancalana didn't appreciate the joke. Neither did his mother, who lashed out publicly at Letterman. But even Biancalana's teammates joked about his hitting. They nicknamed him "Bam Bam." McRae sent some Biancalana-model bats to his 18-year-old son in Florida's instructional league and told his son "there are a lot of hits left in them."

Stepping to the plate this night, though, Biancalana was actually on a tear, for him. He had been hitting a pathetic .119 in mid-July and went on to hit .250 after the All-Star break, emerging as a surprising good-luck charm in the second half and then as a folk hero during the playoffs, knocking in what turned out to be the game-winning run of Game 6.

Up two and one in the count and batting right-handed, Biancalana was in a hitter's count against the lefty Tudor. Tudor was having trouble getting the ball over this inning, and Howser sensed he might just put one over. He signaled for the suicide squeeze play. Howser didn't bunt a lot, but during the September stretch run, he felt Biancalana was at least contributing by getting some bunts down.

Royals' third-base coach Mike Ferraro went through baseball's exotic way of communicating plays through hand signals. Tudor kicked into his windup, slung his left arm around almost sidearm, saw Biancalana squaring to bunt and adjusted in an attempt to pitch the ball outside. It started out looking like a fastball coming right down the middle. For an instant, Biancalana thought, *I got it.*

But he had forgotten the pre game meeting about Tudor. He had forgotten about Tudor's tailing fastball. The ball approached the plate, then began tailing away. Biancalana reached out, then lunged, just trying to foul it off. But the ball tailed out of the strike zone, and Biancalana missed it completely. Motley, coming down from third base, was tagged out. Up in the press box, Denny Matthews

Buddy Biancalana missed a suicide squeeze bunt attempt in Game 1. It was one of several missed opportunities for the Royals' offense in the early stages of the series. *The Kansas City Star*

on the Royals radio network observed, "It's a little different ballgame managing without the DH." The inning died after that.

Against the Cards in the third inning, Danny Jackson fell behind a hitter for the first time and gave up a walk, which didn't bode well for the Royals. A single, followed by a bunt and a ground out tied the game. Then the Royals went quietly in their half of the inning.

The momentum had shifted to the Cardinals. Tito Landrum doubled in the Cards fourth and up stepped right-handed Cesar Cedeno, the Cardinals' late-season hero. Royals' fans quieted to a murmur. Cedeno's bat shattered as he made contact, but he got enough of the ball to send a soft liner over the head of third baseman George Brett and down the leftfield line. Landrum scored for 2-1 Cardinal lead.

Sundberg led off the Royals' half of the fourth. He was so pumped to be there, in the World Series, having never thought he'd reach that pinnacle. He was considered one of the best catchers in baseball, but he was stuck for much of his career on lousy Texas teams, catching in the heat, racking up Gold Gloves and hitting over .270 for five straight years. Then, in 1983 a new manager openly criticized Sundberg and opened the catching job to others. Sundberg moped and hit .201. The Rangers traded him to Milwaukee. He wasn't happy there, so he demanded a trade. The Rangers wanted him back, but Sundberg wouldn't go. The Royals sensed an opportunity and swooped in to acquire him.

"This is the greatest," Sundberg said when he learned of the trade. But he fell off at the plate again, hitting .245 with just 35 RBIs. He then hit under .200 in the playoffs but came up big at the end with four RBIs in Game 7.

In this at bat, Sundberg lined a double down the leftfield line. He advanced to third on a fly out. Then Balboni popped up in foul ground by short leftfield. Royals third-base coach Mike Ferraro quickly instructed Sundberg: "If the left-fielder gets it, stay here. If the third baseman catches it, go."

Third baseman Pendleton caught the ball over his shoulder. Sundberg tagged. He was a below-average runner who hadn't stolen a base in two years. Pendleton whirled and threw the ball right on target. Catcher Darrell Porter caught it and stood by the plate. Sundberg was out by 10 feet, inning over.

The Cards couldn't get much else going, though. Meanwhile, in the Royals' sixth, Willie Wilson singled—the third time a Royals leadoff hitter had reached base to start an inning. Brett popped out, bringing Frank White to the plate. He was one of several Royals ready for redemption in this series. White had made his name as a fielder, winning Gold Gloves and earning All-Star berths. Early in his career, he had little pop in his bat, and he hit eighth. But his bat came to life in the 1980 playoffs. He batted .545 and won the playoff most valuable player award. Phillies scouts found he was a first-ball, fastball, high-ball hitter, so they pitched him low in the World Series. White batted a dreadful .080—just two for 25, with no RBIs—thus making a perverse metamorphosis from butterfly to worm. Since then, though, White had shown much more pop, hitting 45 doubles in '82, collecting 77 RBIs in '83, and swatting 17 homers in '84 followed by a career-high 22 homers in '85. He made a conscious decision to be more aggressive at the plate and drive the ball, even if it meant a lower batting average.

Still, when sportswriters were speculating about who would bat fourth for the Royals with McRae on the bench, White wasn't even mentioned. Howser approached Brett about it before the series, and Brett told him he wanted to bat in the first inning. With Balboni struggling, Howser tapped White. White was a team guy. He would do it. But he wasn't comfortable in the spotlight of the cleanup spot. This was the first time something substantial was expected out of his bat. With sportswriters, White tried downplaying his role. At one point in the series, he made fun of his physique. Flexing his arms in a bodybuilder's pose, he announced: "Look at me. I'm not Steve Balboni."

In the Royals radio booth, announcer Denny Matthews noted a breeze that was drifting in from left field during the misty night. "The air seem heavy to you?" he asked partner Fred White. "It doesn't seem like the ball's carrying very well."

Fred chimed in, "I don't think it's carrying well at all."

Moments later, Frank White cranked one to deep left-center. Leftfielder Tito Landrum stood on the warning track. The ball died and dropped into his glove.

The Royals were scorching the ball all over the park against Tudor. He wasn't looking like the pitcher who dominated the N.L. with a 20-1 streak. He was looking more like the pitcher who started the year 1-7, when he wasn't so accurate with his pitches. What turned his year around was a telephone conversation with a former high school teammate. Out of the blue, the friend mentioned seeing a flaw in Tudor's delivery. A little hesitation in the middle of his motion wasn't there. It was enough to throw off his timing. Tudor made the adjustment. His pinpoint control returned.

But on this night Tudor was off. Cardinals manager Whitey Herzog sat in the dugout thinking Tudor was not getting strikes called on the corners from American League umpire Don Denkinger. But Tudor knew he didn't have his best stuff. And Royals radio announcer Denny Matthews could see that, too. "Tudor's fighting his control," the broadcaster said at one point. The Royals were getting to his pitches just fine. They were hitting—just to the wrong spots.

Now, with a runner on, Sundberg scalded a ball past third base—just foul. It would have tied the game. But instead he grounded out. Fred White noted on the radio, "The Royals aren't getting the most out of their opportunities."

✵ ✵ ✵ ✵ ✵ ✵

In the seventh, the Cards went 1-2-3 again, barely clinging to their 2-1 lead. The Royals pounced in the bottom of the inning, mounting a two-out rally. A pinch-hit triple, a hit batsman, a pitching change and a walk brought up Wilson with the bases loaded.

This was another Royals veteran ready for redemption. No one had been haunted by the demons of 1980 more than him.

He had had a magical '80 season, hitting .326, collecting 230 hits and stealing 79 bases. But his accomplishments were overshadowed by Brett's run at .400. Wilson ached for the recognition he thought he deserved. He got it in the '80 World Series—for slumping badly. At one point, even his wife felt compelled to offer advice: "Stand up straighter, dear." It didn't help. Wilson ended up becoming the only player to strike out 12 times in a single series, his last K coming as the final out of the Series. Fans and the media painted him as the goat, even though he still got on base more and scored more runs than the Phillies' leadoff hitters.

That off season, Phillies reliever Tug McGraw made him the brunt of jokes on the banquet circuit. When baseball started again, fans heckled him. Wilson

Royals starting pitcher Danny Jackson delivered to Cesar Cedeno with the Cardinals threatening in the fourth inning of Game 1. Cedeno would deliver a broken-bat single to give the Cards the lead. *Courtesy of the Kansas City Royals*

had always been a sensitive man; early in his career, he wouldn't sign autographs after hearing a few catcalls from the stands. So after that World Series, with so much attention focused on his failings, Wilson tried to get away from it. He literally stayed at home and didn't come out. He "hibernated," in his words. He was depressed, alone and needed a diversion—that's when he started snorting cocaine.

He didn't become a big-time user, just here and there. After a year or so he decided he didn't like it and gave it up. But in the summer of 1983, one of those pals asked him to find some coke for him. Wilson made a telephone call. The other end happened to be tapped by the FBI. His world spiraled down. The judge handling his case labeled him as a hero who'd gone awry. Wilson spent time in prison and was suspended from baseball for weeks.

It all happened because he was unfairly maligned in the 1980 Series. "I carried it around for about two years," he once said about the effects of his 1980 post-season performance. "We have to go back there (to the world series) and win."

Now in the seventh inning of Game 1 of the '85 Series, Wilson was getting his first shot at parting that lingering cloud over his head. The bases were loaded. Tudor was gone. Fans were on their feet, shouting, egged on by the loudspeakers playing Otis Clay's song "Shout" from the movie *Animal House*: "Yeah-ah-aah-ah-aah-ah. ..."

Out in the leftfield bleachers, Royals fans Joe McConniff and Ron Grace were on their feet like everyone else. The two longtime buddies were in their mid-20s. They had grown up with the Royals. McConniff had gone to the first game in Royals Stadium. Grace collected the team's yearbooks. They had been pumped about getting World Series tickets. Then they found their bleacher seats were smack in the middle of a section of red-clad Cardinals rooters. The guys in front of McConniff and Grace started taunting them before the game even started. "This series isn't going to last very long," one vowed. Now McConniff was watching the action through binoculars. He began daydreaming in his mind, imagining Wilson hitting one into the outfield gap and clearing the bases...

Wilson stood at the plate and wagged his bat from the left side. He was a first-ball hitter—the Cards' scouting report said so. Flame-throwing reliever Todd Worrell challenged him on the first pitch with a 95-mph fastball. The ball was low, dipping toward the ankles. Wilson swung anyway and golfed a pop-up foul ball down the left-field line. It was caught, ending the Royals' threat.

McConniff, peering through his binoculars, screamed out "Nooooooo." Grace yelled, "Why'd he do that?"

In the eighth inning, the Cardinals went 1-2-3 yet again. Brett led off the Royals half. He'd been the Royals superstar for a decade, the man his teammates always expected would do something big. And he always seemed to do it. Just in the past month, when the Royals faced their do-or-die series with California and division-clinching series with Oakland, Brett went on a tear, hitting five homers in those six games. Then the team got down 2-0 to Toronto, and Brett responded with one of the most memorable performances in playoff history—two homers, a double and a run-saving defensive gem.

Now his team was down by one run in the World Series. His teammates had failed to come up with hits in crucial situations. This was likely to be his last at-bat of the game. He figured the only way the Royals were going to score was with a homer. But there was still a heavy mist in the air, just like announcer Denny Matthews noted a couple of innings earlier. Brett got a Worrell fastball and drove it.

It's gone, he told himself.

Worrell knew it, too. *God, I let him hit it out,* he moaned to himself.

Howser was on the bench thinking, *A water-fountain-type ball, way over the fence.*

But just like with Frank White, the friction of the heavy moist air pushed the ball down. Rightfielder Andy Van Slyke leapt and caught it against the wall. The rising roar of the crowd was instantly silenced.

During the ninth inning, the Cards came back to life. A single and a Jack Clark liner off the wall added an insurance run, 3-1. The Royals got their last chance. Outfielder Pat Sheridan pinch hit and led off with a double. Balboni, still in that homer drought, had a chance to tie the game. In the leftfield bleachers, Royals fan Joe McConniff was leaning forward, elbows on knees and fists against his forehead, covering his eyes. He couldn't bear to watch. In front of him, red-clad Cardinals fans turned to taunt him some more: "You're not going to do it."

Balboni got fooled and bounced out to first. Backup outfielder Jorge Orta, pinch hitting, flied out. Reserve outfielder Dane Iorg, also pinch hitting, had the last chance. Fly out, game over.

Royals fans McConniff and Grace immediately got up to leave. Another agonizing loss in the team's playoff annals. "You can't lose the first one at home," McConniff muttered. They scampered up the aisle. They wanted to get out of there. The Cardinals fans in their section were at it again, taunting:

"We're going to win."

"You don't stand a chance."

"We're a team of destiny."

McConniff and Grace were in such a hurry to get away that they left behind their binoculars.

The Royals made their way back to their clubhouse. They had played like they had memorized their press clippings. They tried a suicide squeeze. They tried scoring on a popup. They tried to be aggressive on the first pitch. They tried to hit homers. All were signs of desperation, the desperation of a weak offense. Howser admitted after the game, "We have to take chances." But just about every time they took a chance in a key spot, it backfired.

There was a silver lining for the Royals, however. They knew they had beaten themselves. It's not like the Cardinals had whipped them. Willie Wilson sat with a beer after the game and told reporters: "They haven't proved to us that they're more dominant than we are. Face it, with a break or two, we could be ahead."

It was an attitude eerily like what the Miracle Mets thought after their first series game in 1969. They lost 4-1 to the heavily favored Baltimore Orioles, but as Mets losing pitcher Tom Seaver remembered later: "The feeling we had when we got into our clubhouse was that they had just barely beat us. Never mind the score; a team knows if they've been badly beaten or outplayed. And we felt we hadn't been. … I can very distinctly remember (Donn) Clendenon saying, 'We're going to kick hell out of these guys.' He started talking about it, and the next thing you know we were building more confidence out of having lost a game than if we had won it."

The Royals had that feeling, too.

❊ ❊ ❊ ❊ ❊ ❊ ❊

The next night, for Game 2, was gray and overcast, and it would only get blacker for the Royals.

The Cards went down in order in the first inning against Charlie Leibrandt, a 17-game winner that season. Lonnie Smith started things for the Royals with a single against 18-game winner Danny Cox. Cox was at his worst in the first inning. He went through the season with an ERA of 5.40 in the first inning and a mark of 2.45 for the rest of the game. But Willie Wilson grounded into a rare double play to erase the leadoff single. In the second, the Cards went down 1-2-3 again. For the Royals, Frank White surprised everyone with a drag bunt on the first pitch to reach base. On the national television telecast, ABC announcer Al Michaels observed, "I suppose if anything typifies this Kansas City lineup and attack, it's that your cleanup man bunts." Then White stole second, putting a runner in scoring position with no outs.

Then Pat Sheridan took a curve for strike three. Jim Sundberg swung and missed on a slider for strike three. And Steve Balboni swung at an outside curve and missed—strike three.

Way up in the upper deck, a Royals fan named Brian Burnes was sitting on the edge of his chair with his fists clenched. With the last strike out, he put his head down, staring at the concrete floor in disgust while heaving an exasperated sigh. He had grown up a Cardinals fan, gone to games in Sportsman's Park as a boy, been lucky enough to attend World Series games in 1964, 1967 and later in 1982. By then, though, he had moved to Kansas City and become a Royals fan. Now he liked both cities. He liked both teams. He was conflicted about this World Series. He was merely rooting for a competitive series, because he knew if the Royals made a poor showing, his friends and family back in St. Louis would rib him for living in a city with a team that couldn't win the big one.

So Burnes wanted KC to win this game and even the series. But he was already anxious about it. Watching Game 1 and all the missed scoring opportunities had been like a root canal to him. And Game 2 was starting the same way.

In the third inning, the Cards got a single but stranded the runner with three straight outs. For the Royals, Biancalana led off with a walk, which Leibrandt quickly erased by bunting into a double play. Announcer Fred White in the Royals radio booth moaned, "The last seven times now in two games they've put their leadoff man on there, he has failed to cross home plate."

On the mound, Leibrandt mixed a cut fastball that moved in on right-handers, his regular fastball that he spotted on the outer part of the plate, and a changeup that faded against a righty. One mantra preached in baseball is that the pitcher should "establish" himself inside. That's what Leibrandt did well, throwing in and out, trying to control both sides of the plate. Consider his pitching sequence earlier in the game: Fastball inner half, fouled back. Fastball inside corner, strike. Fastball just outside. Fastball just inside. Changeup low and outside. Changeup inside corner, called strike three.

Now in the fourth, he got two quick outs before giving up a walk. Leftfielder Tito Landrum flicked his bat out at one of those outside changeups and looped the ball into right for a single. In the TV booth, ABC announcer Jim Palmer noted Landrum had gotten his hits so far on pitches away from him. "I think they better change the way they pitch Landrum," he said. It's the Cardinals' first threat. But a soft liner to short ended the inning.

For the Royals, Willie Wilson hit the first pitch between first and second into right for another leadoff batter on base. The Royals Stadium organist began the "charge" cheer with George Brett up, leaning way back in the batter's box, a chaw in his cheek. Wilson took off for second with the hit-and-run on. Howser was trying to pull strings again. This time it paid off as Brett smacked the ball down the rightfield line into the corner. Wilson scored for a 1-0 lead.

White was up next. He faked a bunt, worked a 2-0 count in his favor, then lashed a ball into left-center. It fell in the gap, scoring Brett and giving the Royals the makings of a big inning.

Fans in the stands were now clapping rhythmically on every pitch. But then Sheridan grounded out, Sundberg struck out and Balboni flied out. The middle of the order couldn't come through again.

The game labored on. In the Royals' half of the sixth, Wilson started things with a chopper over the mound. Second baseman Tommy Herr waited on it, gloved it and fired to first, but Wilson was safe. Herr yelled at the first-base umpire, the American League's Jack McKean. Cardinals manager Whitey Herzog jogged out to argue. Meanwhile, the TV replay showed the play was pretty much a tie. With one out, Wilson stole second and White walked. Yet again, another opportunity for the Royals to come up with a clutch hit.

In the Royals radio booth, Denny Matthews detected that "Danny Cox may be on his last legs." Cox had been bothered by a sore elbow off and on since spring training, and lately it was back on. Pain shot through his arm with every pitch.

Sheridan stepped to the plate with a red beard, not having shaved since the last week of the season. After the Royals came back to beat Toronto, a teammate told him to continue not shaving, as a team good luck charm. But it wasn't bringing him any luck in the World Series. This was his third at-bat this game with a runner in scoring position, and he was already 0 for 10 in these situations in the playoffs. Getting baserunners home hadn't been his forte all season. After a .283 average in '84, he had slipped to .228 with only 17 RBIs in 206 at-bats. He chafed at being a part-time platoon player. He couldn't get his rhythm and timing at the plate just hitting batting practice balls a few days in a row. Now he was going so bad that he was getting the pitches he wanted—fastballs away— and still missing them. "I was on a roller coaster going down," Sheridan said that year.

And it hadn't hit bottom yet. The count went in his favor, 3-1. First base-man Jack Clark headed to the mound, picked up the white rosin bag, told Cox, "Come on," and patted him on the butt. Sheridan fouled off a pitch and then swung through strike three for the second out.

Leibrandt couldn't bear to watch. He was sitting in a folding chair outside the dugout in the long tunnel between the dugout and the clubhouse. He'd been doing that all season, collecting his thoughts, going over the next hitters he would face and trying to ignore all the scoring opportunities his teammates were wasting.

Sundberg then hit a tapper back to the mound and Denny Matthews declared, "And the Royals squander yet another chance."

Royals fan Brian Burnes, still sitting on the edge of his seat with his fists clenched in anxiety, again put his head down and let out a sigh. He was a typi-cal Royals rooter, not mouthy and boisterous like Cardinals followers, but stoic and reserved. "Trying to maintain decorum" is how he put it. Suffering in silence might be more appropriate.

The seventh was yet another quick 1-2-3 inning for the Cards. They were going nowhere with Leibrandt on the mound. The Royals got yet another run-ner, Buddy Biancalana, into scoring position. Then Lonnie Smith scorched a ball into left that skipped to Landrum, who came up throwing. As Biancalana head-ed home, Wilson, the next batter, was behind home plate on his knees, waving his arms down, for Biancalana to slide. Biancalana did, his right leg aiming toward the outer edge of the plate. Catcher Darrell Porter caught the ball on the fly, reached over across the base line and lunged toward Biancalana. Wilson spread his arms wide, signaling safe. But umpire Billy Williams of the National League signaled out. Wilson jumped to his feet, spinning around in disbelief before falling to his knees again.

ABC announcer Tim McCarver said after watching the replay, "Not so sure Porter made the tag." Radio announcer Fred White watched too, and told listeners, "I believe Buddy Biancalana scored." But the Royals didn't get an insurance run.

After the Cards went quietly in the eighth, the Royals got another runner in scoring position in their half after a one-out double. Sheridan faced a lefty reliever. Normally, he'd leave for a pinch hitter in that instance. But Howser wanted his defensive presence in the ninth, so Howser went against convention and left Sheridan in to hit. He responded by grounding out to finish the inning. The score remained 2-0, although it could easily have been 4-0 or 6-0 at that point in the game with a timely hit and a favorable call.

❉❉❉❉❉❉❉

Leibrandt returned to the mound for the ninth. He had retired 13 straight batters and had allowed only one runner to get into scoring position in the game. But he had also thrown a lot of pitches—108. Dick Howser and pitching coach Gary Blaylock were sticking with him. Blaylock didn't think pitch counts meant much with Leibrandt anyway, because he didn't throw real hard. Plus, Leibrandt had developed into a workhorse.

It had been a breakthrough year for him, helping resurrect his career. He had won 10 games for the Reds in 1980 with a style that forced batters to put the ball in play. That sometimes led to jams with runners on base. The Reds didn't let him pitch long enough to get out of those jams. Instead, they gave up on him. The Royals picked him up cheap. Leibrandt was brought up in '84 and was Mr. Consistent, working at least six innings in almost every start. Howser was impressed and learned to let Leibrandt get out of his own jams. "It is a particularly strong suit of his," Howser once said. In '85, Leibrandt finished among the top 10 in the A.L. in complete games.

But he had a rocky go of it in the ninth inning in his last playoff start. He had a shutout going, then surrendered a walk and an RBI double before reliever Dan Quisenberry took over and gave up the game-winning hits. So announcer Denny Matthews began the ninth inning in the world Series by noting: "Charlie Leibrandt, being only human, you know very well that in the back of his mind is the fourth game of the League Championship series here against Toronto."

The crowd started chanting "Roy-als, Roy-als." Leibrandt stood on the mound, looking like actor James Caan with his narrow face, high forehead and pointy nose. He held his glove up high, rocked back, bent his torso into his leg kick and threw without much push off the pitching rubber. The Cardinals' Willie McGee popped up toward the Royals dugout by first base. Balboni ran over there, hesitated while checking where the dugout steps were, and the ball bounced a couple of feet from the dugout—a makeable play. Then McGee—as always seems to happen when a hitter receives new life—got on with a bad-hop grounder by third base that bounced off a seam where the artificial turf met the dirt.

But Leibrandt got a ground out and a fly out to pull the Royals within one out of the victory. Fans roared "Char-lee, Char-lee, Char-lee." Denny Matthews reminded radio listeners, "So Leibrandt is trying to fight off that memory of that ninth inning against Toronto." Jack Clark stepped to the plate as pitching coach Gary Blaylock, with his big round glasses and hat askew, headed to the mound.

"He can tie it up," Blaylock reminded Leibrandt. "Don't give him anything he can hit out."

That meant no more fastballs over the inner half. Clark was thinking only one thing: home run. A dead-pull hitter who set up farther away from the plate than just about any other hitter, Clark simply concedes the outside corner most of the time. The first pitch was a changeup outside for a ball. Then came another changeup outside for ball two. Pitch three was more of the same. Clark was given the green light to swing on 3-0. Leibrandt threw another changeup outside. Clark reached out with his 34-inch, 32-ounce Joe Morgan model bat and pulled the ball between short and third, in the hole, for an RBI base hit.

There went the shutout, and with a right-hander at the plate, Quisenberry was warm and ready in the bullpen. Leibrandt was standing on the mound thinking, *Am I going to get the hook?*

Brett stood at third base, peering into the dugout, thinking, *Bring in Quis.* It was decision time for Howser. He was then 49 years old, a five-foot, eight-inch former infielder with short hair, a dimpled chin, a straight mouth and crow's feet around his eyes from too much squinting in the sun. Howser typically had a hands-off style, preferring to let his players on the field decide the outcome of games. But he had a knack for making adjustments, for adapting to situations, when he had to. On his 1980 Yankees squad, he had nine players with double-digit homers, so he played, in the words of one writer, for "one swing, then trot" innings. With the Royals, however, he was reduced to doing the opposite—using speed to set up scoring opportunities—because of his personnel, the far-away walls at Royals Stadium and the artificial turf field. Once he determined his best lineup, though, he stuck with it. Usually he didn't even tinker with the batting order or pitching rotation when players fought slumps. One of his favorite expressions was asking, "What, you want me to get fancy?" Now he was just coming off one of his finest moments, the last three games of the Toronto series, when he seemingly out-foxed Bobby Cox with Quisenberry.

Quis had led the league in saves for a fourth consecutive year, but that was deceptive. He had failed to protect a lead in 12 games. He felt, in his own words, "vulnerable." And one newspaper headline early in the season stated "Quisenberry can't get anyone out." Right-handed hitters started going the other way on his outside pitches, and his typical struggles against left-handed hitters just got worse. Lefties, who had a better look at the ball out of his hand, hit .317 against him that year, compared to .236 by righties. The typical platoon difference was 25 to 30 points, according to the Elias Sports Bureau, so Quis was triple the norm. By the end of the season, Howser was publicly looking for late-game alternatives. Then Quis blew two games against Toronto on hits by lefties. So Howser took special care in Game 6 to start a right-hander, then bring in a lefty reliever early, so the Blue Jays' left-handed platoon hitters would be gone by the time Quis was needed. For Game 7, the Royals were able to work the same strategy again, accidentally, because right-hander Bret Saberhagen was knocked out early with an injury. Leibrandt came in and held the game in check, before Quis finished up.

After the Royals won the pennant and were pouring champagne over each other in the clubhouse, Quisenberry tapped general manager John Schuerholz on the shoulder and pointed at Howser: "There is the man who won this thing." But Howser couldn't employ the same strategy against the Cards because they had too many switch-hitters. And Quis had already shown he had trouble with the Cardinals, giving up a run in the ninth inning of Game 1.

The role of a relief-only ace pitcher was still relatively new to baseball in the mid-'80s. In the '70s teams started developing relief aces but even then most of them tended to burn out quickly because they would throw more than 100 innings a year and pitch nearly every other day. By the '80s the workload of closers was being reduced, but Quis was one of the holdovers, still pitching more than 100 innings a year. He never was overpowering, relying more on deception, changing speeds and his sinker. Was he losing it now? Scouts like the Cardinals' Mo Mozzali noticed something: "He has lost a little off his fastball, and I think it was getting up more than in the past."

Royals coaches never let on, but they recognized it, too. As Blaylock put it years later, "Quis was no longer the dominant relief pitcher he once was. We knew that, but other people didn't know that."

So even at this point in the game, Howser and Blaylock felt good with Leibrandt. Howser was in the dugout, pacing with his arms crossed. He knew that Leibrandt worked out of jams better than any pitcher he had ever had. And Blaylock felt Leibrandt was actually a better pitcher against righties than lefties. The stats bore him out, as Leibrandt did hold righties to a slightly lower average than lefties that year, which went against baseball's conventional wisdom.

The Royals needed just one more out. Fans were still chanting "Char-lee, Char-lee, Char-lee" as Tito Landrum stepped in. Landrum had been getting hits only on pitches away from him. But Leibrandt figured his punch-singles to right were just lucky, that he couldn't keep doing it.

First pitch, changeup fouled back. Fastball fouled back, two strikes. The fans were on their feet whistling and clapping. Fastball outside. Changeup way outside. Landrum's thinking, *React to the ball. Just make solid contact.* Next pitch was another changeup outside, but this time Landrum reached out and punched a flare toward right. It bounced just inside the foul line for a double. Sheridan cut it off, holding Clark at third and affirming Howser's defensive strategy.

Still two out. Cesar Cedeno, another righty, was now up. Quisenberry was done warming up and was watching from the bullpen. Leibrandt had handled Cedeno all night—groundout, soft infield fly, groundout. But, Howser motioned for an intentional walk to set up a force at any base.

In the radio booth, Denny Matthews was told listeners, "It's down to this, folks."

Terry Pendleton was up, a switch-hitter batting right-handed. Leibrandt had been pounding him inside with fastballs, and Pendleton had been fisting them toward the right side. The next pitch would be Leibrandt's 130th and he was laboring. Pendleton approached the plate, telling himself, *Relax. Try to relax.*

First pitch, changeup outside. Then another changeup for a strike. A fastball missed inside, and with a 2-1 count the Royals' outfield was shaded toward right. Denny Matthews observed on radio, "So if Pendleton should hit a ball over Brett into the left-field corner, it would clean off the bases." Leibrandt delivered a changeup over the outer half of the plate. Pendleton was out in front of it. His hips turned, but his bat was still back. At the last instant he turned on the ball and yanked it over third base and down the leftfield line.

The bases cleared, just like Matthews had predicted. 4-2 Cards.

The Cardinals' Cesar Cedeno scored on Terry Pendleton's game-winning, bases-clearing double in the ninth inning of Game 2. *Courtesy of the Kansas City Royals/Chris Vleisides*

The crowd went silent except for scattered cheers from Cardinals fans. In the upper deck, Royals fan Brian Burnes again put his head down and heaved a lengthy sigh. Royals announcer Denny Matthews observed on radio: "Royals stadium still in a state of shock."

Leibrandt bent over on the mound and hung his head as Howser emerged from the dugout. Finally Quisenberry came in. With one pitch he got the last out.

In the bottom of the ninth, the crowd was now seated, drained and in shock. Sundberg flied out to open the inning. But Balboni squibbed one down the third-base line and beat it out, hustling. That brought pinch-hitter Jorge Orta to the plate as the tying run. But he grounded to Tommy Herr, who flipped to Ozzie Smith, who threw to Clark for a game-ending double play.

❋ ❋ ❋ ❋ ❋ ❋ ❋

Cardinals fans throughout the ballpark stood and rejoiced. One group in the bleachers broke out in a chant of "Char-lee, Char-lee, Char-lee," mocking the earlier cheer from Royals' fans. Meanwhile, Royals fans left solemnly, dejected and broken hearted, thinking they had seen the last game of the season at Royals Stadium. The stadium announcer made his typical postgame invitation: "We invite you to relax and watch our colorful water spectacular..." But no one was in that kind of mood.

Royals fan Brian Burnes made the long walk back to his car on one of the farthest edges of the stadium complex. He and most others staggered like mummies, quiet, dazed and traumatized. Suddenly the silence was punctuated by a woman's voice. She was dressed to the hilt, in a suit and hose and heels, but screaming and swearing as she got into her car:

"---- baseball. ---- the Royals. ---- the World Series. I can't believe I sat through that ------ game."

Burnes laughed and thought, *Well, that sums it up.*

Indeed, the Royals appeared doomed. The Cardinals' comeback had been one of historic proportions in the World Series. Never had a team entered the top of the ninth inning down by more than one run and come back to win the game in that inning. And in the history of the fall classic, there had been only six occasions when a team had scored more than two runs in the ninth inning to overcome a one-run deficit and win the game—1908, 1929, 1941, 1972, 1975 and 1980, when the Royals had coughed up Game 5 to the Phillies. In all six of those World Series, the team suffering the agonizing loss in that game also went on to lose the entire series.

So no team had ever won a World Series after losing a game like this, and no team had ever won a World Series after losing the first two games at home. The Royals were doubly cursed now, and even the players seemed to sense that.

In the Royals locker room, George Brett told reporters: "You lose one like this and it's a killer."

Other players openly cursed and some discreetly second-guessed Howser. Willie Wilson told the writers, "Anybody who knows baseball should have known what to do in that situation. I don't want to talk about it further."

At one point, Howser sought out Leibrandt and found him in the trainers room, soaking his arm, alone, disconsolate.

"Don't worry," Howser told him. "You'll get the ball again in the series."

Leibrandt just stared back at him. He couldn't speak.

Then it was time for Howser to face the media himself. He sat composed in his office and tackled all the second-guessing. He didn't complain. He didn't moan. He didn't swear. He didn't blame anyone else. He didn't write off the rest of the games.

He simply explained his reasoning. And like always, he didn't second-guess himself. He made what he thought was the right decision and he lived with it. Of course, in sports, the only truly right decision is the one that works. So sportswriters treated Howser as if, upon returning to the U.S. from Canada where his decisions had helped pull off a playoff upset, the border authorities made him check his brain at customs. He took his lumps, like this one from Tom Melody of Akron, Ohio's *Beacon-Journal* newspaper: "Dick Howser. Now there's a manager who can sit still for defeat. There, too, is a manager who can take defeat without blinking an eye. Without shuffling his feet. Because of all that, his Kansas City Royals might be, well, dead in their tracks."

CHAPTER 4

A LITTLE BIT OF LUCK CAN GO A LONG WAY

The next day, during a travel day in the World Series, the media caught up with Charlie Leibrandt. At one point, someone asked him, "Is it better to be good or lucky?"

"Sometimes," he replied, "it's better to be lucky."

And how. Consider how the Cardinals won the first two games. In Game 1, Cesar Cedeno broke the 1-1 tie with a broken-bat looper inside the left-field line. Then George Brett's mammoth eighth-inning drive, which everyone thought was a game-tying homer, died in the misty air. In Game 2, Pat Sheridan came up four times with a runner in scoring position and couldn't get any of them home. Then during the fateful ninth inning, Jack Clark was trying to hit a homer and instead hit the ball on the ground right between two fielders. And Tito Landrum was just trying to make contact when he reached across the plate and punched a bloop double just inside the right-field line.

As Clark told reporters afterward about his at-bat: "It was a lucky hit, to be honest with you."

That was just baseball. Because in so many ways, "there's a lot of luck in baseball," in the words of Hall of Fame pitcher Bob Feller. Alan Schwarz wrote a book about baseball's fascination with statistics and explained: "This is one of baseball's great ironies—games are played every day, with explanations for everything sought after every one, when most of the time the primary explanation is luck."

✴✴✴✴✴✴

It starts with the process of picking players. Baseball, more than professional football and basketball, is littered with late-round picks who became superstars: Jack Clark (13th round), Jose Canseco (15th), Frank Viola (16th), Don Mattingly (19th), Ryne Sandberg (20th), Paul Molitor (28th), Keith Hernandez (42nd) and Mike Piazza (62nd). Stories of draft mistakes are legendary. Does anyone remember catcher Steve Chilcott, whom the Mets took ahead of Reggie Jackson in 1966? One time, a team drafted a player after seeing him play just day games, only to find he couldn't see well enough for night games.

In the early 1980s, only one in every 11 players drafted ever made it to the big leagues, and most of those got there for a handful of last-season games, without getting another chance. Yet teams spent several million dollars a year on scouting and player development for a hoped-for return of one or two starters. Why was baseball like this? Why did almost every first-rounder in football or basketball end up playing pro ball, while it was highly unusual for a baseball first-rounder to become a star?

The answer was simple: predicting a teenager's eventual baseball skills typically depended on a scout's gut feelings. Baseball scouts for decades discounted performance measures that would later be seen as indicators of future success, such as strikeout-to-walk ratio for control pitchers. Instead, scouts relied on their own eyesight and judgment. And along the way, they built up superstitions and bias. Like light-haired players held up better in summer heat and big legs on an infielder meant limited range. The Philadelphia Phillies' Tony Lucadello, who may have signed more big leaguers than any other scout over his career, used to concentrate on a prospect's body control and how he placed his feet. Lucadello's mantra was: "Eighty-seven percent of the game of baseball is played below the waist"—as if that was a scientific certainty. There were plenty of other corny and accepted evaluation methods, like looking for "the good face" in a prospect, the wide cheeks, square jaw and piercing eyes. As Al Campanis, a former Dodger general manager, told Kevin Kerrane in an early '80s book about baseball scouts: "I never used to sign a boy unless I could look in his face and see what I wanted to see—drive, determination, maturity, whatever. …Some scout would give me a report on a boy, and I'd say, 'Tell me about his face,' or 'Does he have the good face?'"

No matter what baseball men looked for, they ended up being wrong about most prospects. Sometimes that was because of a player's injuries. Sometimes that was because a player just didn't have the mental makeup to succeed. But often, prospects didn't pan out because the draft was, in the eyes of a long-time scout named Hep Cronin, "still mostly a crapshoot."

Kansas City had its share of crap games with the amateur draft. And sometimes during the course of building the 1985 team, the franchise lucked out.

In 1971 the Royals had their sights set on a "can't miss" high school pitcher named Roy Branch. But when he hurt his arm right before the draft, the team debated whether to stay with him or go with a California shortstop with a "hippy problem," that is, with big hips that limited his range. They stuck with Branch, who never made the majors with the Royals, and their second choice—George Brett—fortuitously lasted until the next round.

The next year, the Royals and every other team salivated over another California shortstop. He was "the most sought-after high school athlete in the last decade," according to Lou Gorman, the team's scouting director at the time. But the kid had a scholarship offer to become a future quarterback of the Notre Dame Fighting Irish, so baseball teams shied away from him. The Royals, though, took a gamble, selected him in the first round and gave him a big bonus. That kid was Jamie Quirk, who made the majors but failed to become the star that Gorman envisioned.

The same year that scouts salivated over Quirk, no team gave a second look to another California high school senior. So he went on to play at small colleges. He won a lot of games and toyed with throwing underneath, or submarine style as it was called, where his pitching hand almost rubbed against the ground. He still didn't throw hard, so scouts still didn't pay any attention to him. His college coach, though, had a connection with the Royals and got him signed as an "organizational player," or someone just to fill out a minor-league roster. Within a few years, Dan Quisenberry was still using that submarining style as a dominant major league closer.

Stan Hart, who wrote a book about original scouting reports done on star players, ultimately concluded about the draft: "What is required for success at baseball's version of *Dungeons and Dragons* is good judgment, which is granted to mortals, and the power of prognostication, which is not—plus a hell of a lot of luck."

Once players made it to the majors, luck then played a role in how well they did, too.

In each individual at-bat, there were tiny factors and fractions of inches and matters of milliseconds that separated a hit from an out. A 90-mph fastball traveled from the pitcher's hand to the batter's box in .4167 seconds. A batter had to decide whether to swing or not in the pitch's first eight feet, then he had about two-tenths of a second to make his body do it. And if he happened to hit the ball a half-inch off center, that was the difference between an easy pop fly out and a line drive.

No other sport required such precision. Throw a football a half-inch off its target, and it usually still landed in the receiver's hands. Slap a hockey puck a half-inch to one side or the other of a stick, and the shot would still rocket toward the net as a tough shot on goal. Shoot a basketball a half-inch off the center of the hands, and the shot could still swish. The only thing comparable might be in golf, where a fraction of an inch could be the difference between a perfect drive down the fairway and a bad shank. But a golf ball wasn't moving when it was being hit.

That's why academics and scientists who have studied baseball believe just about every at-bat is a matter of some luck. A home run is a skillful but also fortunate set of circumstances. The batter made the right read of a pitch and swung in a properly fluid motion with his hands in the proper position, and the pitch did exactly what the batter thought it would do. And, within all those milliseconds, he struck the ball on a meaty spot of the bat.

Because of all that, debates have swirled for decades now about whether clutch hitting truly exists. That is, whether a batter truly has ability to rise to an occasion and hit better in pressure situations with any consistency, or whether a clutch hit is a matter of a lucky combination of circumstances that produce a hit. Among baseball researchers who have given the subject some complex mathematical analyses, the emerging consensus is that clutch hitting is not a real skill, but a myth.

This is, of course, heretic to baseball purists. When Reggie Jackson, "Mr. October" himself, was told that clutch hitting was considered a myth, he told *Sports Illustrated:* "That could be the absolute dumbest thing I have ever heard in my life." Sammy Sosa summarized the thinking of many players on the subject: "I really believe some people concentrate better with the game on the line. That's money time. You focus much better. [But] some people don't do great in those situations." Players as well as fans and announcers liked to believe someone coming through in the clutch was a matter of a big heart and extra desire—basically a statement about character.

The only problem is, baseball researchers find no statistical evidence that some players "raise their game," as the saying goes. Certainly, there are clutch hits, moments like Bobby Thomson's home run to win the Giants the pennant in 1951 or George Brett's blast off of Goose Gossage to win the Royals the 1980 pennant.

Yet, Jim Albert of the mathematics department at Bowling Green State University found that while certain players had gaudy clutch-hitting averages one season, they didn't show that ability over their careers. Consider the case of Phillies infielder Manny Trillo. He had an incredible year in 1981, batting .466 in late-inning pressure situations, those in the seventh inning or later in games his team trailed by three runs or less. Trillo, though, was a career .263 hitter, and his average in late-inning pressure situations over his entire career was just .245. Anomalies like Trillo's '81 season, Albert believed, were "due to chance" and "random effects." He concluded: "There appears to be little evidence that players have different abilities to perform well in clutch situations."

He is hardly alone in that judgment. David Grabiner, a statistician formerly of the University of Michigan, ran a mathematical analysis comparing how every full-time major-leaguer hit in late innings of close games over nearly a decade of seasons. He found their consistency over time—in mathematical terms, the correlation—was .01, or statistically insignificant. Players exhibiting more of an "ability" to hit in the clutch got basically one extra hit a year in those situations. "There isn't a significant ability in clutch hitting," Grabiner wrote. "If there were, the same players would be good clutch hitters every year."

Overall, then, what the researchers have come to believe is that whatever happens in the clutch has more to do with a player's inherent skill rather than with some extra ability summoned forth at a particular moment. And usually that skill is at the mercy of dynamics they can hardly control, like a line drive right at a fielder, or a broken-bat looper over the infield, or a long fly just the right angle to elude an outfielder. As Daniel Levitt, a baseball historian who studied the subject, put it in a newsletter for the Society for American Baseball Research: "There is no way to segregate clutch hitting ability from all other factors, including luck."

This luck is something not generally understood about baseball.

That's because fans and broadcasters and everyone else involved in the game want a reason for why something happened—that a batter was "seeing the ball better," or one player "showed more heart" than another, or a team was "destined" to win. In actuality, legions of scientists and academics, after years of statistical study and modeling, have determined that baseball is essentially a series of random, unpredictable events. As one researcher put it: "Nothing ever happened in baseball above and beyond the frequency predicted by coin-tossing models." Think about it: hypothetically, when a quarter is flipped into the air, it has an equal chance of landing on heads or tails. If it's flipped a hundred times, it's likely to exhibit weird patterns, from alternating heads and tails several times in a row, to landing heads seven times in a row. Most events in baseball don't start out with 50-50 probabilities like coin tossing does, but the same concept nonetheless applies. A hitter with a .300 batting average is seen as having an inherent 30 percent chance of getting a hit. Yet rarely does he get three hits in groups of 10 at bats. Sometimes he goes 0 for 10, and other times he goes six for 10.

The same logic applies to baseball teams, too. According to probability theories, a group of players who together score 810 runs in a season, or five per game, could under the same circumstances in any other season likely score anywhere from 730 runs to 890 runs, just by the vagaries of luck and chance. In computer simulations, even the same hitting lineup has been shown to fluctuate by 70 runs from one season to the next solely because of randomness, as opposed to the usual explanations given, such as player slumps or not hitting in the clutch or managerial ineptitude.

All of that, though, is measured over the course of an entire season. Luck becomes even more random over any short period of games, like with any group of 10 at-bats or 10 coin flips—or seven World Series games.

The probabilities of picking a World Series winner involve such mathematical concepts as square roots and standard deviations and sigma ranges. But here's what it all comes down to: The average real difference between two teams is about half a run per game. In an average game, that translates to the better team having a 55 percent chance of winning. In a seven-game series, that better team will win from 2.5 to five games two-thirds of the time. What that means is it's highly probable that the better team won't win four games. Or in the words of

Pete Palmer, a well-known baseball researcher and author of *The Hidden Game of Baseball*, "Basically, it means anything can happen in a playoff series."

❊❊❊❊❊❊❊

Just about anything *has* happened throughout the history of the World Series. Luck has constantly played a role in all kinds of ways—a bounce, an inch, a split-second. And sometimes that's ended up being the difference between winning and losing.

October 10, 1924, Washington Senators vs. New York Giants, seventh game of the World Series:

The Giants led 3-1 in the eighth inning. The Senators loaded the bases with two outs. A grounder was hit to third baseman Fred Lindstrom that looked like the third out. But the ball hit a pebble and careened over Lindstrom's head, scoring two runs to tie the game. It was still tied in the twelfth when the Senators put runners on first and second. A grounder was hit toward Lindstrom again. And again it hit a pebble and took a "big kangaroo hop," as Lindstrom later described it, over his head into left field, scoring the winning run.

October 16, 1962, New York Yankees vs. San Francisco Giants, seventh game of the World Series:

The Yanks held a 1-0 lead in the bottom of the ninth inning. The Giants had runners on second and third base with two outs and the dangerous Willie McCovey at the plate. It was a situation crying out for an intentional walk, as Yankee starter Ralph Terry was tiring and McCovey had tripled off him in his last at-bat. The Yankees, though, not only stayed with Terry but let him to pitch to McCovey. "It was one of the worst strategic decisions in World Series history," Eric Enders wrote in a history of the fall classic. McCovey hit a vicious line drive—but right at second baseman Bobby Richardson for the final out of the series. Arnold Hano, writing in *Sport Magazine* about the game, concluded: "A few inches had marked the difference between a winner and a loser."

October 10, 1968, St. Louis Cardinals vs. Detroit Tigers, seventh game of the World Series:

It was scoreless in the seventh inning, when the Tigers got two runners on and Jim Northrup hit a long shot to centerfield. Gold Glove winner Curt Flood got a late read on the ball, then slipped in the grass as he turned to run. The ball ended up over his head for a two-run triple that broke open the game and decided the series.

October 22, 1975, Boston Red Sox vs. Cincinnati Reds, seventh game of the World Series:

Boston led 3-0 going into the sixth inning. With one out and a runner on base for Cincinnati, Johnny Bench hit an apparent inning-ending double-play roller. The shortstop got it and flipped the ball to second baseman Denny Doyle, who took the ball out of his glove and felt the cover of the ball, which was coming off. Back then, baseballs were made in Haiti, and every once in a while the force of the bat would literally tear the cover off the ball. When Doyle tried throwing the torn ball, it sailed out of his hand and into the dugout. The next batter belted a two-run homer to put the Reds on the board and on their way toward a one-run victory.

As Jim Albert, the Bowling Green mathematician, and Jay Bennett, a scientist, observed in their book, *Curve Ball: Baseball, Statistics and the Role of Chance in the Game*, "Whether we like it or not, chance events have a big effect on the patterns of wins and losses that we observe."

In the 1985 World Series, luck had already made an appearance, almost incognito. It would pay a much more recognizable and celebrated visit later on.

CHAPTER 5

GAMES 3 AND 4:

"EACH OF US FELT ... WE HAD COME TO THE END OF OUR STRING"

For the first time in 11 years, the 1985 World Series was confined to one state. Maybe it was just in the stars for Missouri. One of its greatest figures, Mark Twain, was born Samuel Langhorne Clemens in November 1835, as Halley's Comet was flashing across the sky. He was dying in April 1910, when it was again passing through the sky. The next time the comet came around was the fall of 1985, and his state snagged baseball's biggest stage.

For little Missouri, this was a big deal.

One of then-Gov. John Ashcroft's staffers, Warren Erdman, organized a special whistle-stop train from Kansas City to St. Louis for politicians, chamber of commerce-types and media members. If baseball sentiment was expressed in clothing and anything holding a color, then a hint of the state's leanings came on top of the governor's head. He wore a baseball cap that made a sport out of impartiality. The cap had two fronts and no back, with one side in blue and bearing the insignia of the Royals and the other side in red and carrying the logo of the Cardinals. It was emblematic of most of the state's divided loyalties.

In Boonville, one side of Main Street was painted with a red stripe and the other side with a blue stripe. In a little town halfway across the state, appropriately named Midway, the Auto/Truck Plaza divided its dining room into a blue section and a red section. So when ABC's Al Michaels introduced Game 1 by saying, "Welcome to this little intrastate squabble," a couple of women sitting together in the restaurant looked at each other, incredulous.

"Squabble?" one asked.

"Little?" asked the other.

Howard Johnson, mayor of a southern Missouri Ozark town of Buffalo, noted during the series: "It's just like the Civil War. It's neighbor against neighbor, friend against friend, and husband against wife."

At the University of Missouri in Columbia, it was brother against brother at the Pi Kappa Phi fraternity house.

It started with masking tape down the door of roommates Shawn Link and Jim Deutschmann. Link was from the Kansas City suburb of Independence and lived close enough to Royals Stadium to hear eruptions from the crowd. He lived and died by the Royals. He punched a hole in his bedroom wall after they lost the '77 playoffs. Deutschmann was from the St. Louis suburb of Kirkwood. As a kid, he used to listen to record albums of highlights from the Cardinals' World Series triumphs. Whenever he played whiffleball in his backyard, he always imitated the batting stances of his favorite Cardinals, from Lou Brock to Keith Hernandez.

When the school year started in late summer, Link and Deutschmann cheered on each other's teams and pinned clippings of big games on a corkboard on their door. When both won pennants, though, Deutschmann put down the gauntlet. He divided up the clippings on the door, put tape down the middle and announced, "I'm not rooting for the Royals anymore." Fellow fraternity brothers—two-thirds of whom sided with the Cardinals—took the idea from there. They put tape down the middle of the hallway on the third floor where Link and Deutschmann lived. They put tape down the stairs. They put tape down on the floor of the front hall and out the front door. They even painted a line down the porch steps and down the front sidewalk. On the front door of the brown-brick Tudor-style house was a sign: "To avoid clashes with the brother—Cardinals fans to the right, Royals fans to the left." If someone strayed to the wrong side, invariably a shout rang out: "Hey, get off our side."

The national media, though, saw the state and the series entirely differently than the locals. In their eyes, there wasn't anything cute or quaint about being in Missouri. They considered themselves stuck. The most common statement made by assembled sportswriters at the beginning of the series, *The Chicago Tribune's* Jon Margolis reported, was: "All I want is a four-game sweep so I can go home." Even for that to happen, they had to make one trip across the state, as the series shifted home parks.

So as the governor took some of the media by train, others went by car, along Interstate 70, the ribbon of highway separating the two cities, which gave birth to the series' nickname: The I-70 series. That highway happens to be a down-home stretch, with cafes serving fried chicken and plots of dried cornstalks lining the interstate. Of course, the East Coast media belittled most everything they saw. It was as if they were trying to mimic Mark Twain when he had tra-versed the state by steamboat for the book *Roughing It*: "We were six days going from St. Louis to 'St. Joe'—a trip that was so dull, and sleepy, and eventless that it has left no more impression on my memory than if its duration had been six minutes instead of that many days."

Likewise, when the Eastern press saw red combines and yellow tractors and water towers, it confirmed their suspicions that they were indeed in hick coun-try. Tony Kornheiser of *The Washington Post* wrote about the first silo sighting and a truck stop offering a "Redneck Country Rock N Roll Revival Show." He dripped with East Coast elitism with the question, "How many people at Elaine's would believe the sign saying that Ozarkland is really 'worth stopping for'?"

As it was, coastal residents didn't seem interested at all. TV ratings for the first game drew the lowest prime-time television audience ever for a World Series opener, a 22.1 rating, or 31 percent share of the television audience. In New York, where the media had been trumping a possible subway series throughout September, more televisions were tuned into NBC's Saturday night lineup of *Facts of Life*, *Golden Girls* and *Hunter* than the World Series Game 1 on ABC. A headline in *The New York Daily News* smirked: "Missouri Waltz: 'World' Glides Out of Series." *The Washington Post's* Thomas Boswell opined, "Let's be honest, the St. Louis Cardinals and Kansas City Royals are, by Series standards, drab collections."

As for the baseball aspect of this World Series, everyone was writing off the Royals. Again. On the governor's special train trip, as a Dixie band played, the Cardinal partisans danced with brooms, signifying a sweep. In St. Louis, Royals players looked out their airplane windows when they landed and saw a banner hanging from the control tower: "Welcome to the home of the 1985 World Champions." St. Louis fans drove around the Royals' downtown hotel at night, honking their horns and yelling "Sweep, sweep, sweep." A radio weatherman told listeners not to worry about the forecast for Game 5 because there wouldn't be one. Even the Cardinals players, on their plane ride to St. Louis, talked about closing out the Royals at home. "A little overconfidence might have set in at that point," Ozzie Smith recalled. Reggie Jackson began ABC-TV's Game 3 telecast with the observation: "It almost seems like a match-up of David against Goliath, although this time David may not have a slingshot."

❉ ❉ ❉ ❉ ❉ ❉ ❉

In the Royals dugout, Dick Howser's philosophy remained steadfast. He would field the same lineup and maintain the same commitment to aggressively manufacture runs. Joaquin Andujar was starting for the Cards. He had been awful for the last couple of months. After beginning the season 12-1, posting a 15-4 mark at the All-Star break and reaching 20 wins in August, he won just once more the rest of the year. His ERA approached 6.00 during the season's last six weeks. Up in ABC's broadcast booth, former pitcher-turned-announcer Jim Palmer thought Andujar's arm position was dropping, a sign of being tired from all the innings he had thrown—280 including the postseason.

With one out in the first inning, Willie Wilson bounced a single and promptly swiped second with George Brett at the plate. It was the first time in the series that Brett had hit with a runner in scoring position. The Cardinals didn't push their luck, choosing to walk him intentionally. Up stepped Frank White. He already had more hits in this World Series after two games than he had in 1980's six games. The count went full and the runners took off with the pitch. White responded by lining a sharp grounder up the middle—but second baseman Tommy Herr was running to cover the steal attempt and the grounder headed right to him. He stepped on the bag and threw to first for a double play. "And the Royals must figure, what's going on?" ABC's Al Michaels remarked on TV.

For the Royals, the fate of this game, and really the season, rested on the arm of their ace pitcher, Bret Saberhagen. He was barely out of his teens and looked so young with a brush of hair on his upper lip that was his best attempt at a mustache. *The Los Angeles Times'* Jim Murray commented, "you don't know whether to burp him or buy him an ice cream cone." Saberhagen was happy-go-lucky, too, bouncing around the field before games that season doing quirky things like chasing butterflies. "He looks 18 and acts 15," fellow pitcher Dan Quisenberry said at the time. But Sabes was nothing like that on the mound. "A 20-year-old who pitches like he's 30," Royals scout Guy Hansen said of him. Saberhagen had impressed the Royals brass from his earliest minor league games with something that couldn't be taught—an innate knowledge of how to pitch. He could spot his fastball in different places for strikes, he could change speeds and he had a knack for knowing where to throw a particular pitch in a particular situation to a particular batter. In '85, his second year in the big leagues, he started off well, going 7-4. Still he made an adjustment—he ceased throwing his curves and changeups so frequently and instead threw more of his dipping, moving fastballs. They were the only fastballs that veteran catcher Jim Sundberg had ever caught that seemed to accelerate over the plate. That is, they had so much spin that they didn't decelerate as much. Sabes went 13-2 the rest of the way, mowing down the opposition on the way to becoming, at age 21, the youngest American League winner of the Cy Young award.

Yet, no one was quite sure whether he would be okay for this game. He had to leave Game 7 in the playoffs after his pitching hand was hit by a batted ball and swelled up. Plus, his wife was about to deliver a baby.

Was Sabes nervous? Yeah, he told reporters before the game, who wouldn't be? After all, he hadn't hit in the big leagues before. That's right, he was nervous about hitting. As for pitching? "It's almost old hat," the brash youngster said.

In the first inning, the Cardinals faced the same situation as Royals—runners at first and second, one out and a full count on the cleanup hitter, Jack Clark.

Saberhagen stood on the mound with a wad of seeds in his cheek, holding the ball, continuing to glance back at McGee off second base, freezing him there longer than he had on other pitches. Finally, he delivered the ball to the plate. Jack Clark, always looking to jack inside fastballs, saw the pitch coming inside and stepped into it. But it was a changeup. It froze him. The ball glided over the inside corner for a called third strike. Clark was totally fooled. McGee was going on the pitch. Sundberg fired down to third to nab McGee—double play, inning over.

In the second inning, Balboni, still not trying to think about homeruns, got hold of one. It was high and deep. Leftfielder Tito Landrum had one shoulder against the fence as the ball settled into his glove. Royals radio announcer Denny Matthews told his audience, "Only this huge prison known as Busch Stadium kept that thing in the ball yard."

In fact, contrary to popular belief, both Busch Stadium and Royals Stadium were not pitchers parks, but both slightly favored the hitters. Years of data showed the turfs were fast and produced higher-than-average amounts of doubles and triples. Line-drive hitters thrived and hit for higher averages than on grass fields. The only way the stadiums hurt hitters was with home runs. In the early '80s, Royals Stadium had the second lowest number of homers, behind only Houston's Astrodome. Busch had the sixth lowest. Balboni's blast was just another long out. The Royals went quietly in the second, as did the Cardinals.

At the Pi Kappa Phi frat house at the University of Missouri, Jim Deutschmann and Shawn Link—the roommates who had started the whole tape-down-the middle thing—now sat on separate sides of bleachers outside. Literally outside. Because by Game 3, the fraternity had turned the series' divided loyalties into a game-watching party. A platform was built on the porch for the house TV. A makeshift five-foot-wide manual scoreboard was designed. And on the lawn facing the TV were three levels of wood bleachers—with a line painted down the middle, of course. So far this game, the Cardinals side of the bleachers had been razzing the Royals side, waving brooms and yelling, "Sweep." After the Royals ran themselves out of the third inning—getting three singles and a walk but not scoring because of a caught stealing—Royals fan Link sat there holding his head in his hands while the Cards fans whooped and shouted, "We're going to sweep you."

After the Cards went in order, Sundberg led off the Royals fourth. Andujar's first pitch was a slider at the knees, called a ball. Andujar remained planted on his follow-through an extra second, as if he couldn't believe the call from home-plate umpire Jim McKean of the American League. Andujar had been doing this occasionally every inning, starting with the very first batter of the game. His second pitch to Sundberg was at the knees just outside, again called a ball, and Andujar again stayed planted in his follow-through, with his legs spread wide, a couple more seconds this time. Then he bent down, putting his glove and pitching hand on his knees. Sundberg eventually walked, and Andujar again bent over, hands on knees.

At the University of Missouri in Columbia, the Pi Kappa Phi fraternity split down the middle for the World Series. To separate Cards fans from Royals rooters, the frat brothers put white tape and paint down the middle of the hallways and rooms of their house, and along the front sidewalk, too. It all started between roommates Jim Deutschmann (seated on the left) and Shawn Link (seated on the right). *Courtesy of Shawn Link*

He felt he was not getting calls on the corners. In fact, he was just not used to how American League umps called a game. It was one of baseball's dirty little secrets. The rulebook defined one strike zone, but the two leagues over time developed slightly different ones. N.L. umps were the first to wear a smaller, more compact, wraparound chest protector under their shirts or jackets. Because of this, they could bend down easier. So they set up over the catcher's shoulder on the inside part of the plate and traditionally gave more leeway on the outside corner. Meanwhile, A.L. umps had worn a bulky, mattress-style chest protector over their clothing. They couldn't bend down much, so they stood up higher, directly behind the catcher. That gave them a good view of high pitches, and A.L. umps tended to call higher strikes. This tendency remained even after all umps switched to the smaller chest protector around 1980.

Even within leagues, though, different umpires called games differently. This aspect of baseball wasn't studied much, but when it was, it showed surprisingly wide variations between umpires. *Village Voice*, of all periodicals, once computed umpires' own earned run averages, basically the average number of runs scored by one team when an ump worked home plate. The spread between the lowest and highest umpires was about two runs a game—about the same difference between a pitcher leading the league in ERA and one who gets yanked from a starting rotation. Jim McKean, according to this analysis, was on the low side, meaning he tended to have one of the larger A.L. strike zones.

Andujar and the rest of the Cardinals didn't know this, however.

Balboni stepped to the plate with Sundberg on first. One curveball bent outside for a ball, and Andujar bent over with hands on knees again. Balboni lined out to left. Buddy Biancalana swung at the first offering and chopped it on the infield, but no one covered first and Biancalana was awarded a base hit. Saberhagen then sacrificed the runners over to second and third. Two on with two out.

"So again the Royals with an opportunity for a turning point," ABC's Al Michaels said on TV. Lonnie Smith was up. The first pitch was a slider low and away, and Andujar went through his same routine of nonverbally communicating his displeasure with the call. The second pitch was a fastball inside, and Andujar held his knees and shook his head of thick black curly hair. Herzog called time and walked out to the mound. He stood with his thumbs stuck in his pants, talking with his infielders, until McKean came out to break up the meeting. Then Herzog, without looking at McKean, started jawing at him out of the side of his mouth.

What Herzog didn't say, but surely felt, was that McKean might be intentionally favoring one side. "It's just human nature for an ump to want to see his league do well," Herzog would later write about the game in his autobiography.

That, of course, was asinine. Complaints about umpiring were simply a World Series constant, going back to the very first one. *The Boston Globe's* account of the 1903 Series mentioned: "Pittsburgh had all the luck and a shade the better of the umpiring, as (umpire) Connolly favored (pitcher) Phillippe on strikes…" Nearly a century later, 1985 was the first year under new guidelines for postseason play, in which no umpire could work the World Series more than once every four years. The umps working this series were good, just not perceived as the best—and Herzog began complaining about this even before the World Series started. It really didn't matter who was on the field in navy blue, though, because Herzog railed at the umpiring all year long. It started the first week of the season, when his team lost after a reliever was called for a balk with the winning run on third base. Afterward, Herzog complained, "It wasn't a common sense call," as if common sense was supposed to be a factor. That year the Cardinals developed, in Ozzie Smith's words, "a reputation for not getting along with umpires."

In the World Series, the Cards were whining again, trotting out what would become their recurring chant—they weren't getting the breaks from the umpires. Their complaints, though, usually amounted to a lot of hot air. After Game 1, for instance, Herzog blasted the strike zone of the American League's Don Denkinger. That night's pitcher, John Tudor, heard about it and told reporters, "That wasn't the case. I was awful. He called a good game."

Now, with Lonnie Smith still up, Andujar tried to bear down especially hard. They had once been teammates, friends and drug users together, until Smith left and spilled the beans. When Vince Coleman joined the team and proved his worth early in the '85 season, the Cardinals had an outfield logjam. They traded Smith in May. He was heartbroken. The Cardinals were family to him. He thought about quitting. "Lonnie didn't want to go through with the trade," said Ozzie Smith, a friend since Little League. But he had a family to support. So he came to Kansas City. Then he batted just .145 in his first month in the American League. There were whispers about him. He had checked into drug rehab in 1983, suffered an off year in 1984 and was struggling again in '85—was he not as good a player off drugs?

Smith wasn't buying it. In Kansas City, he was simply adjusting to a new league. And in fact, after Hal McRae helped him adjust to more breaking balls and the higher strike zone in the A.L., Smith got back on track and hit .329 in July. He was tough and aggressive, standing over the plate, not giving in to the pitcher. "His approach to hitting helped everybody," said Royals infielder Greg Pryor. But Smith couldn't shake his past. In September, he was one of several major league players called to testify at a drug trial in Pittsburgh. He talked about using cocaine in the Cardinals clubhouse. He talked about doing cocaine with Cardinals teammates. And he named Andujar as one of those teammates.

Andujar didn't appreciate that. He didn't like being smeared in public. He didn't like having his family read about that stuff. And Andujar had a reputation for brushing back hitters he didn't like. Smith knew that. He knew one of Andujar's pitches could be aimed at his head.

But not now, not with the count 2-0 in the hitter's favor and runners on base. Eventually, the count went full. Smith crouched over the plate. He'd been looking for sliders. In came another one, this time over the outer half. Smith lined it to right. Andy Van Slyke dove for the ball. It hit his glove and bounced out, good for two RBIs. It was one of those World Series plays where an inch was the difference between runs and outs. "The Royals finally get a break," Al Michaels declared on TV.

Outside the Pi Kappa Phi house at the University of Missouri, Shawn Link took his turn to erupt, jumping to his feet and high-fiving his fellow Royals fans on their side of the makeshift bleachers. The Cardinals side booed, but their brooms stayed still. One Royals fan went over to the manual scoreboard and put up the first runs on the board.

The Royals got no more in the fourth, though. In the fifth, Brett led off with a single. White stood in the box in a slight crouch, knees bent, gently swaying his hips and hands. His bat had "20," his number, written on the knob with a smiley face inside the 0. He had produced exactly one RBI as the Royals' new cleanup hitter. Andujar set himself on the mound. White always looked for a fastball over the inner half of the plate. Catcher Darrell Porter set up outside, but as the fastball came toward the plate, he moved his glove back toward the middle of the plate. The ball never got to him. Instead, White connected and mashed the ball, the farthest ball he'd ever hit, for the series' first home run. Royals 4, Cardinals 0.

At the Mizzou frat house, Shawn Link jumped to his feet again on the Royals side of the bleachers and slapped hands with his fellow Royals brothers. Another cascade of "boooooos" rang out from the Cardinals side of the dividing line. And soon, the "We're going to sweep you" taunts were replaced by "We'll let you have one game."

Back at Busch, Andujar was yanked. He had allowed more than half of the hitters facing him to reach base. Other St. Louisans weren't buying the umpiring excuse. The *St. Louis Post-Dispatch's* Kevin Horrigan, noting how Cardinals owner Gussie Busch took his traditional pregame wagon ride with the famed Clydedales horses, sat in the press box and wrote of Andujar: "He followed the Budweiser Clydesdales to the mound. They didn't befoul it, but he sure did."

The Royals didn't get another batter on base the rest of the fifth or sixth innings. Royals announcer Fred White told the radio audience, "They're a long way from chalking this one up because the Cardinals have been a great come-from-behind team all year." Sure enough, the Cards mounted a rally in the sixth with back-to-back singles. The stadium organist pounded out the "charge" chant for the first time since the first inning, then trotted out the "Here Comes the King" Budweiser song. Jack Clark responded to the call by delivering a RBI single. With two on and two out, a curveball slipped out of Sabes' fingers—was he losing his grip on this game? Then Pendleton hit a hard liner—but right at Sheridan in right field.

Bret Saberhagen came to the Royals' rescue in Game 3 after being hurt in his previous playoff start. *The Kansas City Star*

Brett responded in the top half of the next inning with a hit that landed on the foul line. The double was taken away, however, after the right field umpire called it foul. Brett returned to the batter's box and produced a single. A couple of hits later and the Royals grew their lead to 6-1. It was a cakewalk the rest of the way. Saberhagen went the distance on a six-hitter.

❀ ❀ ❀ ❀ ❀ ❀

Game 4 began with a sense of deja vu for the Royals—not from Game 3, unfortunately, but from the games before. In the top of the first inning, the Royals got a runner in scoring position only to strand him. Lefty John Tudor was pitching again for the Cardinals. Only this time he didn't throw his first ball until he had two strikes on the cleanup hitter, Frank White, who popped out.

Buddy Black was on the mound for the Royals. His nickname around the clubhouse was "Ace." That's because he was the team's top starter in '84, going 17-12. He started on Opening Day in '85 and had a 5-3 record with a 2.48 ERA in mid-May. Then inexplicably he lost seven straight and went into a tailspin. He tried throwing harder, but his fastball only became straighter while his curve hung longer. Still Dick Howser stayed with him. Pitching coach Gary Blaylock kept telling the manager that Black was *this close* to getting things back on track. Things finally came back at an opportune time, when the Royals and Angels faced off during the last week of the season. Black threw a three-hit shutout, putting the Royals up a game in the standings. He had a hop to his fastball again and a sharp break in his curve. He continued pitching well against Toronto. He was on a roll again.

In the bottom of the first, Ozzie Smith drew a one-out walk. He stretched to a huge lead off first, with both feet on the turf, like he was ready to reenergize the Cardinals' running game. Black promptly picked him off.

In the top of the second, the Royals went down 1-2-3. In the bottom of the inning, Tito Landrum came up for the Cards with one out and the bases empty. "What a postseason he is having," ABC's Al Michaels said on TV. Landrum was the leading hitter in the series with five hits in 11 trips to the plate, spawning signs in the crowd like "General Tito" and "Tito for President." His performance was taking the steam away from the Cards' excuse that their offense wasn't the same without Vince Coleman, who was now out of the series after a freak accident in the playoffs that chipped a bone in his knee.

Michaels told the TV audience during the last game, "They've been able to put the Coleman story kind of in agate type because of what Landrum has done." He was quickly joining some historic figures in the annals of the World Series. A handful of players had taken over for injured stars and more than made up for their absence. In 1913, after the New York Giants' catcher broke a finger in warmups before Game 2, Larry McLean filled in and hit .500 the rest of the series. In 1978, with Yankees second baseman Willie Randolph on the shelf, rookie Brian Doyle filled in, and despite a .192 batting average during the season, he delivered a .438 average in the series.

With Landrum, the Royals' scouting report said keep the ball outside. But those were the only balls Landrum had hit for base hits. And Buddy Black's strength was pitching on the outer half to right-handers. Black decided to stick with his own strength.

He threw Landrum a couple of curves, both outside, followed by a couple of fastballs that hugged the outside corner. On 3-2, he threw another fastball on the outside corner. Landrum dove across the plate and made solid contact. The ball carried on a line, staying up just enough to barely clear the rightfield fence for the Cardinals' first home run in the Series. *Man,* Black thought to himself, *that was a good piece of hitting.*

Halfway across the country, out in the mountains of Montana, a rag-tag cadre of overachieving softball players screamed at the television between swigs of their Olympia and Rainer beers—"Sh--," "F---," "Son of a -----" and anything else their stylistic literary minds could think of that moment. These players in Missoula, with nicknames like Whiplash and Buddha and Loophole, had adopt-

John Tudor made Game 4 an uphill climb for the Royals, putting them in a 3-1 hole in the World Series. *Courtesy of the Kansas City Royals/Chris Vleisides*

ed the Royals in this series. They saw more of themselves in the American Leaguers, with Steve Balboni, who was bald and portly and struggling to hit homers, with Bret Saberhagen, who was having so much trouble growing a respectable mustache, and with their status as an underdog team still clawing for a championship. These softball players had been that way last year—a lightly regarded collection of mostly budding authors from the University of Montana's writing program, guys almost two decades removed from their high school jocks, competing against mostly younger cops and mechanics and fellow tavern-goers, stumbling through a so-so regular season, then catching fire in the league tournament and, in what seemed like the biggest miracle since buffalo rump became tasty, winning the championship. In 1985, then, these ballplayers calling themselves the Montana Review of Books were the team to beat. They started strong, had their best season, but collapsed in the tournament. Soon after, the team was reeling and disintegrating—the catcher's wife left him, the first baseman's live-in girlfriend dumped him, the starting pitcher announced his retirement, the entire outfield had plans to quit, the shortstop was entertaining offers from other teams and the second baseman expected to go overseas for the next season. So when the entire gang gathered to watch the World Series, they realized it might be the last time the championship crew would be together. They sat on couches or stood next to piles and piles of books in their catcher's now-emptier abode, with the curtains drawn and the air a heady mix of cigarette smoke, fresh pizza, spilled beer and lingerings of marijuana. They didn't like the Cardinals—they were too polished and a bit uppity. They didn't like Landrum either—he was too self-assured and well-spoken. So his homer brought on the cascade of catcalls in Montana.

In the top of the third, the Royals went down 1-2-3 again, all on strikeouts. Tudor, with a home plate umpire from the National League, was getting strikes called below the knees and on the outside edges that Andujar wasn't getting the night before.

In the bottom of the third, Willie McGee was up with two outs. Black quickly got ahead 0-2. The Royals scouting reports on McGee said that he would sometimes chase breaking balls low for strike three. But the reports also said McGee was a low breaking-ball hitter. Two pitches later, Black threw a slider down and in. McGee golfed at it. The ball took off, on a line and cleared the left field fence. Another Cardinal homer. The red-clad fans came alive in an instant to chant "M-V-P, M-V-P, M-V-P" as McGee crossed home plate.

That same inning, Ozzie Smith hit a grounder in the hole. Buddy Biancalana took four steps to his right, dove for the ball, popped to his feet and gunned out his shortstop counterpart. Royals announcer Fred White informed those listening in, "he took a hit away from the Wizard himself…with an Ozzie Smith-like play."

In the Cardinals' half of the fourth, first baseman Jack Clark creamed a ball to left that hit the wall on one hop. Outfielder Lonnie Smith—known for making some of the funniest plays possible, like accidentally throwing the ball behind him or running out of a shoe while chasing a ball—played this ball off the carom, set his feet and threw a one-hop strike to second base to nab Clark, who was trying for a double.

These plays pointed up an overlooked aspect to this series: Both teams were accomplished defensively. The Cards led the N.L. in fielding percentage at .983, which was also the best ever in the club's storied history. Meanwhile, half the Royals' regulars were past or soon-to-be Gold Glove winners, with second baseman White and catcher Sundberg among the players who had won the most in history at their positions. So during all four games thus far, a couple of innings couldn't pass without someone producing a sparkling defensive gem.

In Game 1 Cardinals third baseman Terry Pendleton made an over-the-shoulder grab in foul territory, then threw to the plate to save a run. An inning later, McGee hit a ball into the right-center gap, tried to leg it into a triple, but a perfect relay came to third baseman George Brett, who stood by the base nonchalantly and at the last second reached for the ball and tagged out McGee.

In Game 2 McGee hit a chopper up the middle that pitcher Charlie Leibrandt snared before throwing him out. The next batter, second baseman Tommy Herr, hit a two-hopper into the hole between short and third, but Brett took two steps toward it, dived, nabbed it, jumped to his feet and threw him out.

In Game 3 pitcher Bret Saberhagen grounded a ball up the middle, but Ozzie Smith ranged past second base, got to the ball, turned his body back toward the infield and flipped to first. A couple of innings later, Ozzie stroked a sharp grounder into the hole, Brett again took three steps, reached out and gloved the ball after it had passed him and threw Smith out.

The Royals and Cardinals were on their way to setting World Series records for fewest errors and highest fielding percentage by both clubs. This competition was most surprising at shortstop. The Royals' Biancalana was not well known, but fielding was why he was in the majors at all. Yet with each passing game, as he made a hit or drew a walk, the internal pressure and tension he felt to prove himself dissipated. In one game, after ranging left on one play and then right on another play, Biancalana actually cracked a smile on the field and thought, *I can't do anything wrong.* Meanwhile, Ozzie Smith, considered the best fielder in the game, was not at his best. Right before the All-Star break, he was diving back to first base on a pickoff throw and jammed his right shoulder. A doctor told him it was an "impingement," nothing serious. But it hurt, and Smith tried to compensate by throwing more sidearm, and pretty soon he ended up tearing his rotator cuff. No one knew that yet, however. All Smith knew during the World Series was that he couldn't do anything that required reaching forward, like pulling open a door or turning a radio dial. He also couldn't make strong throws.

This would play a factor later in the series. But in Game 4 it didn't matter at all, as Royals hitters were stymied by Tudor. In the fifth, Steve Balboni finally lined a single, ending a stretch of 13 straight batters retired. Tudor looked nothing like the shaky pitcher of Game 1 and more like the dominant pitcher who won 20 of his last 21 decisions during the season. He was someone whose arm action was so consistently similar between his fastball and changeup that the New York Mets instructed their minor-leaguers to watch him during the World Series.

In the bottom of the fifth, the Cardinals manufactured another run, executing a surprise squeeze bunt with two strikes, the kind of key bunt the Royals couldn't put down in Game 1. That made the score 3-0 in the Cards' favor. The sixth inning passed quietly on both sides. In the seventh, the Royals finally posed a threat. With two on and two out, Balboni stepped into the batter's box. "Is he overdue?" ABC's Al Michaels wondered. With Biancalana on deck, Tudor didn't press his luck, throwing three straight balls outside. Whitey Herzog stood in the dugout and stared out at Tudor, wondering why he was pitching around Balboni. Herzog sent pitching coach Mike Roarke to the mound.

"You walk Balboni and they're going to bring up McRae," Roark told Tudor. *Totally forgot about him,* Tudor thought. *I'm in a lot of trouble.*

McRae had blistered Tudor when he had been in the American League. Hit .464 with five homers against him. So the next pitch was a strike. But then a ball way high put Balboni on first, and sure enough, Biancalana turned back to the dugout and out stepped Hal McRae. "It was an almost incredible miscalculation," *The Kansas City Star's* Joe McGuff wrote later.

McRae entered 1985 thinking that maybe "this could be it," the end of his long career. He had lost his full-time designated hitter job the year before, and during the off season, the front office called him in to ask him about becoming a hitting coach. McRae wasn't ready for that. Then he wasn't in the Opening Day lineup for the first time since 1973. In June he was hovering around the embarrassing .200 "Mendoza line." Howser even pinch hit for him. Right then, McRae put his house up for sale, then moved into the Adams Mark Hotel across from the stadium while his post-career dream house was being built in Florida. But later that June, the Royals chose his son Brian in the amateur draft. That was an emotional lift for Hal—if he could stick it out a couple of more years, maybe father and son could play together. He got hot at the plate. After the All-Star break, Howser made him the full-time DH again. McRae responded by hitting nearly .300 the rest of the way, with 46 RBIs in 56 games down the stretch. It was no coincidence the Royals went on their tear toward the division crown with him in the lineup.

This year he was back in the World Series, where he had a .409 career average in 14 games. But he couldn't play—the DH was not used in this series. Actually, he was elated about that. Unbeknownst to the Cardinals or the media, McRae was hurting real bad. He had pulled a muscle on the left side of his rib cage in mid-September and started just three of the season's final 17 games. It was similar to the injury that had kept Sundberg out of the lineup for a month. McRae then willed himself to play against Toronto, but his body shot with pain whenever he swung and missed. He wasn't even taking batting practice. "I wasn't in shape to play," he remembered.

Now against Tudor, he went to the plate thinking, *Go after the first pitch.* With the bases loaded, Tudor was likely to want to get ahead in the count.

Backup infielder Greg Pryor sat on the bench, thinking, *This is our shot.* Relief pitcher Joe Beckwith, who had taken over for Black, sat nearby thinking, *Shit, he could hit a home run and I could win a World Series game.*

Tudor's first pitch dipped low. But McRae swung at it ankle high over the outside corner, trying to pull it. Instead, he hit a weak grounder. One pitch, two hops to Pendleton and three steps to the bag for a force. Another scoring chance lost.

Outside Missouri, in Missoula, the Montana Review of Books softball gang watched this and slowly felt the air being sucked out of their smokes and good time. Many members of their disappointing team, one year removed from a

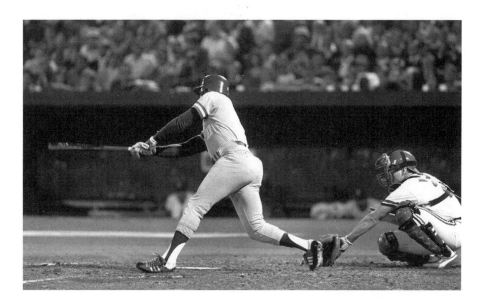

Hal McRae, injured and in pain, swung at the first pitch and tapped out with the bases loaded in the seventh inning, thwarting the Royals' most promising rally in Game 4. *The Kansas City Star*

championship, were headed off in new directions, and the long frigid, insular Montana winter was just around the corner. Rooting for the underdog Royals was the last event of the year keeping them together.

"Each of us felt, knew, that we had come to the end of our string: that we would soon face winter not only as losers ourselves but as backers of losers…a rung lower on the ladder of dreams," one of the players, Bryan Di Salvatore, would soon write in The New Yorker magazine.

The Royals went meekly after that missed chance. Brett struck out swinging wildly at a curve in the eighth, like he didn't have a clue against Tudor. Quisenberry came in to get some work, coughed up two walks and a hit, and looked every bit like the struggling pitcher that Howser wanted to avoid in Game 2. In the ninth, Tudor set down the side in order for the shutout, 3-0.

The Busch Stadium message board flashed Cardinal announcer Jack Buck's trademark saying, "That's a winner." The fans began a chant—"Tu-dor, Tu-dor, Tu-dor"—and it echoed throughout the stadium, carried over the walls and down to Market Street and Broadway Avenue, where gathering multitudes took it and turned it into the opening salvo of a victory celebration, with car horns beeping in a procession around the stadium and fireworks exploding above it. The joy of expectation continued for more than two hours after the last out.

"For the Wearers of the Red," *The Kansas City Times* reported, "ultimate victory surely was only a short 24 hours away." Only four of 35 teams down 3-1 in the World Series had ever come back to win. Not good odds for the Royals.

CHAPTER 6

KANSAS CITY-ST. LOUIS SIBLING RIVALRY

After Game 4, it was looking like St. Louis would get the better of Kansas City. Again.

Throughout the histories of those two cities, that had seemingly always been the case. St. Louis was like the older brother in a family who constantly ridiculed and bullied and outsmarted his sibling as they were growing up. Then in adulthood, even as the little brother grew bigger than him, the older brother still managed to outwit the younger one—and kept picking on him, too.

From the beginnings of both places, St. Louis always seemed a step ahead of Kansas City. St. Louis was founded in 1764 in part by Pierre de Laclede Liguest. Kansas City was established decades later, in 1821 by Francois Chouteau, who was Liguest's grandson and who sprang from French frontier aristocracy headquartered in St. Louis. When Chouteau died, the body of Kansas City's founder was even returned to St. Louis.

Early on in the lives of both places, St. Louis thought it was ordained for greatness. A book published in 1870 hailed the city: *St. Louis, the Future Great City of the World*. Its residents greeted Chicago's tragic 1871 citywide fire as "the inevitable destruction of Missouri's antithesis," wrote Paul C. Nagel in *Missouri: A History*. By the nation's centennial in 1876, St. Louis citizens spoke earnestly about replacing Washington as the nation's capital. Meanwhile, Kansas City struggled to raise money just to pave its roads.

St. Louis did most everything first. St. Louis acquired a big-league baseball team decades before Kansas City. St. Louis reached a half-million in population before Kansas City could dream it. St. Louis became an industrial giant long before Kansas City. St. Louis developed a corrupt boss-system of city government, again years before Kansas City. St. Louis even suffered the pitfalls of urban decay and renewal decades before Kansas City would confront it.

Through this cycle, too, St. Louis was always better at presenting itself and promoting its virtues. St. Louis attracted international attention with its World's Fair in 1904. It included the first Olympics held in the U.S. and the first widespread sales of something new called the ice cream cone. And it endured in the nation's consciousness with a little help later from a Judy Garland song:

> *Meet me in St. Louis, Louis*
> *Meet me at the fair.*
> *Don't tell me the lights are shining*
> *Anywhere but there.*

And the fair occurred even as the city's water was often undrinkable, its smoky air impure and even the cherished Mississippi River filthy. Turn-of-the-century muckraker Lincoln Steffens and other urban critics, according to Missouri author Nagel, "marveled that some St. Louis spokesmen could still boast about their town, despite the ghastly conditions of its jails and hospitals, and the fact that the drinking water seemed to be liquid mud. ...Steffens was simply aghast that St. Louis citizens could not be shamed." At the same time St. Louis was able to hide these faults, Kansas City was crowing about just being able to pave its roads.

A half-century later, in 1954, *Life* magazine ran a 10-page spread of pictures on the two cities. It spotlighted the differences between an eastern-oriented town in St. Louis and a western-oriented one in Kansas City, between a "settled" city and a "striving" one. On the very first pages, one picture showed pinx-coated St Louisans on horseback chasing hounds at a hunt club, while the facing shot was of Kansas Citians, some of them noticeably portly, riding in circles "western-style." This sense of sophisticates vs. bumpkins was the nature of almost all the contrasts shown. The high point of St. Louis's social scene was a ball for "debs," or debutantes. Kansas City's society ball was for "cowgirls." The magazine concluded: "Culturally and socially, St. Louis exhibits its maturity while Kansas City tinges most of its efforts with a self-conscious boosterism."

Then, when St. Louis needed a shot of civic vitality, it proclaimed itself the "Gateway to the West" with a shimmering 630-foot arch designed by Eero Saarinen in the 1960s. Yet, St. Louis had only been the starting-off point for explorers Meriwether Lewis and William Clark. Metro Kansas City had been, according to Josiah Gregg in his 1844 book, *Commerce of the Prairies*, the "gen-

St. Louis's downtown revitalization brought the city lots of national attention during the 1985 World Series. Here, downtown hosted a Cardinals World Series rally. *The Kansas City Star*

eral port of embarkation for every part of the great western and northern 'prairie ocean'"—that is, for the Santa Fe Trail for a route west, for the California trail for the gold rush, plus for the Pony Express mail service just up the road in St. Joseph. So when Kansas City had celebrated its centennial in 1950, city leaders got the Postmaster General to issue a commemorative stamp, which was officially called the "Gateway to the West Midwest Centenary Commemorative Stamp." Years before St. Louis leaders even started building their arch, Kansas City had already been labeled by the federal government the "gateway to the west"—until St. Louis stole the designation.

By the mid-1980s, Kansas City's downtown was in the midst of what some then called "the greatest building boom in Kansas City's history," with a new hotel replacing flop houses on 12th Street and new skyscrapers beginning to rise in the long-neglected loop. St. Louis's downtown was going through a boom, too, with the urban malls of St. Louis Centre and Union Station both opening in 1985. And on the eve of the World Series, St. Louis again was better able to present itself to the nation. *The New York Times* did feature articles on both cities. The article about St. Louis played off the city's new slogan that appeared on Cardinal-red banners around downtown: "What a team! What a town! What a time!" The article on Kansas City played up the tired old "Ev'rythin's up to date" refrain that went back to the broadway show *Oklahoma* four decades before.

❖ ❖ ❖ ❖ ❖ ❖

All this translated into decidedly different civic outlooks. St. Louisans always seemed to relish their history and put a good face on their town. Kansas Citians, meanwhile, always felt embarrassed about the town or its roots—its cowtown heritage, boss Tom Pendergast and the city's former wild ways as a rough and tumble town. Famed expatriated native Calvin Trillin wrote in *The New Yorker* that when reporters covering the 1976 Republican convention in Kansas City were given a list of recommended restaurants, it didn't even include Arthur Bryant's Barbeque. Basically, Kansas Citians tried to put a majestic face on the city—with the American Royal, Crown Center, even the Royals—but they constantly fretted about how they didn't measure up.

It added up to a giant-sized inferiority complex.

And it served as a big scab being picked at during the World Series.

The media jumped on all kinds of comparisons between Kansas City and St. Louis, and in so many ways, KC seemed to come up short. Riverfronts: St. Louis put its to use, while Kansas City left its for an industrial wasteland. Union Stations: St. Louis had renovated its into a hotel and mall, while Kansas City's was on the verge of being boarded up. Even quality-of-life rankings: when *Places Rated Almanac* came out in 1985 with an updated version of its comprehensive rankings of metropolitan areas, which reviewed attributes ranging from climate to the arts, St. Louis made the top 10, at No. 7, while Kansas City fell to an embarrassing 68th.

Kansas Citians stewed. During a party for the national media before the World Series, a chamber of commerce official discreetly complained to an out-of-town journalist, "Our river, the Missouri, is only 33 miles shorter than the Mississippi. But they write all the songs about the Mississippi."

Of course, Kansas Citians tended to overlook the fact that their city already had a St. Louis Centre with Crown Center, or that they had a Mexican food district and St. Louis didn't, or that Kansas City was smarter—it boasted more college graduates than St. Louis. No, Kansas City sports columnist Jonathan Rand observed at the time of the World Series: "When a lot of Kansas Citians think about St. Louis, the chip on their shoulder grows from a toothpick to a redwood."

This insecurity was a wound at which St. Louisans loved to throw salt. So, on the eve of the World Series, *St. Louis Post-Dispatch* sports editor Kevin Horrigan fired a salvo: "People in Kansas City always have been a little bugged about their second-city status. In fact, the whole town suffers from a severe case of what has been called 'rubophobia'—the inordinate fear of being considered rubes." The putdown wasn't original and it wasn't even spelled right. Calvin

Kansas City's Union Station, shown here encircled in fog, was down to its last tenants in the mid-1980s. *Courtesy of author*

Trillin had written in 1976 that Kansas Citians were afflicted with a disease: "rubaphobia—not the fear of rubes but the fear of being thought of as a rube." But neither Trillin nor Horrigan really understood why Kansas Citians felt sensitive about how others viewed their town. *The Kansas City Star's* Bill Tammeus once explained that it had to do with the city's traditional southern-style hospitality and economic interest in welcoming strangers passing through, an interest that went all the way back to the Santa Fe Trail. "It has nothing to do with fear of being considered a rube; it has everything to do with fear of being considered rude," Tammeus quipped.

Still, the acid-tongue zingers against Kansas City, coming from supposed bigger-city erudite, were more like a big brother's hand to the back of his little brother's head.

❊ ❊ ❊ ❊ ❊ ❊ ❊

Really, though, what was going on here?
How in the heck could St. Louisans feel high and mighty about anything?

After all, not only did the Cardinals have baseball's Wizard of Oz, but St. Louis was the modern-day Wizard of Oz city—all bluster and booming voice, until the curtain was opened and the place was exposed for being old and small and meek.

Just look what happened to the city. In 1900, St. Louis was the fourth largest city in the country, behind only New York, Chicago and Philadelphia. It was all downhill from there. By the 1980s, its ranking had tumbled into the 30s, as the city's population was in a staggering free fall, dropping in half from a high of 856,796 in 1950 to a U.S. Census Bureau estimate of 429,295 in 1984. The stain spread to the entire metropolitan area, too, as more people were moving out of metro St. Louis than were moving in.

St. Louis was a city built for the Industrial Age, a macho town known for making beer, cars and fighter jets. Yet its muscles had wilted, and its abandoned factories and rows of vintage smokestacks hulked above the riverfront in a uniform cliff wall of rust and brick. A story in *The Wall Street Journal* earlier in the decade labeled St. Louis a "genuine urban basket case." The U.S. Secretary for Housing and Urban Development had called St. Louis "statistically the most distressed city in the U.S." St. Louis was a wasteland of desolation and abandonment, and it was only getting worse.

Even worse, though, was St. Louisans' posture toward their troubles and downtrodden status. "There was this attitude that this was all a blip in St. Louis's inevitable march to greatness," said Lawrence Larsen, author of *A History of Missouri: Volume VI, 1953 to 2003*. So, the typical approach to problems was often "see no evil, hear no evil, speak no evil." Historically, St. Louis had been tragically myopic—a place where the coal smoke was so thick the city suffered from midnight-at-noon days, yet nothing was done about it for decades. It was a place declared by its own planning commission as an unlivable city in the 1950s, then made worse by planning the nation's largest and worst public housing projects. It was a place characterized as the nation's most distressed large city, and one of the major civic initiatives a few years later was to plant one million flowers. It was a place with the nation's worst population decline, but was deemed by local boosters to be on a roll and revitalized because some buildings were going up downtown. "There was a self-conscious, romantic sense of a grander past that might return," is how James Neal Primm depicted it in his history of St. Louis, *Lion of the Valley*.

St. Louisans were so wrapped up in the past, and snobbish about it, that one of the first questions they asked each other upon meeting was, "Where did you go to high school?"—as if social status as a kid defined them for life and nothing could change it. But that's how they felt about their city, too: once great, always great. It didn't need fixing; heck, the St. Louis Centre and the renovated Union Station both had to be built with out-of-town capital.

Even St. Louis's '80s-era mayor, Vincent Schoemehl Jr., would call St. Louis's pompous attitude of exalting its past and ignoring its present a "morbid fascination with what has become our high-water mark."

If St. Louisans considered Kansas Citians rubes, then Kansas Citians should have considered St. Louisans a bunch of "Arch-y Bunkers"—fixated on the imagery of bygone days to the point of having a bunker mentality toward dealing with the city's chronic distress.

Alas, in 1985 both cities' baseball teams stood as symbols of each town's civic outlook.

For St. Louisans, the baseball Cardinals were one of the only bastions of old St. Louis, of mighty St. Louis, that was still going strong. As Lawrence Larsen explained after researching Missouri over the latter half of the 20th Century: "The Cardinals were more than a baseball team. They were a St. Louis institution that could still beat up on the cities to the east." So the Cardinals team brought out all the age-old prejudices and traditional snobbery in St. Louis fans. Standing in line at Busch Stadium in downtown St. Louis to buy World Series tickets, St. Louisan Stanley Guethle put it this way to a Kansas City newspaper reporter: "Kansas City's boring. It's dull, and the baseball park is blah. Sure, they're all fine folks and all, and I guess it's a nice place, but this is what a big city's supposed to be and Kansas City ain't."

Meanwhile, in Kansas City, the Royals were new and nice, conciliatory and corporate, unflashy and unpretentious, the Hallmark of baseball teams. Kansas Citians, though, were tired of hearing about another "big city" all the time. They got tired of it when it was New York, and the Royals helped the city slay that psychological dragon. Now it was St. Louis, and the city again looked to the Royals to do what civic leaders and the chamber of commerce couldn't—stand up to and outhustle St. Louis.

If only the Royals could act the part of a gentle and submissive little brother who finally had enough of his big brother's bullying and, one day, turned on him, punching him in the face and knocking him down.

Then the family dynamic within the state of Missouri would be altered irreparably.

CHAPTER 7

GAME 5:

"GOT 'EM RIGHT WHERE WE WANT 'EM"

A little after 3 p.m. on October 24, a cadre of Royals players started making the walk to Busch Stadium from the team's hotel across the street. On the sidewalks along the way, Cardinals fans without tickets were already setting up camps with blankets and portable TVs. Souvenir vendors were already out, too, displaying their newest wares. White and red t-shirts with the Cardinals logo and "1985 World Series Champions" emblazoned across the chest. Ball caps with "World Champs" on the front. Red pennants with "1985 World Champions" scripted across them. The Royals players walked by, snickering, silently poking each other to look at yet another sign of St. Louis's smugness.

Then they arrived in their clubhouse and found workmen setting up portable lights and platforms and TV monitors—for postgame interviews with the series loser. Willie Wilson looked at the men and bellowed out, "You might as well stop that right now. You're not going to need that tonight." Soon the players started having a little fun with the setup. They flicked the TV lights on and off. They pretended to give postgame comments—as if they had won the game: "Sorry to spoil your party, St. Louis." They were a feisty bunch.

It was a continuation of the mood set the night before, after the Game 4 loss. Brett walked into the clubhouse and, still in his uniform, shouted out at his teammates: "We've got 'em right where we want 'em. Everybody can jump on my back, because we're gonna do it. We're coming back."

Souvenir vendors outside Busch Stadium were banking on the Cardinals closing out the series in Game 5. World Champion t-shirts, like the one above, and pennants were hot items. *Courtesy of Stu Lewis*

One of the Royals' young pitchers, Mark Gubicza, sat at his locker, staring at Brett, thinking, *Is he crazy? We were fortunate enough to come back against Toronto. But again?* Gubicza thought about it some more. And thought about it some more. And strangely, despite his doubts, he felt better, like he had gotten reassurance from a parent.

Meanwhile, a flock of reporters had gathered around McRae, seeking his insights into his pinch-hit ground out about his team's prospects. He worked a little reverse psychology. "Let me tell you this," he told them. "There will be a lot of pressure on St. Louis to win tonight. They don't want to blow it now." He only partly believed this. He really just wanted to keep up his teammates' spirits so they wouldn't get spooked over their predicament.

But it was an attitude that harkened back to the Toronto playoff series. At that time, after the Blue Jays had taken a similar 3-1 lead in games, Brett had sat at his locker, answering the obligatory questions about the Royals having their backs against the wall, and suddenly he proclaimed, "The pressure is all on Toronto. No one ever picked us to win anything, anyway." He didn't know why he said it. It just came out. He even laughed as he said it. But the media ran with it. They ran to Toronto players and started asking them if the pressure was on them to win one more. Then with each subsequent loss, the Blue Jay players had to answer that question again and again. And Brett's statement, coming from the star of the team, seemed to have a calming effect on his teammates.

So with the team facing the same hole during the World Series, Brett fell back on the same approach. He drummed up another confidence booster: "We've got 'em right where we want 'em." Then, the next afternoon he continued to beat the drum. Out on the field during batting practice before Game 5, Brett stood behind the batting cage as some of the other regulars took their cuts. *Whack* went a teammate's bat on a batting-practice pitch.

"All right, we got 'em right where we want 'em, us down 3-1," Brett called out.

Whack went another pitch.

"Got 'em eating out of the palm of our hands."

Whack.

"Here it is, guys, come'n get it..."

Whack.

"Birdseed."

And everyone laughed.

⁂ ⁂ ⁂ ⁂ ⁂ ⁂

Back in Kansas City, some of the Sisters of St. Pius High School gathered around the only television in their convent to root on their Royals—with prayer.

Their ringleader was Sister Mary Sharon Verbeck, a tomboy in a family of eight Catholics. She had organized outings to Royals games ever since the team's first year in the league. For most games, though, they listened on the radio or watched on their little 19-inch television in their shared living room. In the spirit of the World Series, they decorated the convent's front door with a "Go Royals" sign. This evening, there were five of them, most dressed in their long black "habit" outfits with black veils, but Verbeck was in a Royals sweatshirt and blue jeans with her shoes off. By game time, she had lit a blue candle in the chapel and repeated her Hail Marys for the Royals.

Her boys immediately established a new tone in the first inning. Lonnie Smith fouled off four pitches in between three balls before finally singling on veteran righty Bob Forsch's eighth pitch—about as many as Tudor had thrown in one inning the night before. Wilson followed with a single. Two on, no one out and Brett up—just what the Royals always wanted.

Forsch was a battler, though. He was old school. He came up in 1974, steeped in the "Cardinal Way" of doing things. Bob Gibson was still around, and Forsch even learned to walk to the mound the "Cardinal Way"—firm, brisk and commanding, not loosey-goosey and slouching. By 1985, Forsch had won 20 games in a season, thrown two no-hitters and led his team in victories five times. But the solid six-foot four-inch 35-year-old was nearing the end of his career. He'd been hurt during much of the past two seasons. He'd gone from being the Cards' top starter to their fourth. In this game, he was really an emergency starter because Herzog wanted to give Danny Cox's aching arm an extra day of rest.

Forsch went into the stretch position, extended his long right arm way behind him, then whipped it around while balanced on his straight left leg. Brett hit the ball hard to left-center, but it was catchable. Smith and Wilson both aggressively moved up a base. Frank White stepped into the box. He got ahead in the count 2-0, took a fastball down the middle, then took a slider outside, not that close to the plate, and home plate umpire John Shulock of the American League called it a ball. Forsch stepped forward a couple extra steps after his follow-through, scowled and slammed his right fist into his glove. On the next pitch, White hit a grounder and Smith came home to score. It was the first time the Royals had scored in the first inning in the Series. Pat Sheridan, up again with a runner in scoring position, struck out to end the inning.

The Cardinals came right back in the bottom of the first. Royals starter Danny Jackson retired the first two batters, then back-to-back hard-hit doubles tied the game. Tito Landrum, the Cards' hitting hero so far, who was hitting .571 with runners on base in the postseason, stepped to the plate. He was a favorite with the ladies because, as a part-time model, he posed shirtless for a charity poster, which then became a hot item. The red-clad St. Louis fans start chanting "Tito, Tito, Tito." Back in the St. Pius convent in Kansas City, Sister Verbeck, a small woman with a round face and small round glasses, sat on the floor and repeated over and over, in a Rosary-like chant, "Blessed mother, help my team. Blessed mother, help my team." Landrum fouled off the first three pitches, then fouled out to Steve Balboni by first base.

Maybe some breaks were starting to turn the Royals' way. In the second, Jim Sundberg lined a ball to left. Landrum misread it, started sideways, then rushed straight forward and slid for it as the ball bounced in front and then past him for a double. "So Tito is human," ABC's Al Michaels told viewers. Buddy Biancalana fought and fouled off one, two, three pitches, took a ball that Forsch scowled about again, then hit a grounder between first and second, into right field. Sundberg got a good jump off second, rounded third and saw catcher Tom Nieto setting up by the third-base line for the throw. So Sundberg stayed wide of the base line and dove headfirst toward the back of the plate. Nieto twisted around with the ball and applied the tag. But Sundberg didn't feel the tag. *He didn't get me*, he thought. He was safe, a little redemption for his out at home during Game 1. The fans' crescendo of "aaaaahhhhhs" toward the apparent out turned immediately to "ooooohhhhhs."

Nieto threw down his mask. Forsch ran toward the homeplate umpire waving his arms. Manager Whitey Herzog came out yelling. Meanwhile up in ABC's TV booth, the announcers watched the replay. "It doesn't look to me like (Nieto) touched him until he was on the plate," Tim McCarver observed.

A strikeout and a walk put two on with two out and Wilson up, with another chance for his own redemption.

The stain of his past troubles still followed him. He was appearing in anti-drug TV and radio commercials during this series. But the Willie Wilson who came to bat then was a changed man from the Willie Wilson who spiraled into drug use after his dismal 1980 World Series. He used to come to the ballpark mad. He couldn't play unless he was teed off at somebody. And in the clubhouse, he was morose and angry and so sensitive that when McRae would needle him in the clubhouse he'd explode and shout, "Don't ever speak to me again."

Then prison changed him. "I learned a lot about myself…how to deal with my emotions," he once explained. He knew if he yelled at umpires, people would think he was on drugs. So now he was a looser, happier, more fun-loving Willie. Before this game, even with the Royals one loss from elimination, he had come to the park in a buoyant mood. He had teased the men setting up the television platforms in the clubhouse. He had teased Lonnie Smith about how small his shoes were. And when his name was called during pregame introductions, he had started up the dugout steps, turned to one of the television cameramen and declared, "We're going to shock the house," before doing a little dance step on the top step and heading onto the field.

Wilson felt good, and why not—he was hitting .353 in the World Series coming into this game and had gotten another hit his first time up. He was vanquishing his personal demons from 1980. And he was doing it after such an awful season for him. He had separated from his wife. He was living in the hotel across from Royals Stadium. He had received a penicillin shot from the Texas team doctor in early September and suffered an allergic reaction. His left buttock swelled and required surgery to relieve the pain. He lost a couple weeks of playing time, came back too soon in trying to help the team during its stretch run, and his batting average plummeted. He hit .225 over the last three weeks of the season. Manager Dick Howser dropped him out of the leadoff spot for the first time since 1979. He ended up batting .278 for the year, only the second time in seven years he was under .300. It just wasn't his year.

Through it all, though, Wilson actually was feeling more confident at the plate. He was a natural right-handed hitter, and the Royals had taught him to switch-hit in the minor leagues, to make better use of his speed. But he mostly slapped at the ball from the left side, just to make contact. He even used a lighter bat swinging lefty. However, by late in 1984, his seventh full season, he finally felt he could drive the ball left-handed. He switched to the heavier bat for that

By the end of Game 5, Willie Wilson's hitting and hustle were vanquishing the ghosts of his 1980 World Series performance. *Courtesy of the Kansas City Royals/Chris Vleisides*

side. During '85, he hit a career-high 21 triples into the outfield gaps. For the World Series, though, the Cardinals' scouting report still recommended playing the outfield in on him.

At this moment in Game 5, Wilson stood in the left-handed batters' box holding that heavier, 34-inch, 32-ounce bat—the same size Jack Clark used. Wilson laid off the first pitch from Forsch, a ball. Nieto went to the mound, stalling for time while a reliever warmed up. On the Royals radio broadcast, announcer Denny Matthews predicted, "Forsch, quite likely, is down to his last batter." The next delivery was a fastball over the middle. Wilson lashed it into the right-centerfield gap. The ball rolled all the way to the wall, a triple that scored two runners.

At the St. Pius convent in Kansas City, the nuns shrieked and jumped to their feet. Sister Verbeck yelled out, "Praise be to God," and clapped her hands.

The Cards brought in a lefty reliever, and Brett grounded out to end the inning. But the score was 4-1 Royals and the noise level at Busch Stadium sank to a church murmur. Still, the lead was by no means comfortable. In fact, after the Cards went in order in the second, they loaded the bases with two out in the third on a single and a couple of walks. Fred White reminded listeners on the Royals radio broadcast that even though it was still early in the game, this was "a big, big moment." Pitching coach and pseudo-psychologist Gary Blaylock headed to the mound to talk things over with Jackson.

Jackson was having trouble controlling his stuff again. It was his curse. He'd always been a top prospect. In '82, he compiled a 17-3 record in a couple levels of the minors. In '83, *Sport* magazine projected him as the Rookie of the Year. When that didn't happen, *Sports Illustrated* came right back and named him the top phenom of '84. But he only went 2-6 that year. He had a tailing fastball that moved in toward left-handed hitters, a cut fastball that moved in on right-handed batters and a slider that broke half the width of the plate. His balls moved so much that Royals catchers simply crouched behind the center of the plate. If they set up on one of the corners, the pitch was liable to end up two feet outside.

For much of the '85 season, Jackson was up and down some more. He started the year with $19^{1}/3$ scoreless innings. In September, when the team needed him in the pennant race, he went 1-4 with a 5.14 ERA. It was eating at him. He was trapped, a perfectionist in an imperfect craft. He had expected himself to be the best pitcher in baseball. He had expected to win 30 games a year, no matter how unrealistic that was. By this point of the season, though, he was merely desperate to turn himself around. He thought back to 1982. Back then he had loved the song "Eye of the Tiger" by the rock group Survivor. He had played it constantly. So at the end of the '85 season when it was his turn to pitch in the showdown series against California, he pulled out his "Eye of the Tiger" tape again. He played it at home. He played it on the way to the ballpark. He played it on his headphones in the clubhouse for hours before the game. Play and rewind. Play and rewind. Over and over while closing his eyes and visualizing his fluid delivery. Then he allowed just one run in eight and two-thirds innings, giving the Royals a one-game lead in the division race.

So he kept up that routine before a shutout in Game 5 against Toronto, the close loss in Game 1 of the series and then this game. He had a kind of football player's mentality toward playing—intense and emotional. But Howser and Blaylock thought he got too intense and uptight. They constantly talked to him about showing less emotion on the field, about not getting so upset when he missed with a pitch or a teammate made an error. Sometimes Blaylock went to the mound just to let Jackson calm down and regroup. And that's what Blaylock was doing now. Jackson had just thrown four straight balls to Jack Clark.

"We only need one out," Blaylock told Jackson.

Jackson nodded.

"Let your stuff work," Blaylock continued.

Jackson nodded.

"Let's pound him in," Blaylock went on.

Jackson nodded again.

Landrum was at the plate. The fans kicked up their "Tito, Tito, Tito" chant. The Royals had mostly kept the ball away from Landrum, but he was expecting sliders inside now because that's how Jackson pitched him in Game 1. Landrum stood at the plate slightly bent at the knees and slightly bent forward, pointing his bat toward the pitcher. As soon as Jackson started bringing both his hands over his head in his windup, Landrum cocked the bat behind him. He was a first-ball hitter. Jackson turned his body close to 180 degrees, tucked his right knee up to his belt, stretched his left arm way behind him, thrust his right foot way out forward and then, as he released the ball, bent his torso over that front leg until his body was horizontal. The first pitch came in, Landrum swung and hit it off his foot. Landrum walked around outside the batter's box, pissed at himself. That was his pitch, and he missed it. The stadium organ started up the Budweiser song. Jackson's next delivery was a ball high. "That pitch was up and that's scary," Royals broadcaster Fred White announced.

Next pitch, a foul. Then another foul. Then, yet another foul; but this time it was catchable behind third base, and Brett secured it. Inning over.

At the St. Pius convent, the nuns, holding their hands clasped like in prayer, burst into clapping and shrieks of joy. One blurted out, "Praise God." Sister Verbeck thought to herself, *The Lord is listening to us.*

The Royals got more chances in the fourth. With two runners on, Wilson struck out on a pitch in the dirt. With the bases loaded, White struck out on a changeup. That would be their last threat for a while, as Cardinals relievers began mowing them down. In the sixth, Todd Worrell entered the game for the Cardinals. He was their late-season call-up, just a couple of years removed from a bible college in Los Angeles. He didn't become a reliever until halfway through '85, but quickly became the Cardinals' stopper in September. He pitched two innings in Game 1 without striking out a batter. But on this night his ball was moving. Three straight Royals went down swinging in the sixth. In the seventh, Wilson continued the string, Brett swung wildly at strike three and even lost his grip on the bat, then White K'd on three pitches. Worrell tied a World Series record with the six straight strikeouts.

But the Cards hitters couldn't capitalize on Worrell's success. Jackson had settled down, too. He'd settled into a comfortable rhythm, and in the seventh Jackson struck out the side himself. During one at-bat, a pop-up was hit toward the Royals dugout by third base. Brett ran to it full speed, went into a slide—forgetting it was still turf there and not the rubber warning track in Kansas City that slowed down such slides—and skipped right into the dugout and down the steep steps like a rodeo rider, with his feet up and right hand out behind him. Fortunately, hitting coach Lee May was right there at the bottom of the stairs to catch the fall. Brett missed the ball, but the hustle play keyed up his teammates. An inning later, Ozzie Smith smashed a drive over Wilson's head in center. Wilson turned and sprinted, back, back, back, reaching up with his glove over

Tito Landrum was the World Series hitting star so far and more than making up for Vince Coleman's absence. But starting in Game 5, Danny Jackson and Royals pitchers handcuffed Landrum. *Courtesy of the Kansas City Royals/Chris Vleisides*

his right shoulder to haul in the ball. "Remember '54?" ABC's Al Michaels called out excitedly, referring to Willie Mays's famous World Series catch.

In the Royals' eighth, with two on and two out, Jackson hit a bouncer up the middle. Ozzie Smith got to it as usual, turned and threw across his body. The throw went into the dirt and off Clark's glove. A run scored on Smith's throwing error—"If you can believe that," Al Michaels said on television. In the ninth, the Royals tacked on another insurance run, with Sheridan finally getting a hold of one for an RBI double.

The Cards then mounted one last rally, getting two on with two out. Howser stayed with his starter. Sundberg went to the mound and convinced Jackson to take a deep breath. Two pitches later Jackson coerced a ground ball out to end the game.

At the St. Pius convent, Sister Verbeck exclaimed, "Thanks Be to God." On the radio, Denny Matthews told Kansas City listeners, "There will be no celebration in St. Louis tonight."

✻ ✻ ✻ ✻ ✻ ✻ ✻

How true that was.

Ten minutes of fireworks, set up on the tops of two garages near the stadium, stayed in their boxes. Extra police officers outside the stadium on horseback had no wild revelry to control. "1985 World Champions" t-shirts were slashed in price—"We thought we had made a reasonably secure investment," one souvenir vendor whined. The next day's victory parade, which had been promoted on television before the game, was cancelled. And mock-up front pages, declaring "We Showed Them!" and "World Champs," sat unused.

Meanwhile, at this point in the World Series it was becoming apparent that the Cardinals didn't seem to be enjoying themselves.

Before Game 1, Vince Coleman had snapped at the media after being told that his manager doubted that Coleman would play. "I'm playing," Coleman announced. "You got any more questions, I got an answer: 'Talk to me tomorrow.'" Of course Coleman didn't play. After Game 3, Herzog and Joaquin Andujar had jawed about the umpiring, with Herzog making the ludicrous accusation that Saberhagen's strike zone was a foot wider than Andujar's. Andujar stated: "Hey, everything was working for me tonight but the umpire." After Game 4, Tudor, so graceful and disciplined on the mound, turned graceless and sullen off it. Angered that the media wanted too much of his time and asked too many repetitive questions, Tudor labeled one writer "a shmoo" and called another "dead meat." When one reporter asked why he was acting this way, Tudor fired back, "You want me to swing at you?"—and this was after Tudor had thrown a shutout.

Then before Game 5, the next game's starting pitcher, Danny Cox, didn't show for a mandatory interview session. He stayed holed up in his hotel room, with a "Do Not Disturb" sign on his door. Terry Pendleton went in Cox's place and explained the Cards had become upset at the end of the season because they felt they hadn't gotten much acclaim. Even in their hometown newspapers, Pendleton said, "it was 'Mets lose' across the top of the page and in the bottom corner, 'Cards win'"—which prompted one *Post-Dispatch* writer to quip, "Maybe the Cardinals read their hometown newspapers upside down."

Sports Illustrated simply observed, "The Cardinals seemed to have hauled a collective, paranoid chip on the shoulder into this Series." Tommy Herr remembered: "We just had that air about us that we were on our own."

Now after Game 5, the Cards had to face the "Are you feeling pressure?" and "What's going wrong?" questions. This kept them in a surly mood. Herzog started resorting to the "We miss Coleman" excuse—even with Landrum leading the team in hitting. Never mind the Cardinals had been down 0-2 against Los Angeles when Coleman got hurt and then managed to win four straight without him. Some Cards players weren't even buying the Coleman excuse. After all, the Cards went just 22-18 in the first 40 games after he was called up, a period when he stole 36 bases—making him hardly the difference-maker that Cardinals partisans thought him to be. In fact, one player noted, "We'll never know whether he would have had a good series or whether he would have had trouble against their guys, too. He might have."

So the Cardinals were a grumpy lot who never seemed to loosen up or rinse out the tension from their systems. By contrast, the 1982 Cardinals had been a jovial group and felt like a family. "Every day, it was like being in Pee Wee's playhouse," recalled then-Cardinal Lonnie Smith. So in the '82 World Series, the Cardinals were on their flight home following Game 5, down 3-2 in games after Forsch had lost for the second time. Out of nowhere, pitcher Bruce Sutter called out, "Party at the Forsch's house." Forsch tried to get out of it. But Sutter walked down the aisle telling everyone, "Party at the Forschs'." The plane landed, and the party started about 9 p.m. It went into the wee hours of their off-day. Some of the players didn't show up for the optional practice that afternoon. They had "bad heads," in the words of one. But the team romped in the next game and came back to win Game 7 that year.

In 1985, the Cardinals didn't have such a close-knit clubhouse. They didn't do much together outside the ballpark. And Sutter was gone. Plus, in the World Series, they were ahead and traveling to Kansas City after Game 5. They had no party. They couldn't ride the porcelain bus to glory again.

CHAPTER 8

THE ROYALS' RESILIENCY

Game 5 served as the latest reminder of the Royals' remarkable resiliency. They had been coming back from the dead for months. There was always a standing joke in the organization that if there was a harder way to do something, the Royals would find it, and that was certainly true for 1985.

At the mid-point of the season, the Royals were 41-41. At the All-Star break, they were seven and a half games behind the California Angels. The trend in baseball then was that division winners seldom repeated the following season, and the Royals looked like they would fit right in. But the team was known for second-half surges, and immediately got started, winning seven in a row in late July to pull to within two and a half games by the end of that month. After that they careened on a series of roller-coaster streaks. They lost three in a row going into the players strike that August, but came out of the strike winning 11 of their first 15, then sputtered some more, getting swept by the last-place Texas Rangers.

At the beginning of September, some strange things began happening. A Chicago White Sox outfielder camped under a lazy fly in extra innings, and the ball dropped at his side, allowing the winning run to score. Omar Moreno, an outfielder released by the Yankees and signed by the Royals after Willie Wilson got hurt, hit an inside-the-park homer in his first Kansas City at-bat and proceeded to bat over .500 his first week. Steve Balboni hit a towering shot that was floating 15 feet foul when a gust of wind pushed the ball back across the foul line for a game-winning homer. And the Royals, after taking two out of three games against the Angels, found themselves up by two and a half games.

But the Mr. Hyde side of their split personality emerged again. The Royals went through a 30-inning stretch without scoring a run. They lost nine of 13 games. They dropped out of first place. "They look dead, real dead," Minnesota first baseman Kent Hrbek remarked. And he said that the day before a last-week-of-the-season, four-game showdown series with the first-place Angels.

In the first game, Bret Saberhagen pitched a complete-game five-hitter, capping it with three straight called strikes on Reggie Jackson, for a 3-1 win and a tie for first place. In the second game, Angels pitching shut down the Royals, 4-2. In the third game, manager Dick Howser gave the starting nod to the struggling Bud Black, and Black responded with a three-hit shutout for a 4-0 victory. Then, in the fourth game, Danny Jackson corralled the Angels, 4-1, behind a three-homer barrage. "I didn't think they could do it, but they did it," Angels manager Gene Mauch said afterward. Two nights later, the Royals—having never overcome more than a three-run deficit all season—rallied from four runs down against the Oakland A's to clinch the division.

Baseball analyst Bill James later determined the Royals had a chameleon-like quality, playing up or down to the quality of their competition. From July 19 through the end of the season, the Royals played 32 games against teams that finished the season with winning records, and won 23 of those games. That's a .719 winning percentage against the best, showing they had a propensity to get up for big games.

Then the playoffs started with the Royals in a slumping funk again. In Game 1, they were simply flat, getting just three hits through eight innings, while Charlie Leibrandt got rocked. In Game 2, they made several uncharacteristic blunders—all of Toronto's runs scored with the help of three errors, a hit batter, a wild pitch and a misplayed ground ball. In Game 3, Brett willed the Royals to victory with a box-score line that read—4 4 4 3—but even he needed a single from Steve Balboni to score the winning run. In Game 4, lefty-hitting Al Oliver knocked in the winning run against Royals right-handed reliever Dan Quisenberry for the second time in three games. In Game 5, Danny Jackson kept the Royals alive with a shaky 2-0 shutout. In Game 6 Howser set his pitching trap against Toronto's platoon-laden lineup, starting a righty, bringing in a lefty reliever, then having Quisenberry finish up. Blue Jay starter Doyle Alexander, who had given up Brett's two homers earlier in the series, challenged him again—and Brett hit a tie-breaking homer.

In the seventh game, with two on and two out in the sixth inning, Jim Sundberg stepped into the on-deck circle. After the first pitch to Balboni, who was batting, Sundberg heard a loud voice in his head: "This is the time. Get ready. The bases are going to be loaded." The voice was so loud, Sundberg looked behind him to see if someone was talking to him. Sure enough, Balboni walked. Immediately, Sundberg heard the voice again: "This is the moment." His at-bat unfolded in slow motion as it happened—seeing from pitcher Dave Stieb's

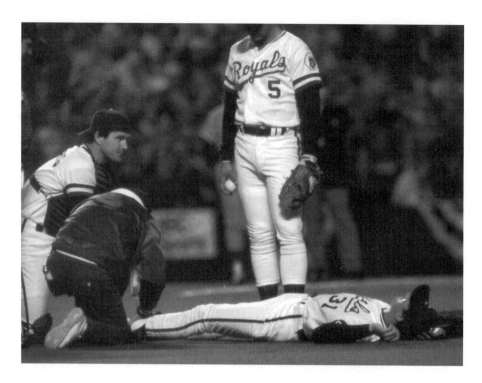

In the 1985 A.L. Championship Series, Bret Saberhagen and the Royals found themselves flat on their backs after falling behind 3-1 to the Blue Jays. *Courtesy of the Kansas City Royals/Chris Vleisides*

motion that the second pitch was going to be a fastball, lining it to the opposite field, seeing it carry, carry and finally hit the top of the right-field fence for a bases-clearing triple. The Royals lead was insurmountable, and the pennant was theirs.

Now in the World Series, the Royals refused to roll over again, despite losing a heartbreaker in Game 2, despite being a game away from elimination, despite St. Louis's home-field advantage. It prompted one out-of-town sportswriter to declare: "This is getting amazing, if not just plain ridiculous." There had to be something about this team—composure, leadership, something—that kept them under control and not pressing in tough times.

What made this team so special?

❖ ❖ ❖ ❖ ❖ ❖ ❖

There is no simple recipe for creating a championship team. The '85 Royals emerged as a tasty stew only after years of experimentation had eliminated several ingredients from the broth.

Throughout the early 1980s, the front office had felt the team, with its core of stars at several positions, was merely a few players away from a return trip to the World Series. But the franchise had floundered in its attempts to find those complementary players. The team tried dipping into the free agent market, sometimes making the highest bids for big names like Pete Rose, Tommy John, Floyd Bannister and Rick Sutcliffe, only to be spurned. As a result, the franchise made some desperate moves for beat-up veteran pitchers like Vida Blue and Gaylord Perry and Steve Renko. When Avron Fogelman bought a minority interest in the team in 1983, "there was a feeling," he recalled later, "that pretty much we had done it, that (1980) was all we could do, that was it."

But the front office methodically got rid of its rotted vegetables and brought in some fresh ones, picked off the farm—the farm system, that is. The Royals had always been pretty careful with the amateur draft. Joe Burke, the 1970s-era general manager, once said: "I'm a strong believer in chemistry. I feel it's better to have 75 percent talent and the right chemistry than 100 percent with the wrong blend." So the team evaluated prospects based on a system passed down from the successful Reds and Orioles franchises—considering the "whole pie" when looking at a player. The top half of the pie was the physical talent. The bottom half was the player intangibles—character, desire, poise and the emotional qualities that would enable him to blend in with teammates and bounce back from the constant challenges of baseball, where three successes in 10 tries at the plate was considered exceptional.

In 1984, the young starting pitchers joined the big league club. The team still had a few gaps to fill, but this time it targeted opportunities, not players. Steve Balboni was a power-hitting legend in the minor leagues who couldn't crack the Yankees lineup and was running out of options. The Royals, needing a power hitter, snapped him up. Lonnie Smith was a proven hitter who became the odd man out in the Cardinals outfield. The Royals, desiring an offensive spark, snapped him up. Jim Sundberg had demanded a trade from Milwaukee but turned down deals to a couple of interested teams. The Royals, wanting a veteran to handle their kid pitchers, snapped him up.

The '85 Royals, then, ended up being a jumbled mix of youngsters and veterans. Most of the younger players had come up through the minor leagues together. The veterans, meanwhile, had progressed past the drug scandal and had been teammates for years now. Between the two groups, there were outgoing flakes and quiet personalities. There were star players who didn't act like prima donnas and subs who accepted their reserve roles. This entire mix ended up blending in a way no one could have predicted.

The locker room in Royals Stadium was shaped in a rectangle, with seven-feet-tall, three-feet-wide dark-wood cubicles lining all four walls. Closest to the entrance were the lockers of Brett, Black, McRae and Balboni. Facing them along the opposite wall were Leibrandt, Gubicza, Sheridan and Biancalana, among others. On one side, White and Wilson occupied one corner. Across the

Hal McRae was the spiritual leader of the '85 Royals. He was convinced that they had more fight in them than previous Royals teams. *Courtesy of the Kansas City Royals/Chris Vleisides*

room, Quisenberry held court in another corner. The room was full of needling—often playful, sometimes pointed.

Quis and Jamie Quirk devised nicknames for everybody. Danny Jackson was "Jason" after the horror movie character because of his explosive temper. Leibrandt was "Rembrandt" because he painted the corners with his pitches, and so on.

McRae was the club's conscience and chief instigator. When Balboni reached 100 strikeouts, McRae had a clubhouse boy set up a silver bucket at the slugger's locker with a bottle of Dom Perignon. Then McRae ribbed the quiet Balboni for not sharing the bubbly with him. Sometimes, if a player was complaining about being hurt, McRae would hide under the towels in one of the oversized laundry baskets, then have somebody roll the basket toward the hurt player's locker. McRae would jump up with a thin fungo bat, hold the bat like a gun and pretend to shoot the complaining player, yelling, "You're no use to us. You're no use to us." The subtle message: play and contribute.

Even the stars weren't immune. That August, as Kansas City's summer heat began draining players of their energy, Brett asked trainers Mickey Cobb and

Paul McGannon what he could do to kick start his body before games. They decided an ice bath would do the trick, just like football players get during training camps. So during batting practice the rest of the summer, the trainers drained the team's mammoth whirlpool—nicknamed the Queen Mary—and filled it with ice water. Then, between batting practice and the game, Brett got in. At first, he only stood, numbing his legs. Eventually, though, he got all the way in, even using a snorkel so he could totally submerge himself. This, of course, brought plenty of hoots from his teammates, who showed up in the trainers room for the rare opportunity to rag on their star. "What, you need to sober up again?" someone invariably joked with him.

At its core, though, this team was very close—"It was a big family," McGannon remembered. Players did a lot of things together. Much of the team participated in gambling pools set up by Leibrandt or Black each week on horse races, car races, golf tournaments, anything. A bunch of guys pored over stock market tables and quizzed each other on what hot investment tips they had heard. On the road, sometimes half the team would get to the ballpark several hours early, strip to their long underwear and t-shirts and play cards, from clubs to bridge, three tables going at once, with players switching partners. "It brought a lot of guys together," Brett recalled. Most of the players even grew mustaches, an unplanned sign of solidarity—"It was a team thing," relief pitcher Joe Beckwith related. And the team went out a lot together as one, instead of breaking off into several different cliques. At home, if someone's kid was having a birthday party and the team was invited, just about everyone showed up. After road games, guys would get dressed and ask around the clubhouse, "What time are we going to lunch?" During the World Series, after the Royals arrived in St. Louis, almost half the players and their wives—about 25 people in all—went to the Hill section for an Italian dinner.

"It was an unusual team," Balboni recollected. "It was different than any team I ever played on."

No animosities, no jealousies, no distractions.

❉ ❉ ❉ ❉ ❉ ❉ ❉

In baseball, chemistry is a word that gets thrown around a lot, but it remains a mysterious concept. On the one hand, baseball executives like John Schuerholz, the Royals' general manager during the early 1980s before rebuilding the Atlanta Braves during the '90s, consciously constructed teams based on character. "I can't quantify it statistically, but it's very important," Schuerholz said. On the other hand, there's no evidence that happy teams win more games than grumpy ones; some tension-filled squads even performed quite well, like the pennant-winning A's and Yankees in the '70s.

Nevertheless, some teams feed off their chemistry. Consider the 1959 Go-Go Chicago White Sox, one of the few teams to trip up the Yankee dynasty of the 1950s. Those Sox had future Hall of Famers like Early Wynn, Luis Aparicio and Nellie Fox. But the Sox had more than talent. Outfielder Jim Landis recalled once: "It was a good blend of young and old. …The best part of it—and I've always said this was a big part of our winning—was we got along so well. Maybe seven to 10 guys [would] go out and have a bite to eat together on the road. Just relax and enjoy each other. And even when we were at home, four or five couples would go out for dinner together. There was great unity."

On the opposite end, some teams are notorious for not having that. Of the Boston Red Sox teams of the 1970s, it was said that when the team plane landed, the players quickly dispersed on their own—"25 players, 25 cabs." Of the Angels teams of the early '80s—squads filled with big-name veterans like Reggie Jackson, Rod Carew, Bobby Grich, Doug DeCinces, George Hendrick, John Candelaria and Don Sutton—George Brett once said: "They never win the big games. They've got the big stars, but they can't win the big games."

So how does chemistry translate into winning?

Certainly, it's teammates pulling for each other, encouraging each other, and playing smart, fundamental baseball that puts the team's goals first. For example, in Game 5 of the playoffs, right before the first pitch, Brett ambled to the mound to speak to one of his buddies on the team, starting pitcher Mark Gubicza. Gubicza was known for a granite-faced demeanor. "Now give me a smile," Brett teased. And the tension of starting an important game evaporated.

Yet, the Royals' teams of the '70s were tight-knit, too, and it didn't get them over the hump. In fact, after three straight playoffs, Yankee third-baseman Graig Nettles observed about the Royals: "They try harder to beat us. Therefore, they don't play as well. We're a little bit looser. Sometimes, when you try too hard, things don't go your way."

Likewise, after the Royals finally reached the World Series in 1980, the pressure ate them up. They had leads in five of the six games. In the last five games, they batted .340 with the bases empty and .191 with runners in scoring position. Mere coincidence? One team official said at the time: "We're so tight we squeak." In his book *Seasons in the Sun: The Story of Big League Baseball in Missouri*, author Roger D. Launius summed up the conventional wisdom about the Royals during that time: "They were a consistent, almost mechanical team that churned out victories like General Motors churns out cars … (but) when one looked deep down into the soul of the Royals for the inner strength out of which champions came, however, there was not much there."

Now, years later, what had changed? For one thing, the manager.

Whitey Herzog had been the kind of manager who became irate over ignominies. So, during all three playoffs in the 1970s, Royals players complained to reporters about being wronged by umpire calls that snuffed out potential rallies. Later, Jim Frey was known for lashing out at his players, and during the 1980 World Series he called a team meeting in which a Howard Cosell imitator came into the clubhouse and insulted and ridiculed every Royal there, to try to loosen them up. Dick Howser, though, was totally different than Herzog or Frey. He didn't fly into furies. He didn't whine to the press. He seldom held team meetings. He also didn't pat players on the back. He didn't banter around the batting cage. He didn't go drink with the players after games. He didn't even acknowledge his team's shortcomings. And this temperament exasperated some fans and baseball people. George Steinbrenner criticized Howser during his 100-win season as Yankees manager because he was never thrown out of a game.

The top managers in the game at that time were outspoken like Earl Weaver and Herzog, or featured fiery tempers like Billy Martin and Sparky Anderson, or were flamboyant like Tommy Lasorda. With Howser, though, there was nothing flashy. If he had any shtick, it was as a stoic, patient, unflappable figure always on top of a situation—just like his favorite actor, John Wayne. John Wathan, a backup catcher who himself would go on to manage the Royals, thought Howser reminded him of a "captain on a ship who just always keeps everything real, real steady. No matter how big the waves got, he was always there to steady the ship."

Howser's hallmark as a manager was his consistent approach and level-headedness toward the game. He stuck with his lineup once he decided on it. One of his favorite expressions was, "You don't want to get too fancy." And he remained calm during the nail-biting moments of ballgames. "You never saw any panic out of him," reliever Steve Farr recalled. Howser once said he never wanted his players to think, "When things get tough he goes south on us." Instead, after tough losses, Howser's habit was not to rant or rave, but to announce in the dugout or clubhouse: "Piss on it. We'll get this thing done." He gave encouragement to struggling players: one day in '85 ace reliever Quisenberry and struggling reliever Joe Beckwith were walking off the field together and Howser saw them and said, "My No. 1 and No. 2 guys in the bullpen," a subtle but powerful show of confidence that would stay with Beckwith his entire life. In all these ways, Howser instilled an even-keel mindset.

Veteran players in baseball come to believe that teams eventually take on the personality of their manager. And that certainly happened with the Royals. They shed their prickliness. They lost their tenseness. And they became laid-back, professional and confident.

"You've heard people use the term 'loose' in describing us," Howser said after one of the World Series games in St. Louis. "It is more confidence than being loose. A lot of people may not expect us to win, but our players expect us to win. When you have players that feel that way, there is no telling what you can do."

That was another thing different about the '85 Royals: fortitude.

They didn't have a "we are the best" swagger of a dynasty team, but a "we can beat anybody, anytime over a short period" kind of self-assurance. When Jim Sundberg joined the team, he couldn't understand it at first. Here he was finally playing for a contender. He expected to win. But the team struggled during the first half and seemed blasé about it. After back-to-back losses in May, Sundberg

Manager Dick Howser was the quiet, even-keeled general whose motto was "Just get it done." *Courtesy of the Kansas City Royals/Chris Vleisides*

sat glumly in the clubhouse, telling Frank White he knew the Royals were doomed when an error was made at a critical time.

"You can't think like that," White told him. "Here, when someone makes a mistake, you think we're going to get out of it."

And Sundberg began to see for himself. McRae always talked in May and June about where the team should be at certain points, less than 10 games out at the All-star break, a couple of games out going into September. Then the team followed McRae's prescription. Stay close and we'll overcome—that was the mindset.

So in the playoffs, even down 3-1 against Toronto, the Royals knew they matched up well against the Blue Jays and felt they could come back. Before Game 5, backup catcher John Wathan was sitting in the dugout when a Toronto announcer struck up a conversation. "It'll be tough for the Royals to win three in a row," the announcer remarked. Wathan was taken aback. "A three-game winning streak in baseball is nothing," Wathan retorted. "We've won three in a row before."

When that actually happened, even McRae was impressed.

"I've never played with a team that fights better than this one," he said then. "Other teams had more talent ... but I've never been on a team that took the roller coaster we did this year. This team showed more character than any of them. They fought and fought and fought, and it seemed like the more people said they couldn't win, the more they did win. ...It's the best I've felt in any season here because it's the best fighting instinct we've had."

That fight and desire became especially evident when the going got tough. In the seventh game of the ALCS, a hard-hit ball struck Saberhagen's pitching hand. He stayed in at first, but after a couple of innings, pitching coach Gary Blaylock went back in the clubhouse to check on him. A bunch of the other Royals pitchers were in there, too, hovering. Blaylock looked at the swelling and knew Saberhagen would have to come out of the game. Blaylock didn't say anything but started looking around at the other pitchers, trying to determine who to send out during the final game of the playoffs. Leibrandt was reading his mind. As Blaylock looked around, Leibrandt looked right at him and, without saying a word, shook his head up and down. Blaylock sent him out to warm up. It was the only time Blaylock could ever remember telling Howser who was going to pitch—not who should possibly pitch but who *was* going to pitch. Leibrandt ended up the winning pitcher.

Of course, it helped the Royals that throughout the playoffs they were the underdogs. They could play without feeling the heavy hand of postseason stress tightening their shoulders or churning in their guts. The pressure to perform was always on the other team. As shortstop Biancalana explained: "Anytime you're the underdog, it's easier to go out and play." And the Royals didn't put pressure on themselves. No player spouted to the media or sat around the clubhouse saying, "We gotta win this game."

Still, for all their looseness and confidence and fighting spirit, the Royals still had to get things done on the field. And they just so happened to be in the midst of a stretch—covering the showdown series with the Angels, then the ALCS and World Series—in which their pitchers would hold opponents to three runs or less in 14 out of 18 big games.

That can work wonders for the psyche, too.

CHAPTER 9

GAME 6:

"MAYBE THE ROYALS HAD ONE OF THOSE COMING"

The World Series returned to Kansas City for Game 6, where the locals were feeling a bit piqued at the continuing comparisons between the two teams' fandom.

During the first games in K.C., red-clad St. Louis fans had been all over Royals Stadium, even chanting "Oz-zee, Oz-zee" at times just like they did at home. During the games in St. Louis, Royals fans stuck out like blueberries in the bowl of cherries that was Busch Stadium. Busch ushers, when asked if they saw any K.C. fans, answered, "Yeah, I saw a guy..." The *St. Louis Post-Dispatch* kept up their pokes at Royals fans, with one story observing that "at last count about twice as many Cardinals fans had died their hair red as Royals fans who had opted for the blue look."

The national press seemed impressed. Frank Dolson of the *Philadelphia Inquirer* summed up the perceptions about St. Louis: "Hardly a storefront in the recently rebuilt downtown area of this city on the Mississippi could be found without a pennant or a sign pledging allegiance to eastern Missouri's favorite sons. Hardly a native walked the streets without displaying something, anything Cardinal red in color. A person not decked out in bright red was instantly seen for what he/she surely was: a foreigner. ..."

So Kansas Citians, because of their inimitable inferiority complex, started going out of their way to show their spirit. Julie Cluckey, then a secretary with

Coldwell Banker real estate, called the firm's 20 offices and tacked up fliers at supermarkets to announce a rally on the morning of Game 6 in a shopping center parking lot, complete with a high school band. "I was just so disgusted hearing that stuff about the Kansas City fans not having any spirit," Cluckey told the local newspaper. Across town, Daniel Carlson painted a four foot-by-eight foot sign with the words "Go Royals" and propped it up in his front yard. "I've been reading in the paper all too much about how St. Louis supposedly has more team spirit. Friday afternoon, I came home and decided I'd make a sign," he said. In a quiet subdivision in a Kansas-side suburb, residents put blue scarves and blue streamers around little statues in the roadway islands that marked the entrance to the neighborhood.

All this was understandable to some observers of fan behavior. Authors Dan and Kieran Dickinson visited different cities for their book, *Major League Stadiums*. In Kansas City, they observed: "More than in most places, being a Royals fan is an expression of solidarity not just with a team, but with a community and, indeed, a way of life."

Kansas City fans just had different ways of expressing this. Their ballpark wasn't downtown, so they didn't have street scenes of camped-out fans and souvenir vendors. Royals Stadium sat on the edge of a highway amid a sea of parking lots, so Kansas City fans had to devise more inventive ways to be outside the ballpark but still near the action. For a big game like this one, they did. Out beyond the leftfield fence, dozens of cars sat parked on the shoulder of Interstate 70, their orange hazard lights flashing on and off, on and off, in the darkness. Between the highway and the stadium was a grassy knoll, and dozens of fans sat on blankets with radios. And a few agile fans even scaled trees and sat there with portable televisions.

Inside the ballpark, Royals fans got their chance to respond to all the "fat lady" signs that had popped up at St. Louis' stadium. There, Cardinals partisans had spoofed the old opera adage, "The show's not over until the fat lady sings," with signs like "The fat lady is warming up" and "The fat lady is clearing her throat." Now, K.C. fans unfurled their own signage: "The fat lady is only humming" and "The fat lady has laryngitis." And one portly woman in an opera-like costume walked around holding a sign exclaiming, "I'll sing tomorrow."

As all this was unfolding, the Royals were finishing up batting practice. Pitcher Bret Saberhagen was prancing around the field twirling a cigar in his mouth. He and his wife had finally had their baby, a nine-pound boy named Drew. Saberhagen wasn't pitching, so he spent the afternoon passing out cigars and describing how the boy's hands were already big enough to grip a ball. Over by the batting cage, a few other Royals were teasing ABC-TV announcer Reggie Jackson about his pants being too baggy and too long. "I guess that shows you they are a very relaxed ballclub," Jackson told his TV colleagues once the broadcast began.

From Game 3 on, Cards fans (top) trotted out signs predicting the Royals' demise by playing off the old opera adage, "The show's not over until the fat lady sings." She wouldn't make an appearance until Game 7, however. Meanwhile, Royals fans (bottom) got into the act for Game 6. *Courtesy of the Kansas City Royals/Chris Vleisides*

Over in the visiting team's clubhouse, Cardinals players were dressing for the game quietly, seriously, as if they felt the weight of the world. There were fewer jokes, more pursed lips, more gazing at nothing. Their lineup had been posted. It included a major tweak—Ozzie Smith was leading off, despite the fact that he was one for 16 in the World Series. It was his first time in that spot in this series. It was his first time in that spot during the season. In fact, it was his first time in that spot since 1983. What message did this convey to the rest of the team? That manager Whitey Herzog wasn't comfortable with what got them here.

Television actor McLean Stevenson from *M.A.S.H.* visited both clubhouses. Then he paid a quick visit to the Royals radio booth. Announcer Denny Matthews had once played for Stevenson on a youth baseball team in Illinois. Matthews gave him a headset. "I was down in the locker room before the game, I must tell you, I was down with the Royals and down with the Cardinals," Stevenson told the radio audience, "and the Royals were 10 times more loose than the Cards. Really, the Cards are really uptight."

By game time, a full moon appeared on the horizon behind the stadium.

❀ ❀ ❀ ❀ ❀ ❀

Herzog's lineup switch accomplished nothing in the first inning, as the Cards went down 1-2-3 against Charlie Leibrandt. For the Royals, Lonnie Smith started things off with a double against Danny Cox, an intimidating-looking player with a short fu manchu mustache that curved around the sides of his mouth. Cox's right arm was so stressed from a season pitching in pain that it was almost bent in a permanent handshake position off the field.

Willie Wilson, in a situation calling for him to pull the ball instead of hitting to the opposite field, pulled the pitch to advance the runner to third. That brought up George Brett. The Cards had been consistently walking him with a runner in scoring position, so Brett was expecting a walk here. But the Cardinals decided to pitch to him. Not only that, but the infield was playing back, conceding the run. Brett, though, was antsy. He swung and missed at a ball at his armpits for strike two. The fans reacted with an "ewwww." The next pitch was a slider that started inside and tailed back toward the plate. Brett jumped away. Home plate umpire Jim Quick, who hailed from the National League with its wider strike zone, called strike three.

"You used to get that pitch all the time," ABC's Jim Palmer, a former pitcher said on TV. "Very rarely do you get that pitch [now]."

The Royals didn't argue, though. Frank White then grounded out, and the Royals were immediately zero for three with a runner in scoring position. It looked like another one of those nights for the team in blue.

And it was. Just about every inning, the Royals got baserunners on but couldn't do anything with them. In the fourth, White laid down another one of his surprise bunts for a single. Howser relayed the steal sign. White didn't get much of a lead, then took off for second. The throw was in time, but Ozzie

Smith caught it well in front of the bag. White slid under and around the tag. The umpire, however, was positioned behind White and didn't get a good look. White was called out. Again, the Royals didn't argue. The next batter, Pat Sheridan, singled—and another possible run was lost for the Royals.

Meanwhile, Leibrandt continued retiring the Cards 1-2-3 over the first five innings, the first time that had been done in the World Series in 18 years. If there were any doubts whether Leibrandt was feeing some lingering effects from his Game 2 loss, he dashed those the first time he faced Jack Clark. Leibrandt challenged him with three inside fastballs and induced Clark to pop out.

As usual, Leibrandt wasn't getting outs the way Ring Lardner once described Walter Johnson: "He's got a gun concealed about his person." Or the way Red Smith once wrote about Lefty Grove: "He could throw a lamb chop past a wolf." Still, Leibrandt's usual mixture of speeds on the inside and outside corners made batters look like they were swinging jockey whips. He was a control pitcher, and that fit his personality perfectly. He was the most meticulous guy on the team. Nothing was out of place in his locker. And he always stood in the same spot on the mound to receive the catcher's signs.

The Cards finally collected a hit in the sixth and mounted their first threat: runners on first and second with no outs and the pitcher up in an obvious bunting situation. Cox tried to get the bunt down but popped it up instead. Ozzie Smith, still with only one hit in the series, stepped to the plate, which prompted one of the Royals announcers to state, "That scares you a little bit. He's about due to take off." But the Wizard hit into a double play, and as Leibrandt walked off the field, Royals fans resurrected their Game 2 chant of "Char-lee, Char-lee, Char-lee."

Still scoreless in the seventh, the game began to turn on managerial tactics. The Royals got runners on first and second with two out and Leibrandt due up. "Now Dick Howser has a decision to make, doesn't he?" asked Royals announcer Fred White on the radio. Leibrandt was probably a sure out; when he was batting, he couldn't even tell the difference between a fastball and a breaking ball. But he was pitching a shutout. Howser usually put pitching first, and he stayed that way here. So Leibrandt strolled to the plate. "This is one that'll get talked about," Fred White opined. It was already being second-guessed on the Royals bench. Most of them were thinking Howser should pinch hit. *How many more opportunities will we have to score a run?* thought reserve outfielder Dane Iorg.

That's what statistics guru Bill James was thinking, too. Sporting his customary ear-to-ear beard, he was out in the rightfield bleachers with his wife and friends. James grew up and lived just outside of the Kansas City metropolitan area. He'd always been a Kansas City baseball fan, even of the dreadful A's. By now he had evolved from a night watchman at a baked-bean plant to a big-selling baseball author. With his annual *Baseball Abstracts,* he was changing the way fans viewed baseball and he was turning much of baseball's conventional wisdom on its head, by demonstrating, for instance, that stolen bases were almost inconsequential as an offensive strategy because of a high percentage of caught stealings. So here at Royals Stadium, James knew from the work of sabermaticians like himself that the chances of scoring a run increased from around three percent with Leibrandt batting to 25 percent with a pinch hitter.

With Leibrandt at bat, James turned to a friend and grumbled, "This is an atrocious percentage move." Then Leibrandt struck out meekly.

In the top of the eighth, after the Cardinals got a single and a walk, Whitey Herzog faced the exact same situation as Howser had the previous inning: with two on, two out and a pitcher throwing a shutout due to bat. It was baseball tradition to play for the win on the road, and that's what Herzog did, sending up a pinch hitter.

Of all people, it was little-used Brian Harper, who had gone hitless for almost two months, since September 3. Leibrandt quickly got ahead 0-2. On his third pitch, he let loose a fastball over the inner half of the plate. Harper swung, striking the ball near the handle. The bat broke but the ball carried out over the infield and looped into left-center, scoring the game's first run. It was the kind of timely and lucky hit the Royals couldn't seem to get in this series.

The next batter walked as Leibrandt screamed to himself on the mound. Dick Howser came out and removed him from the game. Howser brought in Quisenberry for the same situation he avoided using Quis in during Game 2—facing a left-handed hitter with the bases loaded. This time, the hitter was soon-to-be-league MVP Willie McGee. But Quis jammed McGee and got a bouncer to second to end the inning.

Hard-throwing lefty Ken Dayley took over for the Cards in the bottom of the eighth. Lonnie Smith struck out. Wilson walked, bringing Brett to the plate. "George, throughout his career, has thrived on moments like this," Royals announcer Denny Matthews asserted optimistically. The fans in the stands were on their feet, screaming on every pitch. Strike one. Strike two. Ball. Strike three. All 95-mph fastballs. With stuff like that, Dayley remained in to face the right-handed White, who flew out.

The Cardinals went quickly in the top of the ninth. They were now only three outs away from the championship.

❋ ❋ ❋ ❋ ❋ ❋ ❋

As the Cards took the field for the bottom of the ninth, streams of fans headed up the aisles and out the exits—essentially giving up. In the rightfield bleachers, stat man Bill James thought about joining them.

He knew the Cardinals were undefeated that year—88-0—when leading after eight innings. And he remembered being at Game 2 as the Cards fans jeered "Char-lee, Char-lee, Char-lee" after the Royals loss. He didn't want to be there when boorish behavior broke out after the last out.

But he had a rule—never leave the ballpark until the game is over. So he decided to stick it out.

Up in the press box, hundreds of sportswriters were composing their accounts—the fall of Kansas City in the playoffs once again, Charlie Leibrandt's miserable luck in the postseason, the Cardinals adding to their glorious tradition, Herzog cementing his status as a legend, and on and on.

Nearby, in the separate suites of the Royals' owners, Ewing Kauffman and Avron Fogelman got up to stretch. They met each other out in the hallway. They were both self-made multimillionaires, Kauffman in pharmaceutical sales, Fogelman in apartment development. Fogelman had been a savior of sorts for Kauffman, taking half the team off his hands and splitting the monetary losses, which Kauffman had been growing tired of. Fogelman was only too happy to do it. He had grown up a baseball fan, and his office in Memphis had all sorts of signed baseballs. He had joined the franchise during its darkest year, 1983, and brought new energy to it. He came up with the creative idea of lifetime contracts, to tie the best players to the team so they wouldn't leave by free agency. Now the two stood in the hall in their coats and ties, surprised the team had even gotten this far and knowing that this could be the end.

"Things don't look good," Fogelman said.

Kauffman patted his partner on the shoulder and reminded him, "We're still awfully proud."

Dick Howser started the frame looking for any edge. The Cards' Dayley, a hard-throwing lefty, returned to the mound. So Howser sent out righty Darryl Motley to pinch hit for lefty Pat Sheridan. Whitey Herzog had a choice to make with his bullpen by committee—have Dayley pitch to the slumping Motley, who was one for seven in the series, or bring in righty Todd Worrell, who had struck out the side in his last two World Series innings. Bringing in Worrell would risk that Howser would counter with a better pinch hitter. Bob Broeg, the dean of St. Louis sportswriters, sat in the press box thinking Dayley should be left in, considering he had pitched 12 innings in the postseason without allowing a run. But Herzog went with Worrell, with his own intimidating fu manchu-like mustache. Howser countered with one of his better pinch-hitters, Jorge Orta. He was zero for two already in the series in this role, but the quiet 14-year veteran could still rocket line drives with his chiseled arms and chest. He had batted .267 during the season but he no longer had the speed to leg out many hits and steal 20 bases like he once did.

Worrell kicked his left knee up almost to his shoulder, like Nolan Ryan, and delivered. Fastball strike. Fastball fouled back. Worrell needed just one more strike to set a World Series record for consecutive strikeouts. His next pitch was an off-speed curve. Orta swung. He was out in front on it and hit a dribbler toward first. The noise level in the stadium rose with each step as he ran. Royals announcer Denny Matthews raised his voice on the radio: "He's got a chance to beat it out."

First baseman Jack Clark fielded the ball as Worrell raced over to cover first. Worrell readied for Clark's toss, fishing for the bag with his foot, picking it up and moving it back down until he felt the base. The throw came from Clark,

The Royals' Jorge Orta landed on Todd Worrell's foot while crossing first base, as umpire Don Denkinger (foreground) decided how to call the play. Denkinger ruled safe, while television replays showed Orta was out. *The Kansas City Star*

Orta hit the base, stepped on Worrell's heel—almost pushing Worrell's shoe off—and stumbled over the bag.

Right behind the base, near the coaching box in foul territory, was umpire Don Denkinger. Usually on a play like this he was waiting for sounds—the ball hitting the glove and the runner hitting the bag. But on this play, the crowd was too loud. He had been running toward the bag, watching the ball and the runner. But then six foot, five inch Worrell had to reach high and wide for Clark's toss. The ball and runner were now out of Denkinger's sight line, forcing him to look for the ball in the glove, then look down at the runner.

In the split second he did that, Orta's foot was on the bag.

Denkinger signaled safe.

Worrell turned toward Denkinger. "I was on the bag," he implored.

"You didn't have your foot on the bag," Denkinger told him.

Worrell kicked first base, pointed down to his foot and screamed, "He stepped on my foot."

In this situation, some managers would avoid the controversy and just head to the mound, calling his infielders together, calming them down and reminding everyone they have a one-run lead. Not Herzog. He jogged out to argue, hardly the gait of a man who felt victimized. That was because he thought Worrell's foot might have come off the bag, too. But he had to back up his players. Worrell was still shouting, "He stepped on my foot."

Herzog asked Denkinger, "How was he safe?"

"He beat the throw," Denkinger told him.

"How could he," Herzog countered, "if he stepped on Worrell's foot?"

Up in the right-field bleachers, Bill James and his wife and friends were watching this as just another Cardinal eruption. The play looked close, but Royals Stadium had no video board. A man a few rows behind them had a portable television, an early model with a screen the size of a baseball card. Everyone looked over at him. The replays come on. "He probably was safe," the man blurted out after one angle.

In fact, another angle showed Orta was clearly out.

To the fans at the stadium, though, the play seemed like no big deal.

The argument on the field continued for barely a minute. Denkinger, a 17-year veteran of the major leagues working his eighth postseason series, had overruled another umpire in a past playoff—in the deciding fifth game of the 1982 American League Championship Series, when Milwaukee's first baseman tagged a batter with his glove while the ball was in his other hand. The first base umpire called the batter out, but Denkinger came out from behind home plate and changed the call.

But on this night, none of Denkinger's colleagues overruled him. Besides, Denkinger, ranked in the top third of American League umpires by league managers that year, believed he made the right call. As Herzog ended his argument, he told Denkinger, "We just can't catch a break"—which was ludicrous, of course.

Bad umpire calls like this had happened before in the late innings of World Series games.

In Game 3 of the 1925 series, with the Washington Senators clinging to a 4-3 lead in the eighth inning against the Pittsburgh Pirates, a Pirates hitter launched a deep fly to right. Senators outfielder Sam Rice tumbled over the wall of the temporary bleachers trying to make the catch. After several seconds in with the Senators crowd, he reappeared with the ball in his glove. The umpire ruled a catch. The Pirates were furious, believing a fan had retrieved the ball for Rice—something hundreds of Pirates fans later claimed to have seen. But the catch saved the game for the Senators.

In Game 1 of the 1948 series, with the Cleveland Indians in a scoreless duel with the Boston Braves in the eighth inning, Indians pitcher Bob Feller whirled

Cardinals manager Whitey Herzog conferred with umpire Don Denkinger after "The Call." From his vantage point, Herzog originally wasn't sure whether Orta was safe or not, but he didn't accept Denkinger's explanations. *Courtesy of the Kansas City Royals/Chris Vleisides*

around and threw to second base on a pickoff attempt. He caught the Braves runner napping. Unfortunately, he caught the umpire napping, too. The ump called the runner safe and held firm despite the Indians' objections. The next batter went on to punch a hit that scored the only run of the game.

In both of those major controversies, the beneficiary of the bad call won the game. It remained to be seen whether the same fate awaited the Royals.

The Cards finally got back to their positions. Steve Balboni came to bat. It was a bunting situation, and Balboni looked for the bunt sign from the third-base coach, even though he couldn't remember bunting in a game before. But there was no bunt sign. He was on his own. Balboni was still homer-less in the playoffs, a streak that had become his second longest drought of the season. "Balboni turns into baloney in the fall" read one newspaper headline during the series. He thought to himself now *I have to come through.* But he was not trying to hit a home run—only trying to hit the ball hard.

He swung at the first pitch and lifted a foul over by the first-base dugout. Catcher Darrell Porter and first baseman Clark both ran over there. It should have been the first baseman's play. But Clark thought he heard Porter call out, "I got it, I got it." That was fine with Clark. He was still unsure of himself as a first baseman. Sometimes Whitey Herzog replaced him defensively in ninth innings with the more reliable Mike Jorgensen, but not this night. Now Clark looked over at Porter, who was by the home-plate side of the dugout. Then Clark looked up and noticed the ball was spinning down toward the opposite end of the dugout. Clark backpedaled a couple of steps, but the ball was over his head. It bounced on the rubber warning track and into the dugout.

Clark turned away and yelled, "Goddammit."

"It was a catchable ball," he would admit later. But Porter had run to the wrong spot, and "it made me look like a horse's ass." His teammates, though, would forever think it was Clark's ball.

Lucky gifts like this one also happened before in the late innings of World Series games.

In 1912, with the New York Giants ahead of the Boston Red Sox by one run in extra innings of the deciding game, Boston star Tris Speaker popped a foul ball by first base. Pitcher Christy Mathewson, catcher Chief Meyers and first baseman Fred Merkle all ran toward it. Mathewson could have made the catch, but for reasons never explained, he called on Meyers to make the play. Meyers couldn't get to it, and Merkle stood by as the ball dropped.

In 1934, with the Cardinals ahead of the Detroit Tigers by one run in the bottom of the ninth of Game 2, the Tigers' Gerald "Gee" Walker hit an easy foul pop-up between home and first base. Both the Cardinals' catcher and first baseman were there in time, but they got crossed up, and the ball fell harmlessly.

It's one of the clichés of baseball that when a hitter is given a second chance, he usually delivers. Speaker did, and his hit with two runners on base tied the deciding game, and two batters later his team won it. Walker delivered, too, scoring a runner and tying the game, which his team then won in extra innings.

Now Balboni had his second chance. On the next pitch he whiffed at a fastball, 0-2. Next pitch, he bent down for a low pitch and stroked a sharp single to left between short and third, moving Orta to second.

First the Denkinger call and then this. Clark stood by first base thinking, *Now some s---'s going on.*

Inside the Royals clubhouse, Frank White couldn't move. He had come back into the dressing room because he couldn't bear to watch the end. Before the game, he and some of his teammates had been talking about how, if they could just win tonight, they would win the whole series. So he was pissed the Royals were losing again, despite outplaying the Cardinals. ABC's Reggie Jackson, who had the job of interviewing the probable series losers, was watching the end of the game on a little television inside Dick Howser's office with a couple of clubhouse attendants, laundry boy Frank Gilman and Charlie Leibrandt, who already had his pants, socks and shoes off. Jackson had motioned White, who was pacing by the lockers, to join them. So White was sitting with them with his jersey unbuttoned and belt undone. After Balboni's hit, White got up to leave, to head back into the dugout during the rally.

"Don't move," Jackson called out.

"I gotta go," White protested.

"You gotta stay," Jackson told him. "You're going to break the karma."

Ballplayers are that superstitious, so White stayed put.

McRae had been in the on-deck circle, but it was a bunting situation now with two on and no outs, so Jim Sundberg kept his at-bat. The fans were standing and clapping in quick rhythm. The stadium organist played, "When the Saints Go Marching In." Sundberg bunted two balls foul. Then, even with two strikes, he tried again. He got a bunt down, toward the mound, Worrell hustled to it, hesitated, then threw quickly to third. It was close. But Orta was called out.

McRae was sent to the plate to pinch hit, putting the team's usual cleanup hitter in a position to knock in at least the tying run. Denny Matthews told the radio audience, "Mac, knowing him as I do, is still thinking and stewing about his swing against John Tudor in St. Louis the other night [in Game 4]. He was not a selective hitter at that point. He went after the first pitch." This time, McRae didn't go up looking to swing at the first pitch. It was a ball. On the second pitch, catcher Darrell Porter expected a fastball and kept his glove over the outside corner. But the pitch was a slider breaking outside. At the last instant, Porter reached out and stabbed at it. The ball glanced off his glove and rolled to the backstop. It was scored a passed ball. The runners moved up to second and third.

Howser had pinch run for Balboni when he represented the winning run. Now Sundberg was in scoring position as the winning run, but Howser didn't pinch run for another of the team's slowest runners. McRae was intentionally walked to load the bases and allow a force out at any base. The fans booed.

Ironically, Howser still had a left-handed pinch hitter left when he didn't bat for Leibrandt in the seventh inning. Denny Matthews told the radio audience, "The next man on the spot will be Dane Iorg."

Iorg had starred in 1982 series for the Cardinals, hitting .529 in those seven games and tying a World Series record for most hits by a DH, with nine. Yet, with no DH in the National League, Iorg could never break into a full-time starting job. He was more of a good-hitting utility player. And after '82, his at-bats shrunk. By '84 he was the odd man out of a crowded Cardinal outfield. The Cards sold him to the Royals that May. The Royals needed a left-handed bat. Iorg got to play because of some injuries. He felt needed. Even when the injured starters returned and Iorg was reduced to pinch hitting again, he came through with some key hits. He felt he contributed. Between the two teams, he achieved a career-high in at-bats.

Iorg expected more in '85. He didn't get it. He started the year getting the bulk of the DH at-bats. Then in midseason, McRae was given the job again. Iorg played sparingly. Howser liked to stick with a set lineup. Iorg felt lost. "It'd be better if I could go someplace where I could play," he told the media at one point. He wasn't signed for the next season, so he knew he wouldn't be back with the Royals. He ended up with just 130 at-bats and batted a career-low .223. Then in the playoffs, adding insult to injury, his parents rooted for the Blue Jays and his brother Garth because Garth was playing more.

In the Royals' close-knit clubhouse chemistry, Iorg was somewhat of an outsider. He was a Mormon, so he didn't go out drinking. He also didn't come in early for card games. But there was no other pinch hitter his teammates wanted up right then. "Because he wanted up there," fellow reserve Greg Pryor remembered.

In this World Series, Iorg had only batted once. But he was a professional pinch hitter. He knew how to get himself ready. So starting about the fifth inning of this game, Iorg had shuffled out of the dugout and down the tunnel to the clubhouse. There, in the empty room, he took his stance, held his bat and swung. And swung some more. "Keep the shoulder in. Don't pull off," he told himself. And soon he announced his rising confidence with every swing.

Swish—"Jeez, I've got my stroke back."

Swish—imagining the pitcher, "You gotta be kidding. Jeezo, peezo, that guy's a clown."

Now in the ninth, as Iorg watched ball four to McRae, a flash of terror entered his brain. *They've got pitchers warming up. What if they bring in a lefty? I won't get to bat.* Quickly, though, the flash passed. *No, Whitey's going to stay with his closer.*

That was an edge for Iorg. He knew Todd Worrell. They had been best friends in the Cardinals organization, even while being almost a decade apart in age. And Iorg knew how Worrell pitched—no changeups or big breaking balls.

Iorg walked toward home plate. The crowd was on its feet, yelling and clapping and raising hands up in prayer. Iorg looked over at the Cardinal dugout. A coach, Hal Lanier, held up two fingers toward the infield, which meant set up for the double play.

Don't hit into a double play, Iorg thought to himself. *You won't be able to live with yourself.*

Then he caught himself. *Don't think negative. Stay positive.*

Baseball researchers might believe there was no such thing as an ability to hit in the clutch, but baseball players didn't believe that. They thought that ability existed. They thought that ability consisted of focusing on pitches, tuning out distractions, relaxing instead of tensing up and not thinking at all about pressure. That was no trouble for Iorg. Pressure was trying to make a big-league team. Pressure was being at the plate in spring training knowing you had to get a hit to keep playing. Pressure was staying in the big leagues. And Iorg was way past that now.

This was a moment he craved, a moment with the game on the line. He knew he would hit the ball. He hardly ever struck out. He went to the plate telling himself, *Look for the ball down.*

A base hit could win it, a double play would end it. Iorg, with his actor's good looks, took a couple more practice swings with his 34^1/$_2$-inch, 32-ounce bat, an old Davey Johnson model. He dug in the batter's box, getting into a slight crouch and swiveling his shoulders a little for rhythm. The Royals dugout was quiet. Reserve outfielder Lynn Jones sat on the bench thinking, *If we could get this hit, it would really be unbelievable.*

Ball one outside. The crowd roared and clapped and stomped. Iorg stepped out of the box. So much in baseball depends on how the ball-strike count goes. It's like in blackjack, where the odds change and the tone shifts with each card dealt. In baseball, the Oakland A's once found that a first-pitch strike lowered a hitter's batting average by 75 points. A first-pitch ball raised the batting average by the same amount. That's because the hitter could begin looking for the pitch he wanted. And that's what Iorg was doing now as he stepped back in. He told himself, *Look for the ball down.*

Worrell threw. It was low, thigh high.

Iorg leaned into it.

His bat struck the ball near the handle, breaking the bat. But the ball carried out over the infield and looped into rightfield. "Very much like Brian Harper's base hit to score the first run," ABC's Jim Palmer observed.

Balboni's pinch runner, Onix Concepcion, scored easily with the tying run. Sundberg, who wasn't pinch run for, got a good jump from second, came around third and saw Porter was far in front of the plate awaiting the throw, just like Tom Nieto during Game 5. So Sundberg went for the back corner of the plate again.

He dove head first.

The throw arrived.

Safe.

"The game is over," exclaimed Royals radio announcer Denny Matthews.

❈ ❈ ❈ ❈ ❈ ❈

Kansas City fans instantly swung from hell to heaven.

In the rightfield bleachers, Bill James hugged his wife and high-fived fans around him, as others tossed beer in the air, pounded the seats, jumped up and down until the stadium shook, screamed and, in the case of one woman, wet her pants.

In the owners' suites, Avron Fogelman swung his arms out and in, out and in, in an exaggerated safe sign, while screaming, "Let's do it. Let's do it."

In the bottom of the ninth inning of Game 6, Jim Sundberg dove head-first with the winning run as his hand touched home plate before Cardinals catcher Darrell Porter could apply the tag. *The Kansas City Star*

In Howser's office, White and Leibrandt pulled their pants on and finally got to escape, leaving the laundry boy and the clubhouse attendants to slap hands with Reggie Jackson.

The rest of the Royals charged onto the field from the dugout and jumped on each other. Pitcher Mike Jones barreled into Iorg with such force that he bloodied Iorg's nose, decorating his jersey with, ironically, a cardinal smudge.

Soon, Leibrandt made his way out. Iorg intercepted him. "Charlie," Iorg shouted, "I knew we were going to win it. I knew you couldn't lose another heartbreaker."

Up in the radio booth, Denny Matthews and Fred White tried to make sense of what they had just seen.

Matthews proclaimed, "If you ever doubted a team was destined to win, all you have to do is roll the tape of this ninth inning, and you can see that someone was smiling down on the Kansas City Royals here tonight."

White chimed in, "I will offer to you perhaps proof that the Royals had one of those coming in championship play—Paul Blair's looping single to center in 1977 in Game 5, perhaps Roy White's home run in '78 to the short porch in

Yankee Stadium…and maybe to an extent, Brian Harper's pinch-hit single, it wasn't really whacked, but it was a clean base hit…and I'll go back to Game 2 here, to the Landrum double and (Pendleton's) bases-clearing double.

"Maybe the Royals had one of those coming. Maybe tonight the Good Lord said, 'Ah, what the heck. Let's let them have it right here.'"

Under the stands, the umpires hustled to their dressing room. Commissioner Peter Uebberoth was there, having fled the Cardinals clubhouse with the World Series trophy. Denkinger asked him if he got the call right at first base.

"No," Uebberoth answered.

Denkinger felt sick. He and his wife had been invited to a party after the game. Now he didn't feel like going.

It was among the most legendary miracle finishes of a World Series game. Only three other times in history had the home team gone to bat in the bottom of the ninth inning behind and then scored multiple runs to win. And this was the first World Series with two ninth-inning comebacks—the Cardinals had done it in Game 2. *Sports Illustrated's* Ron Fimrite later observed, "The sixth game Saturday had that magical combination of excellence, luck, foolishness, irony, courage and gut-wrenching suspense that seems to find its way into this great sporting event year after year. But not since the sixth game of the '75 Series between the Reds and the Red Sox [won on Carlton Fisk's 12th-inning homer] had all these ingredients been present in such rich abundance."

Inside the Royals clubhouse, resiliency floated through the room like the aroma of the victory cigar that Willie Wilson lit. He puffed and roared: "I might sleep here tonight. I might not go home. I've got Tudor on the brain, man. We're going to kill him." He and Hal McRae and a bunch of others started parading in a congo line around the clubhouse, shouting "Tu-dor, Tu-dor, Tu-dor." Howser retreated to his office with a beer. Since Game 2, he had been getting plenty of mail with lines that started like "You are a …". This time the moves worked out.

Inside the Cardinals locker room, a cart filled with dozens of bottles of champagne had been wheeled out, and plastic tarps over the lockers had been ripped down. The players hardly moved. Second baseman Tommy Herr and outfielder Willie McGee sat on the floor, ignoring reporters' questions and plates of barbeque that had been placed before them. Worrell stared out blankly, "in a dead zone," as he put it. Tudor, the next day's pitcher, sat looking shell-shocked. The Cardinals had checked out of their hotel that morning, not expecting to have to stay another night. The mood was morose, full of what St. Louis sportswriter John Sonderegger called "negative vibrations" and "doom and gloom." *The Los Angeles Times* described it as a "morgue. It was as if the Redbirds were dead birds."

Over in his office, Whitey Herzog couldn't avoid the umpiring again. He cursed and moaned and harped. "We're not getting too many calls," he complained—despite the fact that the Royals had been robbed of scoring opportunities in the early innings because of questionable calls. Herzog, though, was so perturbed, he was already writing off the seventh game: "We've got no more chance of winning [the next night] than a man on the moon because that guy is behind the plate," referring to Denkinger.

It wasn't like the Cardinals were the first team to have to shake off a late-inning bad call or a heartbreaking sixth-game loss in the World Series.

In both 1925 and 1948—the other World Series when games turned after a bad call—the victimized teams lost those games but still went on to win the series.

In 1982, the last time the Cards were in the World Series, they self-destructed during one game, much like they did here. They were ahead 5-1 in Game 4, ready to go up 3-1 in the series, when a little roller was hit to the first baseman, and pitcher Dave LaPoint dropped an easy throw covering first. Then there was a broken-bat single, a bloop double, a check-swing single and before it was over, the Brewers had scored six runs in the inning—all unearned—to win the game. Still, the Cards came back to take that series.

And consider the most famous sixth game in history, in 1975, with Fisk's 12th-inning dramatics. In the loser's clubhouse afterward, the Reds' Joe Morgan could be heard inspiring his teammates, saying things were in their favor, that they had the best players, that they had a great pitcher on the mound the next day, that they were right where they needed to be, everything was going to be fine. And as Reds manager Sparky Anderson left the locker room for his office, Pete Rose put an arm around Anderson's shoulder and told him, "Listen, Skip, I'll tell you what. Relax. We're going to win it tomorrow."

In the Cardinals clubhouse after Game 6 of 1985, no one did anything like that. During the season, Ozzie Smith had kept a wooden train whistle at his locker, and when the team was winning, he'd toot on it a few times—"whooooo-whooooo"—and then yell out, "Let's keep the train rolling." But his locker was back in St. Louis. He hadn't pulled out the whistle during the World Series, and he didn't have it with him. No one else tried to lighten the mood, either.

"There was nobody who made an attempt to say, 'Let's get our heads up and go get 'em tomorrow,'" recalled Cardinals television announcer Jay Randolph. Instead, the Cardinals wallowed in their misfortune.

It was reminiscent of one other improbable World Series collapse. In 1941, the Brooklyn Dodgers were one strike away from evening their series with the hated New York Yankees. On a full count, the Yankees' Tommy Henrich swung and missed at a curveball for strike three, but the ball glanced off Dodgers catcher Mickey Owen's glove. Henrich sprinted safely to first. The next batter singled. After that, a double. Then a walk. Then another double. The Yankees took the lead and the game.

Back then in Brooklyn's Ebbets Field, the two teams' locker rooms were next to each other, separated only by a wall. As the Dodgers sat in stunned silence in their room, the Yankees' Joe DiMaggio told his teammates, "Listen to that clubhouse over there. They'll never come back from this one."

And they didn't. The Yankees won that series.

CHAPTER 10

GAME 7:

"THE TEAM THAT TOOK ITS PLACE IN HISTORY AS THE MIRACLE ROYALS"

The Cardinals arrived at the ballpark with a hangover—they were still feeling it from the previous night. Players dressed and talked quietly, like everything was forgotten. But they knew better. There wasn't any spark, any spunk, any outward display of excitement about playing in a seventh game of the World Series.

"I thought the atmosphere was definitely different in terms of guys trying to get up for the game," reliever Todd Worrell recalled.

Ozzie Smith put it this way: "After we lost Game 6, we knew we had no business even going out on the field for the seventh game. We had had the Series won, and we knew that we had blown our chance."

But had they really blown their chance? Were they doomed, as Whitey Herzog suggested the night before? Up to that point in World Series history, 28 series had gone down to a deciding game, and the road team ended up winning 17 of them. Plus, the team that had lost Game 6 came back to win the seventh game 10 of the last 15 times. What's more, in both the 1925 and 1948 World Series—the ones in which a blown umpire call had an impact on a game—the team victimized by the umpire's call went on to win the series.

The '85 Cardinals, though, remained agitated from Denkinger's call. The team had been bothered by the umpiring throughout the World Series, and that was the capper. No one said anything about it, but Herzog knew. Before the team left the clubhouse for the start of the game, he tried a pep talk. "It happened and there's nothing you can do about it now," he told them. "Let's give ourselves a chance to win." But Herzog could tell he wasn't getting through. "There was no fire in their eyes," he remembered. Yet, the players' emotional state merely mirrored their manager's. Herzog was still pissed off himself. Upon presenting the lineup card at home plate, he told the umps, "Try to have a good night."

On the other side of the field, the Royals were quiet, too, but looser. A couple guys worked on crossword puzzles. A couple guys went through fan mail. A few guys read the newspaper. They were treating it like it was just another game. Except they all knew it wasn't. Even George Brett was already tied up in knots inside.

Brett had been on a mission all year. During the previous off season, after Brett's second injury-plagued sub-par year in a row, team co-owner Avron Fogelman had his star out to his yacht in Florida. Fogelman challenged him: "You know, you spent 43 days on the disabled list and I'm paying you more money than anybody else on this team. What I want you to do next year is go get yourself into the best shape you possibly can, and you come to spring training and go out and help us win a World Series." Brett had taken that to heart. He'd been frustrated, too. The manager had been lifting him in the late innings for a defensive replacement so he wouldn't get hurt again. So Brett got an old high school buddy to be his personal trainer. He lifted weights, he rode bikes and he ended up losing 25 pounds and four pant sizes. The first day of spring training, during stretching exercises, Brett could touch his head to his knee—he hadn't been able to do that before.

The end result was obvious. Brett had what he considered his best all-around year, reaching a career-high with 30 homers and becoming a Gold Glover with quicker feet in the field. And when the team needed him most at the end of the year, he had gone on one of his patented hot streaks. The last week of the season, when the Royals put away California, Brett had five homers in six games. Then against Toronto, he had carried the club with his legendary four-hit, two-homer performance in Game 3.

In the World Series, however, he hadn't delivered any magic yet. He was overanxious. He was out of rhythm. He was striking out. He was hitting just .273 with one extra-base hit. It was tearing him up.

Last night, after all the celebrating following Game 6, Brett finally made it home in the wee hours of the morning. He was still wired. He finally turned off his television at around 2 a.m. He slept some, woke up and looked at the clock.

It was 2:30.

He shut his eyes. He kept seeing negative images in his head—striking out in the seventh game, a ground ball going through his legs. He got back to sleep, woke up and looked at the clock.

It was 2:45.

This went on all the night, in and out of sleep. He woke up for good and decided he needed a diversion, something to take his mind off the upcoming game. He and Jamie Quirk headed to that afternoon's Kansas City Chiefs football game across the parking lot from Royals Stadium. They ended up in the same suite as Whitey Herzog. The three of them avoided World Series talk. But at halftime, Herzog told them, "Well, it's time," and they all walked over to the baseball stadium and shook hands.

Brett still needed to release his nervous energy, and his swing needed tweaking. So he rounded up someone to throw him pitches and a kid to shag balls, and he took some early batting practice. At times during the season, he took extra BP just for five swings, merely to check his fundamentals. This time, he started off hitting to leftfield, then to center, then to right, spreading the ball around. Then homers over the walls. Line drives off the walls.

Brett, of course, was talented—his golfing buddies told a story about once, on the Lake Quivera course, when an errant shot was coming toward him, he took a golf club, swung at the errant ball and sent it flying back toward its shooter. But another reason why he remained at a superstar level was that he was never satisfied. He took so much batting practice that his hands looked and felt like, in the words of one writer, "pads on a gorilla's feet," with thick calluses stained orange-brown from a season's worth of pine tar, dirt and tobacco juice all rubbed in.

That work ethic was something he learned from his dad while growing up. Jack Brett had been an accountant. He'd been in the military, and he demanded that things be done right. And he'd criticize and literally kick George in the butt if George messed up. Even when George became a star, Jack would ask him why he couldn't have gotten another five measly hits to reach .400 in 1980. This lasting fear of not being good enough for his father kept George striving.

So, there he was before the biggest game of his life, alone in the batting cage, working out the kinks, launching sharply hit balls, striving for perfection. When he finally left, his hands were bleeding.

Back in the Royals' clubhouse, Brett wasn't the only one with jitters. Starting pitcher Bret Saberhagen sat at his locker quietly, a far cry from his normally chatty self. He didn't have the baby to distract his mind anymore. He was the youngest pitcher to start a seventh game. He felt the weight of the team, of an entire city, on his shoulders. He felt that if he messed up, if he didn't have his best stuff like usual, that he'd be letting down so many people. "It's probably the most nervous I've been before a game," he remembered. Brett and a few teammates came by to try to loosen him up. "It's only the most important game of the year," they teased. Then Brett got serious. "Get out there and do what you've been doing all year long."

Around the corner, Dick Howser was camped out in his office. He hadn't gone out for regular batting practice. He was staying put. An hour or so before game time, team co-owner Fogelman ducked in. "If you're ever thinking of giving a Knute Rockne kind of speech, this is the time," Fogelman said, ready to hang out and hear it.

Howser told him: "I don't want them to see me or feel the pressure, and I don't want to say anything to them that they may take the wrong way. What I want to do is stay out of their hair." Fogelman left thinking, "Now that's a great management style."

When it was time to play, Howser finally emerged, looked at his players around the clubhouse and in the dugout and thought they had "fighter pilot eyes"—the intense look one gets before going in for the kill. It was just what he had hoped for.

Up in the stands, it was a thirsty crowd, an expectant crowd. Some fans unfurled a banner that read: "We want it and we want it bad." It was a crowd in a retaliatory, bullying mood, too. One fan walked through the stadium parking lot with a dead bird, spray-painted red, being dragged on a rope. Seeing that, other Royals fans Dave Colgan and Jeff Driver laughed and pointed. Colgan and Driver had grown up together in suburban Johnson County, gone to college together at Kansas State University and now lived together near the Westport bar district. They were in their early 20s, representing a generation of Kansas City baseball fans who had grown up solely with the Royals. It was the only team they truly followed, as the Chiefs were stuck in mediocrity, the NHL had left the city long ago and the NBA had just abandoned K.C., too. Colgan and Driver were young and single and often had made the leftfield bleachers at Royals Stadium their evening's entertainment. They must have gone to four or five dozen games that summer. For the World Series, Colgan had camped out at the stadium with his brothers to get tickets. Before this game, in the parking lot with a load of beers, the two buddies were getting into the spirit of the night.

When some red-clad Cardinals fans walked by, Colgan saluted them: "Hey, Cardinal fever." And when they yelled back, "Yeah," he added: "Die from it."

❋ ❋ ❋ ❋ ❋ ❋

The sun had set by game time and the temperature dropped to 66 degrees. Game 7 pitted Saberhagen vs. John Tudor, a classic matchup of 20-game winners. Tudor was trying to do what just a few pitchers in history had done—win three games in a single World Series. And like others who had done that, Tudor was pitching on three-days' rest, one day less than normal. But for him, that was the norm. He'd been pitching on three-days' rest for the past month.

In the first inning, Ozzie Smith led off again for the Cards. They went 1-2-3 after three fly ball outs. Royals radio announcer Denny Matthews declared that Saberhagen's fastball was "hopping" and hitters were getting under it. In the Royals' half, Brett's extra batting practice paid off. He tomahawked a line-drive single on a high pitch. But the Royals got nothing more.

The next inning, Jack Clark took a strike and mumbled an obscenity after the umpire's call. He ended up singling, but three straight outs ended the frame. For the Royals, Steve Balboni came up with one out. ABC's television announcers had been all over him this series, saying things like, "Sooner or later it has to happen," as if the only way Balboni could contribute was with a home run. He pulled one pitch long, but foul. The count went to 2-2. He laid off a changeup low. Then he laid off a fastball outside for ball four, a rare Tudor walk.

Darryl Motley was next. Back in Little League in Portland, Oregon, Motley had played in an all-star game, struck out and failed to knock in runs as his team lost. Afterward, he stood behind a car in the parking lot, crying. His mother, Brenda, found him there and put her arms around him. "Well, honey," she told him, "you have to remember, there will be days like this." Motley thought of that day often during 1985.

He'd had a hard time getting the Royals' attention in the minors, then responded to his chance in 1984, hitting .284 with 25 doubles, 15 homers, 70 RBIs and 10 stolen bases—looking like the team's next outfield star. He was just five foot nine, but he had an upper body befitting a weightlifter. In '85, he improved in power, with 17 homers, but his average sank to .222. He was platooned, then put pressure on himself to produce and lost his stroke. "I never knew if I would hit the ball hard," he said that year. Often he came home disgusted. Fortunately his mother lived with him during the summer in his new house. She reminded him, "There will be days like this."

During the World Series the platoon continued, so Motley played in the games that Tudor pitched, which wasn't helping his batting average. He was one for seven in the series. But before this game in batting practice, he had hit some balls out. He was feeling good as he stepped to the plate, carrying the bat he'd used in BP.

Tudor missed with a couple of changeups. He didn't throw curveballs to right-handed hitters, so the changeup was his only off-speed pitch to them. But he was not getting that pitch over this night. So he was throwing more fastballs than he usually did, being somewhat more predictable in his tactics.

Up in the Royals radio booth, announcer Denny Matthews observed, "Two hours ago during batting practice, there was no wind at all. At the start of the game, the breeze began to stir, and now it's blowing quite hard toward the left-field corner. It will help a right-handed batter should he pull the ball and get it up."

The count went full. Then Motley fouled a pitch off. The stadium organ got the fans clapping. Next pitch, "A long drive to left," Matthews announced, as Motley jumped sideways up the first-base line, watching the ball down the line, a la Carlton Fisk in the 1975 World Series. "If it stays fair," Matthews continued, "it's gone. It is ... foul ball."

The crowd's collective shouts audibly dropped from "ahhhh" to "ohhhh."

Motley picked up his bat by the barrel in his right hand and, walking in front of home plate, tapped the handle on the ground, once, twice, a little harder now, even harder now. Did he hear a crack? He stepped into the batter's box, gripped the handle with both hands and held it up to his face. Sure enough, a crack. Just his luck, breaking the bat he'd felt comfortable with.

In the superstitious world of baseball, where managers don't step on foul lines and players don't move during rallies, Motley had two curses on him. One: Once you hit a home run foul, you're generally going to make an out. And two: Once you break your bat, you're going to strike out.

Motley picked out another bat, a black model, and got back in the batter's box. He took a deep breath. ABC's Jim Palmer had talked with Royals hitting coach Lee May before the game, and Palmer told the television audience, "I said, 'What's the key? What have you advised your hitters to do against Tudor?' He said, 'We have to hit the ball up the middle. We have to go the other way. If we try to pull him, we don't have a chance.'" Motley, though, was pulling him. He was sitting on the fastball, because that's what Tudor had been primarily throwing.

The next pitch was a fastball that Motley pulled again. "And there it goes," Matthews called out.

The stadium erupted. Royals fans Dave Colgan and Jeff Driver couldn't see the ball. They had standing-room tickets and were perched along a lower-deck railing on the third-base side. They turned to the tiny portable TV they had set up on a waist-high trash can. Motley raised both arms above his head. The ball hooked down the line, then disappeared in the bleachers, and the three-deep crowd around Colgan and Driver burst out with wails of joy and high-fives and spontaneous, high-stepping, arms-flapping dances in the crowded concourse.

It was 2-0. The Royals' bench loosened up. In 10 of the last 12 World Series seventh games, the team that scored first eventually won.

In the third inning, the Cards went down in order on nine pitches. For the Royals, Lonnie Smith led off with a walk—the first time Tudor had walked a leadoff hitter in 14 games. As ABC's Jim Palmer had observed earlier, "He [Tudor] is all over the place with his control so far tonight." It wasn't his night. With one out, Brett leaned back on a high inside fastball, accidentally tapped the ball toward third, and it slipped out of Tudor's hand for a single. Then Frank White walked to load the bases after being down in the count 0-2.

Jim Sundberg worked the count full. The fans were on their feet screaming and clapping. Sundberg took ball four low, walking in a run to pad the Royals lead, 3-0. Brett, standing off second base, jumped in the air and thrust his fists up. After completing his follow-through, Tudor bent down, grabbed some dirt from the mound and flung it.

Herzog went to the mound. He had been squawking about strike calls again from the dugout. Now he asked Tudor, "What was that last pitch?"

"A ball," Tudor told him.

Darryl Motley connected with his new black bat on a two-run homer that started the Royals' avalanche of runs in Game 7. *The Kansas City Star*

Herzog motioned for a reliever. Tudor walked off the mound. Stewing and needing a release, he headed toward the tunnel; as he passed the dugout fan he exploded, taking out his aggression with a single punch to the fan. His hand went through the metal frame and was cut by the whirling blade. He was taken to the hospital for stitches.

The new pitcher was side-armer Bill Campbell. Balboni, still without an extra-base hit but at least hitting the ball, bent down in an awkward swing, yet connected solidly for a ground ball single for two more runs and a 5-0 lead. But that was it in the inning.

In the fourth, the Cards went down 1-2-3 on eight pitches. In the fifth, Saberhagen set down the first two batters for 11 straight outs before allowing a single. He recorded the third out of the inning on his ninth pitch.

In the bottom half, the Royals turned it into a laugher. Single, single, single, sacrifice, double, single, and it was 9-0. Brett was four for four, becoming just the fourth player to have four hits in a series Game 7, duplicating what another future Hall of Famer, Willie Stargell, had done in 1979 to help carry his team to the title.

Then the Cardinals came completely unglued. Joaquin Andujar, who had been warming up an inning earlier, entered the game—and he was not happy about it. He won 20 games during the season. He was a starter. Now he was mopping up in a humiliating loss.

The count went even on Frank White, then White fouled off five straight pitches. On the next pitch White connected for a chopper that bounced over Pendleton's head for another hit, boosting the score to 10-0. "I don't know what the definition in Webster's is of extreme agony," ABC's Al Michaels said, "but I think one definition would have to be being a St. Louis Cardinal at this moment, knowing you're down 10-0 and you're only in the fifth inning."

Sundberg stepped to the plate. He took a curve inside, and Andujar pounded his glove. After a fastball inside, Andujar stepped forward off the mound, tossed his gloved hand above his head in frustration, pointed a finger toward Porter and then back toward his body, telling Porter to come out. But Andujar took a couple more steps forward, causing umpire Don Denkinger to come out from behind home plate. Denkinger shouted, "They weren't strikes. Get back on the mound."

Instead, Andujar walked closer to the plate and pointed at Denkinger. The two came together until they were jawing nose to nose. Herzog jogged out of the dugout and picked up his diatribe from Game 3, that Andujar wasn't getting the corners. Denkinger just stood there, listening, as Herzog ended his rant with this zinger: "We wouldn't even be here tonight if you hadn't blown that call last night."

Denkinger still hadn't seen a replay of his call from the previous night. He hadn't read the paper or watched TV. He went to that afternoon's football game, just like Herzog had. "I had no idea at all what (my call from the night before) had stirred up," Denkinger said later. But he was not going to let Herzog blame him for the Cardinals' demise.

Herzog started walking away, and Denkinger snapped back at him: "You wouldn't be here either if your team was hitting."

That really set off Herzog. He came back at Denkinger and called him a----sucker. Denkinger ejected him. A group of Cardinals surrounded Denkinger. Cardinals coach Nick Leyva ran out of the dugout and got between them. "I have never seen a team come this unraveled," Al Michaels said on TV. His fellow announcers went over the replay. "That ball wasn't a strike," Tim McCarver opined in reference to Andujar's last pitch.

Andujar got back on the mound. The count was full on Sundberg. The next pitch was called another ball inside. Andujar pumped both hands toward the plate. Denkinger immediately threw him out. Andujar proceeded to run right at Denkinger and bump him. Terry Pendleton and Leyva ran over to the screaming Andujar and wrapped their arms around him.

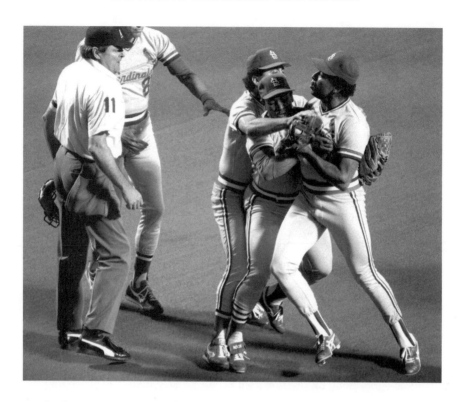

Cardinals pitcher Joaquin Andujar screamed at umpire Don Denkinger and had to be restrained by teammates and coaches after being thrown out of Game 7. *The Kansas City Star*

In the stands, along the lower-deck railing, Dave Colgan and Jeff Driver and a three-deep throng of standing-room ticket-holders were screaming at Andujar, despite their distance from the field: "You're done, go home," and "Sit down, you loser." Nearby, some of the few fans dressed in red behind the Cardinals dugout were beginning to make their way up the aisle for an early exit—but not without catching some grief from the long-suffering Royals faithful: "Byyyyye, Cardinals fans" and "Have a nice trip home."

One of the fans leaving was Deanne Porter, wife of the Cardinals catcher. She went out to her car and cried.

Andujar finally left the field, headed into the clubhouse and took a bat to a toilet and a sink, knocking both off their stools and causing an explosion heard all the way back to the Cardinals' dugout.

There was a 10-minute delay while Bob Forsch entered the game and warmed up. His entrance caused the Cards to tie a World Series record for most pitchers used in an inning. His first delivery was a wild pitch that scored another run. It was

11-0 now, and the national sportswriters started pounding on their typewriters and pounding the Cardinals. The *St. Louis Post-Dispatch's* Kevin Horrigan wrote: "They played like chumps. Some of them acted like chumps." The *Los Angeles Times'* Scott Ostler added: "Not since 1919 (when the Black Sox threw the World Series) has a Series team made such a complete collective ass of itself."

Indeed, it was a meltdown of historic proportions. Not since 1931 had a team self-destructed like this in Game 7, when the Philadelphia A's botched a ball, threw a wild pitch, gave up a passed ball and missed a couple of pop-ups, leading to two runs in an eventual 4-2 loss. Not since 1935 had a manager and a player both been ejected from a Series game, and that was in the Tigers-Cubs series when umpire George Moriarty was accused of bias because he had once played and managed for the Tigers. And not since 1960 had a Game 7 starter been sent to the showers so early, when the Yankees' Bob Turley was knocked out.

Now in 1985, it was just a matter of time for the Royals—waiting through more three- and four-minute innings. The Cardinals swung early in their at-bats, trying to get the game over with. Saberhagen was trying not to walk anyone, so he threw nothing but fastballs.

With the outcome not in doubt, the fans turned their attention from the field to the stands. They marched a parade of signs through the aisles:

"The World Series—A foul beginning and a Royal ending."

"The heat is gone."

One portly woman decked out in an opera-like gown—representing the ubiquitous "fat lady" in the fans' battle of signs—traipsed around the stadium carrying a poster reading, "I'm ready to sing."

The 11-0 margin was the most lopsided win the Royals had all year. And it tied the World Series record for the most lopsided win.

Before the last better in the last inning, Brett approached Saberhagen on the mound to remind him, "Don't forget about me after this out. I want to be next to you."

A fly ball was hit to leftfield. Saberhagen watched the ball as he and Brett converged. Brett puts his hands out, palms down, telling him, "Not yet. Not yet."

Then Motley made the catch, and as Al Michaels announced in TV land, "To Motley, for the title," Brett yelled on the field, "Now," and he and Saberhagen jumped into each other's arms. It was 10:10 p.m., October 27, 1985.

❈ ❈ ❈ ❈ ❈ ❈

Swarms of fans were poised at the front-row railings, eyeing a few dozen police officers guarding the field. A few courageous fans climbed over first. As the officers gave chase, a couple hundred others—including Dave Colgan and Jeff Driver—followed over the railings like a flotilla of barrels popping over a waterfall.

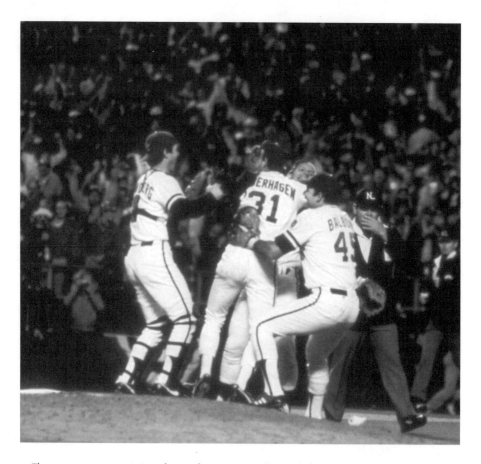

The wait was over! Royals catcher Jim Sundberg (left) and first baseman Steve Balboni (right) converged on pitcher Bret Saberhagen and third baseman George Brett as they embraced to celebrate the final out of the 1985 World Series. *Courtesy of the Kansas City Royals/Chris Vleisides*

There wasn't any grass to tear up, so a mass descended on the pitcher's mound. Fans took handfuls of dirt and tossed them up into the air like confetti. Colgan and Driver walked around the infield with their hands stretched out above their heads in a victory salute, Kirk Gibson-style, as dirt landed in their hair. Some fans slid into second base. One man made a running full-body slide into home plate with his miniature television still in his hand. Others headed into the outfield and threw themselves up against the padded outfield wall, pretending to make leaping catches.

Up in the stands, Bill James, the baseball analyst who dug into baseball games for shreds of enlightenment, stood at the same seats he had occupied for

Game 6, hugging strangers and basking in a new revelation, about how a base-ball game "could make you feel so good." Joe McConniff, the fan from Game 1, was in the upper deck with this 63-year-old father, who had never seen a Kansas City championship and who now, amid all the raucous high-fiving, softly declared, "We finally did it." Brian Burnes, the fan at Game 2, sat at home watching on TV in his typical near silence, simply relieved that he could now relax. Shawn Link, who had watched Game 3 at the University of Missouri frat house, was rejoicing at a bar in Kansas City, certain his Cardinal fan roommate was spiraling into depression. Out in Missoula, Montana, the literary softball players, who had watched Game 4, had gathered one last time and, with the final out, let loose a string of guttural sports-fan colloquialisms: "They did it." "God d---." "No sh--." "Motherf---." Sister Mary Sharon Verbeck, who had watched Game 5 at the St. Pius convent, was in front of the TV again, letting out one final "Thanks be to God."

Down in the clubhouse, the Royals whooped it up in that time-honored baseball tradition—showering each other with champagne, even spraying some down their pants. When the white bucket of champagne was empty, they did the same thing with beers. And all the while, they roamed back and forth across the room, embracing each other in bear hugs and high-fiving until their hands hurt. Together, they opened the spigot of steam that had been boiling inside all year and, for some veterans, from years of playoff frustrations. Danny Jackson, usu-ally soft-spoken, stood in the center of the room screaming over and over, "We shocked the house. We shocked the house." Willie Wilson danced with that high-pitched cackle of his while holding another victory cigar and yelling out, "We shocked the world. Yes, we shocked the world."

And there was George Brett, the club's one superstar, holding court for the media: "A lotta people said we weren't any good on paper, and that's really great because paper never won a baseball game. What paper doesn't show you is what you saw tonight, what is in the heart and the pride and the determination to win that we had. Now we are the best team in the U.S.—and the world. We won the World Series, even if people said we weren't from a big enough city in the world to do it. ...

"For all the people on the West Coast who didn't get to see the powerhouse Los Angeles Dodgers, too bad. And for all the people who didn't get to see the powerhouse Mets or Yankees, we're sorry. But we gave the country something none of them had as much as we did—inner strength and desire and a team that came back like nobody ever before. ...

"I'm proud to be a Kansas City Royal. I used to be a California boy, but [now] I'm a Kansas City boy, and I have never been prouder to say so than tonight."

Meanwhile, the town was going nuts. As early as the fifth inning, police closed off the intersection of Westport Road and Pennsylvania Avenue in the Westport bar district. Tom Jackman, a reporter for *The Kansas City Times* news-

Bret Saberhagen, covered in confetti, waved to the crowd during the Royals' victory parade in downtown Kansas City. *Courtesy of the Kansas City Royals/Chris Vleisides*

paper, watched as the streets swelled with several thousand blue-capped and white-shirted fans, becoming a whirling, swirling mass, drinking beer and high-fiving and shooting off fireworks and chanting "We're No. 1. We're No. 1." Westport was still relatively new as a gathering place in the city, and this was before St. Patrick's Day had grown to gargantuan proportions or the days of Red Friday pep rallies for the football Chiefs. The city hadn't popped its cork like this before.

There were other, smaller celebrations everywhere: in a midtown neighborhood, where residents flicked their porch lights on and off up and down a block; in the Country Club Plaza, where cars paraded with horns honking and drivers hollering and passengers hanging out of windows; even in the little Cleanarama Laundry in the suburb of Independence, where a packed house stopped doing their laundry and screamed and clapped and jumped on tables and on top of piles of newly folded clothes.

Of course, all that was only the beginning of the city's celebration. The next day, for the victory parade, schools let out early, businesses closed up and downtown got dressed up like never before. Fifteen arches containing 600 blue-and-white balloons were draped across Grand Avenue. Blue crepe paper was wrapped around parking meters. The city's parks department prepared 2,200 bags of confetti and delivered them out of cherry pickers to windows of businesses along the parade route, some 40,000 pounds of confetti in all—double what was used following the 1980 World Series. The Royals rode in donated vintage cars as the shredded paper rained on them, sticking on their shoulders, getting caught in their hair, covering up car seats, piling up four inches deep on the street—and in some cases starting fires under the cars. When smoke billowed around the car carrying the Howser family, they fled so fast that their daughter left her shoes in it. (It was the last time the city would allow confetti for a parade.)

Spectators pressed right next to the slow-moving cars, shaking hands, getting autographs and yelling out "way to go." The players were still numb from all they had been through. "Sometimes I still think we need to play someone else. It's hard to believe we don't have anyone else left to beat," Dan Quisenberry said from the back of his convertible.

Inside the offices of *The Kansas City Star* and *Times* on Grand, a reporter happened to be on the telephone with someone from New York and apologized for the noise coming through the open windows from the parade outside. "What's the parade all about?" the New Yorker asked.

In the ensuing days, it was time for various Kansas Citians to collect on bets. Cabbies from St. Louis's Laclede Cab Co. drove across the state with 50 cases of beer for KC's Metropolitan Transportation Services. Gene McNary, the St. Louis County executive, came to town, donned a Royals jacket and sang the "Everything's Up to Date in Kansas City" song on the courthouse steps in Kansas City. The director of the St. Louis zoo made a trip to KC's zoo to clean up dung in the elephant area.

And one nine-year-old St. Louis boy named Tim Graeff went to his piggy bank and tearfully removed his only dollar. He and his Kansas City cousin had each earned one that summer for helping out their grandfather. Then they wagered it on the series. So after the Royals won and Graeff realized he had to pay up, he stuffed his dollar into an envelope and sent it away, without any note, to his cross-state cousin. "That one precious dollar," Graeff remembered years later, "was the most difficult debt I ever had to pay."

❀ ❀ ❀ ❀ ❀ ❀ ❀

America loves an underdog, so the series finally caught the nation's attention. TV ratings progressed as the series progressed. While Game 1 had drawn a 31-percent share of the viewing audience, Game 7 was up to a 47-percent share. Overall, the average rating for the entire series was about 10 percent higher than for the previous two World Series.

Yet as the series got tighter, it actually widened statistically. In the end, four Royals hit over .300, led by Brett's .370, while only Tito Landrum did so for the Cardinals. Four Cards regulars hit less than .200, with Ozzie Smith the worst at .087, with two hits in 23 at-bats, something he subsequently did not mention in his autobiography. Before the seventh game, the Royals were outhitting the Cardinals as a team, .270 to .190. After the seventh game, the differential had climbed to .288 to .185. That 103-point margin was by far the largest ever for a seven-game World Series. As for the pitchers, the Royals had a staff ERA of 1.89, led by Saberhagen's 0.50 for allowing one run in 18 innings, while the Cards were more than two runs higher at 3.96.

By any comparison of the stats, Kansas City creamed St. Louis. Still, the Cards wouldn't give much credit to the Royals. Herzog badmouthed the team that beat him: "I'm not taking anything away from them, but I don't think they could win our division." The sour grapes sounded a lot like those coming out of California's clubhouse at the end of the season, when manager Gene Mauch complained, "I am bewildered how they contained our lineup. I know they are good, but the Celestial All-Stars couldn't do this." And those complaints sounded a lot like the ones coming out of Toronto's clubhouse after the playoffs, when Blue Jays relief pitcher Dennis Lamp lamented, "We're a better team but we didn't win. It's ridiculous."

The nation's sportswriters, too, hardly gave the Royals their due for a stunning triumph. In *The Sporting News*, still baseball's paper of record then, there were no columns extolling the Royals' miraculous comebacks or remarking on their place in history. No, the consensus was the Royals had won because of "the horrendous performance of the Cardinals," according to one article, or because of umpiring—ignoring the umpiring lapses that had stopped the Royals from leading or tying Game 6 before the ninth inning. National League columnist Bill Conlin remarked: "The fact remains [the Cardinals] should have been home in St. Louis, nursing their hangovers and picking confetti out of their hair from the joyous parade downtown. They were not outdone by the precocity of 21-year-old Bret Saberhagen or the swinging sword of George Brett. The pivot of this World Series was not provided by a player of either team. Instead, it radiated from American League umpire Don Denkinger."

Even the sportswriters who had bashed the Royals' chances early on in the series didn't produce any mea culpas afterward. Consider this from *The Washington Post's* Thomas Boswell: "Could the Royals have won the World Series if The Tarp That Ate St. Louis hadn't broken an itsy-bitsy teeny-weeny bone on Vince Coleman's knee? Of course not. Don't be silly. ...Could the Royals have won without Don Denkinger? Maybe so. But maybe not, too."

What should the nation's writers have said? Look at what had been presented in *The Sporting News* after other unexpected series upsets. For the Amazin' Mets of 1969, the front page featured a cartoon on its cover of a small man, with Mets on his shirt and a rock slingshot in his hand, slaying a gigantic warrior. An article inside gave the Mets all the credit, explaining that "the laws of improbability has been rest asunder and the Mets enthroned as baseball's No. 1 team." The year before, when the Detroit Tigers had completed a comeback against the seemingly invincible Cardinals, an editorial praised the Tigers' resiliency, not their lucky breaks: "During the season and in the World Series, the Tigers often were on the floor, but they always got up, and when they did, it was lights out for the opposition. If everybody loves a winner, everybody [except St. Louisans] adores the Tigers, whose trademark was the comeback." And even after Mickey Owen's dropped third strike gave the Yankees new life to win a game and the momentum to seize the 1941 series from Brooklyn, renown baseball writer Fred Lieb noted that the Dodgers team had batted a "feeble" .182 and concluded: "A review of the final tables of the Series shows the victory of the American League again was earned and deserved."

In 1985, however, no one in the national press came up with a snappy one-liner celebrating the Royals accomplishment, something like "K.C. now stands for Kings of Comebacks." No, the sportswriters couldn't get past Denkinger's call or Herzog's blind rage about it. This stubbornness and wrong-headedness on the part of the media would not have surprised Missouri legend Mark Twain. In an 1870 essay entitled "How I Edited An Agricultural Paper," he took a swipe at the credentials of critics: "You turnip! Who wrote the dramatic critiques for the second-rate papers? Why, a parcel of promoted shoemakers and apprentice apothecaries, who know just as much about good acting as I do about good farming and no more." Maybe the same could have been said of some of the nation's sportswriters.

The fact is, the Royals took their place as the greatest postseason comeback team of all-time. No team had ever rallied from 3-1 deficits twice in one postseason. No team had lost the first two games at home in the World Series and come back to win it. No team had lost a series game like the Royals did in the ninth inning of Game 2 and still won the series. And no team facing elimination had rallied to win a game in the ninth inning and then gone on to win the World Series.

Yet, no one in the national publications properly hailed these accomplishments. So it was left to the hometown paper, *The Kansas City Star*, and sports editor Joe McGuff: "For better or worse, there is a time in human affairs when events assume a momentum of their own and overwhelm any attempt to control them. Perhaps that is the only rational way to explain the team that took its place in history … as the Miracle Royals."

PART TWO

1985 IN
MEMORIES AND LORE

CHAPTER 11

THE AFTERMATH

Sitting in the stands of Royals Stadium on Opening Day 1989, esteemed baseball analyst Bill James looked out at his favorite team and saw a starting lineup that quite possibly—with the right development and a little luck—had a future Hall of Famer at every position.

At first base was George Brett, a no-brainer. At second was Frank White, whose credentials were close. At shortstop was Kurt Stillwell, coming off a season with 28 doubles and 10 homers at age 22, certainly better at that age than Alan Trammell. At third base was Kevin Seitzer, who had a .315 lifetime batting average at age 26. At catcher was Bob Boone, whose career longevity was close to Hall standards. In leftfield was Bo Jackson, who had unlimited potential. In center was Willie Wilson, in a pattern of decline, but who at age 33 could still bounce back. And in right was Danny Tartabull, who had two 100-RBI seasons behind him already at age 25.

"What happened, of course," James later wrote, "is that *all* of their chances took a turn for the worst over the next three years, all except Brett."

And that was symbolic for what happened to the entire franchise after 1985. The Royals fell back into a spiral of bad luck, from a freak illness to a freak injury, from young players and prospects not panning out to the franchise suffering under the game's widening salary disparity.

Bo Jackson, with his prodigious home runs, blazed like a comet through Kansas City in the late 1980s, before flaming out due to injury. *Courtesy of the Kansas City Royals/Chris Vleisides*

What had been the most successful baseball expansion franchise would start, with the conclusion of the '85 World Series, a drought of at least two decades without making the playoffs. A lot of it had to do with unforeseen calamities.

Just look back at those first ensuing years.

In 1986, the Royals stood eight and a half games behind the Angels at the All-Star break; they had been seven and a half games behind in mid-July of 1985, so they were within their usual striking distance. Then right at the break, manager Dick Howser complained of headaches and got diagnosed with a brain tumor. A monsignor was ushered into the team clubhouse to tell the players the tumor was malignant. Steve Cameron, in his history of the Royals franchise, observed: "The Howser tragedy tore at the heart of the Royals—from the top on down, from owner to batboys, pitchers to secretaries. [It] rocked Kansas City, too, washing the community with a sense of loss and the feeling of being left without its baseball rudder. The man seemed to stand for everything the franchise believed, everything it had worked to achieve, and suddenly he was gone."

In 1987, college football Heisman Trophy winner Bo Jackson, who shocked the sports world by choosing baseball over football, appeared in a blaze of glory, hitting 16 homers and knocking in 42 runs by early July. Then he slumped, got upset about being lifted for a pinch hitter and cleaned out his locker, only to come back when ownership allowed him to play pro football, too—for the hated Los Angeles Raiders. That unsettled his teammates and fans who believed Bo when he had promised to concentrate on baseball. With two-sport Bo turning into a media circus and the fans booing him when he came to bat, the team went into a second-half tailspin.

By '88 and '89, Kansas City seemed to have its next generation of stars in place—the ones Bill James thought could be establishing Hall of Fame credentials. The '89 Royals even won 92 games—more than in 1985—and Bret Saberhagen won another Cy Young award. In past years, this would have been good enough in their weak division. But no longer. Oakland had turned into a juggernaut, with the Bash Brothers of Mark McGwire and Jose Canseco, plus consistent pitching stars like Dave Stewart and Dennis Eckersley. They began to dominate the division.

So Royals owner Ewing Kauffman—who had sworn off costly free agents starting, ironically enough, at an owners meeting during the 1985 World Series—decided he wanted another winner and opened his pocketbook for free-agent pitchers Mark Davis, Storm Davis and Richard Dotson. All three were disasters, particularly Mark Davis, who had won the National League's Cy Young award the previous year but then suddenly couldn't save games anymore, as he lost confidence and got homesick for the West Coast. The team finished with a losing record in 1990.

Of course, the Royals problems during this period went beyond mere rotten luck and bad karma.

A thin Dick Howser (middle, wearing a tie) visited with the Royals during spring training of 1987 after undergoing cancer surgery. *Courtesy of the Kansas City Royals/Chris Vleisides*

Most of the players who put the Royals over the top in 1985 never performed to that season's level again or were frustratingly erratic. George Brett never hit 30 homers in a season again. Neither did first baseman Steve Balboni. Darryl Motley never hit double-digits in homers again. Willie Wilson never hit .300 again. Lonnie Smith never stole 40 bases again. Closer Dan Quisenberry never saved 20 games again—proving Howser probably was right in his World Series hunch that Quis was losing it.

Then there was the starting rotation. In '85, it had been one of the few staffs over the previous quarter-century with three starters 24 years old or younger who each won at least 10 games. Other such staffs had included Hall of Famers like Jim Palmer and Fergie Jenkins, or hotshots who flamed out like Baltimore's Steve Barber. The Royals ended up with the latter. Saberhagen started his weird odd-year, even-year pattern of good and bad seasons. Mark Gubicza was almost as inconsistent. Danny Jackson never had a winning record again for the Royals. Charlie Leibrandt never won 17 games in a season again. Buddy Black never won in double digits again for K.C.

Like in the early '80s, the Royals tried in the late '80s to patch things up with trades. They still made a few gems, landing slugger Danny Tartabull and reliever Jeff Montgomery. But more often they gave away up-and-coming talent for next to nothing. David Cone went on to win nearly 200 games after he left the Royals for catcher Ed Hearn, who got 35 at-bats the rest of his career. Greg Hibbard and Melido Perez each won double-digit games four times after they were traded for Floyd Bannister, whose career was about through. Even Danny Jackson finally fulfilled predictions for a 20-win season right after the Royals traded him.

Bill Veeck, the maverick baseball owner whose "Go-Go" White Sox had stopped the Yankees' string of 1950s pennant winners, summed up the plight of surprise teams trying to bring back their pennant-winning magic: "You can't recapture the rapture."

❄ ❄ ❄ ❄ ❄ ❄

So the '85 Royals had no last hurrah. There was no defining end of their era, either. They just sort of petered out.

Dane Iorg left right after the World Series. Platooned rightfielders Motley and Pat Sheridan didn't last another season with the Royals. Catcher Jim Sundberg was gone after '86, Buddy Biancalana left during '87, Balboni during '88.

At the same time, the Royals handled the decline and departure of their stars clumsily. The front office nudged McRae to become the team's hitting coach, then offered him the manager's job late in '87—but only on a trial basis, which didn't appeal to his heightened sense of pride.

Lonnie Smith was released at the end of '87 and felt the Royals blackballed him when no other team offered him a job. So he went out, bought a gun and imagined using it on Royals general manager John Schuerholz, but of course never did.

Quisenberry couldn't bear his reduced pitching role, moaned about it publicly, asked to be traded—despite having a lifetime contract—and finally was released in 1988.

White was not treated with the respect he expected, either. He wasn't even put in the lineup for a fan group's "Frank White Day," and he was unceremoniously released after the '90 season.

Wilson was called out publicly by his manager for having a "bad attitude" and was released after the '90 season, too.

Saberhagen, with two Cy Young awards, was traded in a 1991 deal that shocked the city and didn't pan out.

Even Brett's ending had its rocky moments, as he felt the team didn't want him back for one final bon voyage season. Still, he finished up in memorable fashion by kissing home plate in front of the home fans in 1993.

Owner Ewing Kauffman saved the team twice before his death in 1993. He and his wife, Muriel, often showed their devotion to the team with royal blue outfits. *Courtesy of the Kansas City Royals/Chris Vleisides*

A decade after the '85 series, then, no one was left on the team who had played in the 1985 World Series. And by then the Royals, once one of baseball's "model" organizations, had deteriorated into an ownerless, hapless and penniless club.

Ewing Kauffman saved the team twice. First he bought out his financially floundering partner, Avron Fogelman, before Fogelman could sell his majority-interest option. Then, Kauffman devised a complicated ownership succession plan in which the team would be held in trust until a local owner could be found. Well, after Kauffman's death in 1993, no one locally stepped forward. After major-league owners rejected the sale of the club to a group headed by East Coast lawyer Miles Prentice, Wal-Mart CEO David Glass of Arkansas thankfully stepped forward as the savior, stabilizing the franchise.

At the same time, a string of high draft picks blew up on the team. There were horror stories like Jeff Granger, the No. 5 overall pick in 1993. He was a 6-foot-3 college pitcher, a lefty with "major league stuff right then and there," a Royals official once said. Granger made it to the majors, but his stuff wasn't major league. He ended up pitching just $31 2/3$ innings and giving up 32 runs. After him, in one stretch at the end of the '90s and into the '00s, the Royals used seven first-round picks in five years on pitchers, and none developed into a reliable major-league starter.

They couldn't afford such a dry spell because the economics of the game had turned against them. The 1985 Royals would be the last team to appear in the World Series without a player making more than $1 million. When that team won it all, it was during the most competitive time in baseball history, with small markets enjoying their biggest successes. Some disparity existed between high-salary and low-salary teams—the top-spending team in 1985, the New York Yankees, had a payroll almost three times higher than the lowest-spending team, the Seattle Mariners—but the spread between them was just about $10 million. By 2004, the top-spending team, again the Yankees, had a payroll almost seven times higher than the lowest-spending team, and the spread had grown to an astronomical $155 million.

Big bucks didn't guarantee success, but it sure made a difference in competing. Teams like the Yankees or Red Sox could populate their rosters with a dozen big-name, high-priced free agents. The Royals couldn't. And if the Yankees or Red Sox made a mistake with a player, they could just buy a replacement. The Royals couldn't. They were stuck with their young players who didn't pan out.

So every year, it seemed, the Royals hit a new low. The team finished in last place for the first time ever. Then last place in consecutive years. Then they cracked 100 losses for the first time. Julia Irene Kauffman, daughter of Ewing, stopped wearing her mother's diamond-encrusted World Series ring. "We were losing when I wore it," she said.

Eventually expectations dried up as closer Jeff Montgomery acknowledged to a Kansas City television station: "If we could be a .500 ball club, I think that would be the equivalent [of] the Kansas City Royals winning the World Series." Finally, even prominent long-time fans like Bill James threw up their hands in frustration and emailed *The Kansas City Star's* Joe Posnanski to announce, "I give up on them."

Then something special happened. In spring training 2003, manager Tony Pena handed out t-shirts reading, "We believe what we can do." It became an attitude and a rallying cry. The Royals shocked baseball by getting off to a 16-3 start, with some improbable come-from-behind victories. The team soon hit the skids, like everyone expected, but bounced back, stayed in the pennant race into September and finished with the franchise's first winning season in nearly a decade.

The next year, that bubble of joy burst. Everything that went right in 2003 went wrong in 2004. The team didn't get off to a fast start, didn't exhibit a "believe" attitude, didn't get as many clutch hits, didn't produce as many comeback wins and didn't get big years out of newcomers like Juan Gonzalez. The team ended up losing a club-record 104 games—a mark up there, too, with the worst Kansas City A's squads.

Kansas City is again a baseball town that's become numb to losing.

* * * * * * *

Every so often, the stadium rocks again, for at least a moment.

The team may be down, they may be in the midst of a losing streak, but suddenly on the Jumbotron in left field, it's the fall of 1985 again: That Moment, Game 6, when Dane Iorg lofted a flare over the infield and Jim Sundberg chugged around third base and slid just out of reach of the tag. Seeing that again, the usually sedate Royals fans freak out. They stand up. They bang seats. They scream. Sometimes, it's the loudest cheering of the night.

That's about all Royals fans have as a visible reminder of the '85 World Series, because nearly all the players are no longer around. They're not in the organization, not in the broadcast booth, not even in the community. Instead they're scattered all across the country.

McRae—in Florida. Sheridan—Michigan. Sundberg—Texas. Jorge Orta—Illinois. Iorg—Utah. Joe Beckwith—Alabama. Balboni—New Jersey. Steve Farr—North Carolina. Biancalana—Nebraska. Lynn Jones—Pennsylvania. Onix Concepcion—Puerto Rico. Leibrandt and Smith—Georgia. Saberhagen, Gubicza and Black—California. Wilson—he moves around.

Just a handful of '85 Royals remain around the Kansas City area full time—Brett, Jackson, John Wathan and Greg Pryor. Jamie Quirk, White and Motley spend parts of the year in town.

Almost all of the '85 players are still involved in baseball in some way—Balboni, White, Jackson, Motley, Wilson and Orta at minor-league levels; Brett, Black, Sundberg, Jones, McRae, Wathan and Quirk with big league teams; and Saberhagen, Gubicza, Leibrandt, Beckwith and Biancalana working with youths.

Only Brett, White and Wathan have any connection with the Royals organization anymore. For most of the rest, they may look up the Royals in the standings every so often, or pause at a Royals game on TV to catch the score. Other than that, they've lost touch with the team. As Lynn Jones put it, "The ties have been broken."

They've lost touch with each other a little, too. Half the team used to get together every winter for about a decade for a golf trip, just to keep the group together. Even guys like Balboni, who wasn't much of a golfer, would go. At night, as the players took over a hotel restaurant and the beer and wine flowed, they talked about what their kids were doing or how many strokes they deserved for the skins game—but hardly ever about 1985, the season, the playoffs, the series. They just didn't bring it up, except for an occasional amusing recollection, like before Game 3 when Cardinals owner Gussie Busch's wagon almost tipped over as the Clydesdales pulled it over the pitcher's mound. But they didn't talk about the games or the clutch plays or the controversial calls. They were like veterans who had been to war, had fought together and won, and didn't need to hash it over much again.

Make no mistake, however, the 1985 World Series represented the high-light of those players' baseball lives. Only Jackson ever went on to play for another championship-winning team. For almost everyone else, a mini-replica World Series trophy from 1985 sits in a case or on a shelf in their homes. For a bunch of them, like Leibrandt and Sheridan, their display includes World Series balls and bats signed by the team. For a few of them, like Balboni and Sundberg, a team picture hangs under glass. And for a couple of them, like Beckwith and Jones, the diamond-encrusted World Series ring remains on a finger.

For several key participants, though, the 1985 World Series stayed with them in more worldly ways.

For some of them, it helped define their baseball legacies.

For a few, it had a significance that extended into their family lives.

And for others, it became something they struggled to get past.

Chapter 12

BRET SABERHAGEN:

"It's Time to Catch Up on Some Things"

A lanky boy stands on the pitcher's mound. He's a pro prospect. The star of his team. Starting a tournament game. He knows only a little about spotting hitters' weaknesses or setting hitters up or staying composed on the mound. Can't really blame him. He's only a high school senior. Besides, he's got someone on his side who knows a lot more about all that stuff.

Bret Saberhagen sits in a corner of the tin can they call a dugout at this Los Angeles high school field. Out in front of him, the grass is as lush and green as a country club golf course. It's an early evening in March. The sun dips below scattered palm trees. The sky is cloudless. The San Gabriel Mountains form a jagged horizon beyond right field. The game has started. It's the bottom of the first inning. The catcher stands and turns toward the dugout. Saberhagen, wearing a black pinstriped uniform like the rest of the team, touches a spot on his face, then a part of his thigh. The catcher turns away, goes into his crouch and puts down fingers for his pitcher to see. The boy on the mound throws. Ball one.

Saberhagen spits a sunflower seed. He's tan and trim—doesn't look like he's gained many pounds since his playing days. The only signs of aging are the crow's-feet lines angling out from his eyes. He sits there, chewing a mouthful of seeds, gesturing to his face and thigh, then spitting out one seed at a time. All the while watching, plotting, directing. No expression on his face. Even as the boy on the mound gets in trouble.

The second batter lines a single to left field.

The third batter rips a single to right field.

The fourth batter takes a curve and both runners take off. No throw from the catcher. Double steal.

Saberhagen orders an intentional walk, loading the bases with just one out.

The fifth batter steps in and quickly falls behind 0-2 in the count. A change-up just misses the outside corner. The count goes full. Saberhagen touches one side of his face, then one side of his thigh. Fastball on the outside corner. Foul ball. Saberhagen touches the same side of his face, then the same side of his thigh. Fastball on the outside corner. Foul ball. Saberhagen repeats the same gestures two more times. Finally, a pop-up is induced for the second out.

The sixth batter comes up. Saberhagen gestures differently. "Keep your weight back," the runner at second base yells to the batter. The pitch is a change-up. Fouled off. Saberhagen repeats the gestures. "Keep your weight back," the runner at second calls out again. Another change-up, ripped foul.

Saberhagen doesn't like what he's seeing. He calls time.

He pops out of the dugout and crosses the base line, still walking with his shoulders bent forward slightly and the bouncing, quick-stepping strut familiar to Royals fans from long ago. He reaches the boy on the mound.

"We need to change the signs," Saberhagen tells him. The runner at second has broken his code, deciphered his gestures. "Keep your weight back" is a universal tip for a change-up. "Here's what we'll do…," Saberhagen begins. They stand there on the mound. Coach and pitcher. They're nearly the same height. With the same high cheekbones. Same thin nose. Same pointy chin. In fact, people say they're mirror images.

That's because the boy on the mound is Saberhagen's son, Drew William Saberhagen. He's the baby that was born during the 1985 World Series.

❖❖❖❖❖❖❖

It was 18 years before when the Baby Bret Watch became a World Series subplot, played out before millions of people on national television.

There was Bret in St. Louis, pitching the Royals back into the series in Game 3, cruising along with a big lead, mugging for the camera late in the game, patting his tummy and mouthing to his wife Janeane through the TV screen, "Hold on. I'll be home." Bret was just 21 years old. This was his first kid. He had been to Lamaze classes. He wanted to be in the delivery room.

The next two days in St. Louis, ABC's announcers reminded viewers the baby was coming "any day now." They even promised to convey the news during a college football show if the World Series ended before the delivery. Not since the birth of England's Prince William to Prince Charles and Princess Diana had there been such anticipation over a new arrival.

After Game 5, Bret made it home. At 6:30 a.m. on the day of Game 6, his wife's water broke. The doctor at St. Luke's Hospital assured Bret the baby would be born by game time that night. Bret settled by his wife's bed, watched hours of

The arrival of baby Drew Saberhagen turned into such a media event that his mother, Janeane, showed him off a day after giving birth. *Courtesy of St. Luke's Hospital*

Saturday morning cartoons and nervously coached—breathe in through your nose, out through your mouth. The contractions quickened. Bret stayed quiet. He let Janeane crush his hands.

At 11:38 a.m., the baby came out: nine pounds, three ounces and 20½ inches—a big boy. The doctor unwrapped the umbilical cord from around his neck, and Bret snipped it off. Bret and his wife had already chosen the name Drew. It had no family significance. They just liked the sound of it.

Bret stayed at the hospital, making the obligatory phone calls and buying cigars. The team sent over a gift. It included a t-shirt with "Future Royal" printed on it. Around 3 p.m., he headed out to the ballpark and played the proud daddy, bouncing around the clubhouse, passing out the cigars and chomping on one himself. He reported the baby had "good fingers for a split-fingered pitch."

Of course, TV passed along the news to the rest of the nation that night of October 26. And when Jim Sundberg was called safe at home, Bret led the charge out of the dugout. He would get to pitch again, in the biggest game of the season. He headed back to St. Luke's to bid good night to his wife, then finally made it home. He got 10 hours of sleep.

The next night, Game 7 was another whirlwind. The Royals scored early, the Cards came unglued, Bret breezed and fans held up a sign asking, "Drew Saberhagen: World Series MVP 2005?" Bret stayed at the ballpark for hours afterward, still dressed in his baseball pants and cleats, spraying champagne and boogeying over and over to the song the Royals played before games: "There she was justa walkin' down the street, singin' do-wah-diddy-diddy-dum-diddy-do... ."

Then it was back to the hospital in time for Drew's 2 a.m. feeding. Then home for a shower and change. Then back to the ballpark at 5 a.m., Monday morning, to appear on *Good Morning America*. Then back to the hospital. Then back to the ballpark in mid-morning to catch the team bus to the downtown ticker-tape parade.

Going here, going there, go, go, go. It was madness. But Bret didn't mind. He loved to keep moving. And he did that for the entire off-season. There was a visit with President Reagan. A sit-down with Johnny Carson. A jaunt to the Virgin Islands for a golf tournament. A stop in New York for a holiday TV special. Another hop to New York to collect his Cy Young award. Charity events around Kansas City. Dinner banquets on both coasts. Yet when he was home, Bret was changing Drew's diapers, taking him to doctor checkups, giving him baths, holding him in his arms. He loved being a Dad.

Then it was time for the next baseball season. Bret hadn't prepared. In his first spring training game of 1986, he came out smoking, throwing almost 95 mph. As if there had been no winter. As if his arm didn't need to gradually build strength. His arm started hurting. When the season started, he got knocked around. One day in June, he gave up eight runs before getting an out in the second inning. In July, he was sent to the bullpen. His arm kept hurting. He ended up with a 7-12 record and an earned run average of 4.15, right near the league-average ERA of 4.18. He was merely average.

That next off-season, Bret stayed home. He wasn't called to pick up awards or chat with celebrities. He took a 20-percent pay cut. He stewed. He had an exercise station installed in his basement. He lifted weights. He ran on a treadmill. He prepared. It worked. Bret was 15-3 at mid-season. He became the first Royal to start the All-Star Game. Then he slumped. Drew had been accidentally burned. A pot of steaming beans had fallen on him. Bret was distracted. His pitching motion got out of sync. He won just three of his last 15 starts. His final numbers—18-10, with a 3.36 ERA—were still good enough for American League Comeback Player of the Year.

The arc of his career had been set. Not a smooth arc, but a jagged, up-down, stock market-like trend line. Stretches of greatness. And stretches of mediocrity. In 1988, Bret started 10-6, then went 4-10 the rest of the way, finishing with a 3.80 ERA, close to the league average of 3.97. In 1989, he was 3-4 in late May, then went on a magical tear—20-2—to win his second Cy Young award. In 1990, Bret felt something go "pop" in his elbow and eventually had surgery, finishing with a 5-9 record. In 1991, he bounced back, posting a 13-8 mark, including a no-hitter against the Chicago White Sox.

In the process of remaining the ace of the Royals staff through the rest of the 1980s, Bret Saberhagen (middle, leaning forward) went through many peaks and valleys.
Courtesy of the Kansas City Royals/Chris Vleisides

Through it all, little Drew picked up the baseball bug. Bret and his wife took Drew and little sister Brittany to games. Royals Stadium, like other big-league parks, had a room under the stands stocked with toys for players' kids. Brittany stayed there. Drew wanted to sit in the stands. After games, Bret had him brought down to the clubhouse. Drew invariably came in, whizzed past Bret, went up to whoever played well and offered congratulations. One time, after an error by shortstop Kurt Stillwell led to a Royals loss, 5-year-old Drew found Kurt at his locker and told him, "Don't worry about that error. You'll get 'em next time." Once the Royals hit the road, however, Bret was an absentee parent. Drew started T-ball baseball in suburban Kansas City. Bret hardly saw a game.

After the 1991 season, the Royals did the unthinkable. They traded their two-time Cy Young winner. He was still in his 20s, but general manager Herk Robinson considered him "frail," liable to break down. Bret was dazed. Janeane cried. The Royals seemed like family. Players called. They said they were going to miss Drew around the clubhouse. But it was the Royals' big chance to acquire some hitting. So Sabes was shipped off to the Mets, to the East Coast.

The wife and kids, meanwhile, moved full-time to the West Coast, to Los Angeles, where Bret and Janeane had grown up high-school sweethearts. Within a year Bret broke up with his wife and took up with a singer. Now Bret was really apart from the kids. They visited him only three times during the six-month baseball season. He started putting down roots on the East Coast. He got married again. He rehabbed a house on Long Island and invested in a sports academy and video arcade. His new wife sang in a band.

All the while, his career slowly crumbled, just as the Royals had suspected it would. He came down with one injury after another. In 1992, it was tendonitis in a finger. In 1993, it was knee surgery. In 1995, he had shoulder surgery. In 1996, he had another shoulder surgery. He kept making comebacks. The talent was still there, winning 14 games after one surgery, 15 games after another surgery. But his durability was gone. He never pitched 180 innings a year after leaving the Royals. He bounced around to a couple more teams. He thought plenty about retiring. But nearly half of his multimillion-dollar salaries was going to alimony.

On the West Coast, Drew was getting into real baseball. His mom, Janeane, signed him up, took him to games, sat in the bleachers. If Bret got to see him play twice a season, that was a lot. Drew started pitching, but youth baseball coaches shied away from offering him advice. What could they say to the kid of a major leaguer? Occasionally, Drew sent videotapes of his pitching to Bret, and Bret called with tips. All the while, Drew harbored a dream. He knew the stories of his birth. He had his own videotapes of the '85 World Series. He had a photograph of his Dad on his bedroom wall and snapshots from father-son games in a photo album.

But he just wanted Bret to retire, come back to L.A. and coach him.

Then Bret did.

He retired in 2001, after another two shoulder surgeries. By then, he was divorced a second time. So, he moved back to L.A., to the hilly, outlying suburb of Calabasas, where 16-year-old Drew and his other kids lived with their remarried mom. As soon as Bret came back, Drew moved in with him for a while. They did regular father-son stuff they hadn't done much of, like sit and watch sports on TV. "I've missed a lot of birthdays, I've missed a lot of things," Bret said at the time. "I can't make up for the stuff I've missed. I owe everything to baseball … but now that it's over, it's time to catch up on some things."

Bret started going to Drew's high school baseball games. The next season, one of the coaches left the team. Head Coach Rick Nathanson asked Bret if he'd like to help out.

"Shit, yeah," Bret told him.

❋ ❋ ❋ ❋ ❋ ❋ ❋

So there was Bret out on the mound with his son in the first inning of a high school baseball tournament. Based loaded, two outs, two strikes on the batter, with the runner on second having stolen Bret's signs. This happened some-times. Stealing signs was part of baseball. But Bret, ever the competitor, didn't like the opposition showing him up. One time, a parent stood behind the back-stop, yelling out "fastball" or "curve" based on Bret's gestures. After the inning, Bret went up to the parent and hissed, "You keep doing that and one of your players is going to get one in the ribs." In a high school game.

This time, there's no room to put someone on base. Bret tells Drew what to throw on the next three pitches. The first one's a fastball. The batter flies out to centerfield. End of inning, no damage.

In the bottom of the first, the Saberhagens' Calabasas team scores a run, giving Drew a lead. He goes back out for the second inning. He faces the plate, standing with both feet on the rubber, shoulders slightly hunched forward, mitt held up by his face, his left hand gripping the ball inside it. Then he takes a quick little step backward, turns, hoists his right knee up to his chest, tucks his mitt toward his body, thrusts forward off his left foot and delivers the ball overhand. If not for the shaggy blond hair and stout hips, you'd think you were watching a left-handed Bret Saberhagen. That's how similar Drew's pitching motion is to what Bret's was.

"A spitting image of Bret. It's scary," says Mark Gubicza, Bret's long-time friend and teammate with the Royals, who coaches a rival L.A. high school team.

The similarities hardly end there. Drew looks like his Dad.

"The mirror image. It's eerie," says Janeane, Drew's mother and Bret's first wife.

Drew's a jokester like his dad. He's been known to stick a wad of chewing gum on a teammate's back, just like Bret was known to light a coach's shoe on fire or plant a rubber snake in the grass where an umpire stood.

Drew's the same type of pitcher his Dad was, too, although he relies more on control and guile than a blazing fastball. And Drew's likely to get picked in the major-league draft just like his Dad was, although Drew wants to go to col-lege first. Tonight, a couple of pro scouts are here behind the backstop to watch him. They've got their radar guns out. The pitcher facing Calabasas is hitting 87 mph on the guns. That's major-league caliber. But he's wild, too. He's already walked in a run. Meanwhile, Drew's only hitting 80-81 mph on the guns. That will change as he gets stronger. But already he's got some skills the gun can't measure—instincts, poise and confidence. "He knows how to pitch and throw his pitches for strikes," says Mike Baker, a California-area scout for the Atlanta Braves.

Drew is obliging the scouts this night against traditional L.A. powerhouse El Camino Real. El Camino is the champion of last year's tournament and a team coming off back-to-back 10-0 mercy-rule wins in opening rounds of this year's tournament. In the third inning, Drew throws five pitches and sets down the side in order, 1-2-3. In the fourth inning, he gives up a couple of singles, then picks off a runner and ends the threat with a strikeout. By the sixth, he's faced

Spitting image: Bret and Drew Saberhagen pose during the spring of 2004. Bret was the pitching coach for his son's high school team in Calabasas, California. *Courtesy of Bret Saberhagen*

just two batters over the minimum since his shaky first inning. He's throwing a shutout. He's showing why he anchored a suburban L.A. all-star team the previous summer, a team that played for the national championship in the Little League Big League World Series. He's showing why he's been named to "all-area" teams in one of the nation's hotbeds of baseball talent.

Of course, he's got a long way to go to match his Dad. Even at the high school level.

❊ ❊ ❊ ❊ ❊ ❊ ❊

The field where Drew's pitching this night is off Balboa Boulevard in the heart of Los Angeles' San Fernando Valley. Bret grew up just a few miles from here. He used to ride his bike past this field on his way to Little League games sometimes. Back then, the Valley embodied the American Dream for millions of Americans, because it was the suburbia they saw on television.

Beaver Cleaver and his family lived in the lily-white San Fernando Valley. So did the Brady Bunch in a neighborhood of split-levels. The Valley legally belonged to Los Angeles and contained half of the city's land area, but it was its own world. The Valley was swimming pools, bridge games, backyard barbeques and kids on bikes. It was where people left the keys in their cars. Where teenagers drag raced down the main streets. And where, too, by the dawn of the 1980s, suburbia was being spoofed. The Valley became where drug-dazed airheads attended high school in the movie *Fast Times at Ridgemont High*, and where Frank and Moon Zappa immortalized the "fer sures" and "ohmigods" they heard at the Sherman Oaks Galleria for the song "Valley Girl."

That song came out in 1982—Bret Saberhagen's senior year.

Bret was a point guard on his Cleveland High School basketball team. By the time that season ended, the baseball team was already practicing. Bret tried to catch up. He aired out his arm and injured it. Pro scouts had been following Bret for several years. They called the coach to ask if Bret was pitching. "No, but he is playing shortstop," the coach told them. The scouts stopped coming.

Bret went to a doctor. The doc dragged out an X-ray and put it on the wall. "I suspect it's a rotator-cuff problem," the doc said. The most dreaded pitching injury. The doc proscribed a shot. Bret hated needles. The family sought another opinion. Bret wound up with a chiropractor. That doc thought Bret merely suffered from improper conditioning. The doc massaged the arm. Bret started pitching again. His velocity was down, from the mid-80s to the high 70s. He looked like he was pushing the ball, not throwing fluidly. Still, Bret was winning.

Toward the end of the season, Bret started against El Camino Real. The Royals' Guy Hansen was the only scout there. He had stuck it out during Bret's season. He couldn't believe Bret's ability had disappeared. As usual, Hansen was behind home plate. And as usual, Bret looked like he was floating the ball in there, throwing slightly sidearm. Then in the middle of the game, Hansen started hearing the ball go "pop" in the catcher's glove. Bret's arm was coming more overhand. Hansen pulled out his radar gun. It showed 86-87 mph. When Bret came off the mound after the inning, Hansen went over to him.

"You got it back, don't you?" Hansen asked.

"I think I do," Bret replied.

A week or so afterward was the major league draft. The Royals weren't too interested in Bret. The Major League Scouting Bureau had turned in reports on him. The marks were pretty low. Two days after the draft started, Bret was still available. Hansen pleaded. "Draft him as an infielder." The Royals did. In the 19th round.

Less than two weeks later, on June 14, Bret played his last high school game. It was in Dodgers Stadium for the L.A. city championship. Bret was in a zone. His fastball was darting. His curveball was biting. Wherever the catcher put his mitt, that's where the ball went. But he had other things going for him too—poise, a maturity "beyond his years," as one coach put it.

One batter reached base in the first inning, on an error. Meanwhile, Bret's Cleveland High teammates piled up runs. Two in the first. Five more in the second. In the fifth inning, a teammate approached Bret on the bench. "Hey, Sabes," he bellowed, "you're throwing a no-hitter, dude."

Among baseball superstitions, that's about as taboo as it gets. No one in the dugout is supposed to utter the words "no-hitter" while one's in progress.

But it didn't matter that night. When Bret's catcher fielded a bunt and threw the last batter out at first, Bret had the only no-hitter in the history of the L.A. championship game. It was a resounding 13-0 win. He retired the last 20 batters and surrendered no walks. Take away the error and it was a perfect game.

After that, Bret spurned college, turned pro and left home. Then after his career ended, he returned for good and rejoined the San Fernando Valley's suburban exodus, this time out into the hills beyond. Calabasas, with its swimming pools and manicured lawns and serene lifestyle, is where the Brady Bunch might have moved when they grew up. Even with the price of a split-level hovering around $1 million.

These days, the old-time Valley is an entirely different place. All around the Van Nuys business district are pupuserias and mueblerias and travel agents specializing in discount tickets for international carriers. Granada Hills High School, once a bastion of the all-white Valley, has students who speak 28 languages other than English. In the old section where Bret grew up, 43 percent of the residents are foreign-born. The Valley is known today as the place where police beat Rodney King. Gangs leave their marks on street signs.

And the school where Drew is pitching is surrounded by a 10-foot-tall chain-link fence.

❉ ❉ ❉ ❉ ❉ ❉

It's the top of the seventh inning now in Drew's game. It's the final inning. Calabasas is leading 2-0. Drew's got the shutout going. Seems like old times in the family. A Saberhagen beating El Camino Real again.

Then the leadoff batter hits a bouncer to third. The throw goes over first base, advancing the runner to second. The next batter pops a fastball foul, behind first base. Drew's the first baseman when he's not pitching. Now his back-up overruns the pop-up. "Get in the game," Calabasas head coach Rick Nathanson yells out from the dugout. Drew comes back with a changeup on the outside corner. Strike three. One out. Up comes the eighth-place hitter in the lineup. He gets hold of one. He sends it deep, deep, over the centerfield's head, up against the fence. That breaks up the shutout. Now the tying run stands at second base.

No one's warming up for Calabasas. Drew has to finish this game. Bret spits a seed, gets up out of the dugout again and heads to the mound.

Bret's committed himself to this high school team. He's not working. He's got the time. So he waters the school's ball diamond. He rakes the infield after practices. He got up mornings and built bullpens with raised mounds and permanent home plates by the dugouts. He could have hired others to do all that. Instead, he spends his money on other stuff for the team. He makes sure water jugs are filled with Gatorade. He bought every player a pair of spikes.

"I've known other former major leaguers, and they can be full of them-selves," says Howard Hirsch, father of Calabasas's centerfielder. "He's not like that. He's a real nice man, real generous."

For Drew, having Bret there has meant everything he thought it would. Bret's been the pitching coach. He's tinkered with Drew's delivery, getting him to keep his torso turned sideways longer, so he has better control with his pitch-es. Bret's called the pitches, too, giving Drew confidence that he can throw any pitch in any count. And Bret's not been shy about jumping on Drew sometimes, the first time someone's really done that to him. "Him being here and getting on me a little bit has been good for me," Drew admits.

But Bret's not getting on him here, not on the mound, not with the game on the line. No, this trip to the mound is a primer on poise. The infielders gath-er around Bret and Drew and the catcher. "Don't worry about the error," Bret tells them. "Keep your head up. All we need is two outs." Then he turns to Drew. He reminds his pitcher that the coaches are trying to limit him to 90 pitches, so his arm stays fresh and strong. And the count is now past 80.

Bret heads back to his seat in the tin can dugout. He chews, gestures and spits. Batter up. Strike. Strike. Foul. Strike three. Two out. Next up. Grounder to short. As the throw goes to first, Drew walks off the mound pumping his left fist up and down. Teammates surround him and throw their gloves in the air. Half of the 200 spectators in the metal bleachers erupt, jumping to their feet, clapping and roaring. It's Drew's first win of his senior season.

"We rule the Valley," Coach Nathanson declares afterward.

"My hat's off to Drew. And his Dad called a great game for him, too."

❀❀❀❀❀❀

Drew's team finished the season 12-11. He had a 4-5 record with a 2.05 ERA, completing his high school career with a 1.69 ERA. He was picked in the 38th round of the June 2004 major-league amateur draft, but didn't sign and instead took a scholarship to Pepperdine University.

CHAPTER 13

DANE IORG:

"THAT STUFF DOESN'T MEAN MUCH TO ME"

He faithfully follows his Mormon values. No alcohol, no smoking and no drugs, of course. Not even any coffee or flashy clothes. But the core beliefs go beyond the cosmetic. They require not just morality but modesty and selflessness, too. So life is built around close and long-lasting relationships—with God, with family, with friends. How many years you played big-league ball or how many hits you got doesn't matter much. "Often the achievements that matter most are not those that are public or highly valued by society," the church proclaims.

That explains Dane Iorg's home in the south suburbs of Salt Lake City. Walk in and to the left is a living room, with a few stuffed chairs opposite the fireplace. To the right is a converted dining room, mostly empty except for the family computer. Through the short front hallway is a sparsely furnished family room, with a leather couch, love seat and easy chair arranged diagonally to a big-screen TV in the corner. Opening into this room, on the right, is the kitchen and a family eating table with wood benches.

It all looks simple and tasteful but slightly bare. Even the walls are mostly blank. Lining a mantle above the family-room fireplace are small portraits of each of Dane's eight children. And hanging on the wall of the front hall are a half-dozen family pictures next to a painting of Jesus Christ. But that's it.

Dane Iorg (No. 9) walked off the field after being mobbed by teammates following his game-winning hit in Game 6. *Courtesy of the Kansas City Royals/Chris Vleisides*

Nowhere is there any photo, any memento, any glass case, any indication at all that Dane played baseball, starred in the World Series or delivered the most famous hit in Royals team history.

A World Series ring? In a bedroom drawer, not on his hand. The baseball from his game-winning Game 6 hit? Somewhere, he thinks. The broken bat from that hit? Not sure what happened to it. Photos of him at bat or in uniform? Tucked away. An old jersey? Given to a baseball school to display.

One evening after grilling steaks for dinner, Dane sinks into the family room love seat. His Hollywood-actor looks have evolved from *Quantum Leap's* Scott Bakula to the *Rockford Files'* James Garner now. He's still stout with his lumberjack-thick arms and round, wide blue eyes, but years out of baseball have added a paunch under his golf shirt. His longtime wife and college sweetheart, Gay, sits on the edge of the couch, her blond hair in a bob and her figure still trim for someone who's given birth eight times. As a humble and devout Mormon couple, they allow themselves a few trappings of Dane's success—like a pool and hot tub in the back. But as for baseball, that's something that others may see as glamorous or special, worthy of special rooms or walls filled with memorabilia, but it's part of the past for the Iorgs now, another life long ago.

"It's like we moved on," Gay says. "I see people sometimes and they're still living that. It's just not that important to us.

"It's almost like that world doesn't exist anymore."

Dane shakes his head. "That stuff doesn't mean much to me."

Besides, how would he look with an oversized, diamond-encrusted ring on his finger every day? "That's kind of extravagant," Gay states, "for a lumber sales-man."

❈ ❈ ❈ ❈ ❈ ❈ ❈

Dane became a free agent after the Royals' glory of '85. He had been unhappy with his lack of playing time. It was a constant theme in his career, and Dane was still itching for a starting job, just one opportunity to show what he could do over a full season. His clutch World Series hit gave him a new chance. That winter was the first year of baseball owners' collusion toward free agents. All-star Kirk Gibson couldn't get a nibble from other teams. Dane Iorg, though, got feelers from a handful of them. He signed with San Diego. But it didn't work out there, either. He received just 106 at-bats and batted only .226. He lost interest in the game. It was time to hang it up and spend time with his growing brood at home.

He ended his 10-year career with a .276 batting average. His best years, like the two years he hit over .300 and two others he hit over .290, all came with the St. Louis Cardinals.

Now he was 36 years old with no idea what to do with his life.

"Players like myself, it's a pretty tough transition. Most people are into a career. After baseball, man, you're figuring out what you're going to do next. You didn't make enough money that you were financially secure. You have to go to work."

Former baseball players sometimes have trouble with this. Many hadn't gotten an education past high school. And they didn't have skills that transferred to the working world. Ex-pitcher Dick Bosman, upon leaving the game after his 11-year career, once said: "It hits you every day. If you play a kid's game for years, really give it your life, then have to walk away—well, anybody that says it doesn't rip 'em apart … 90 percent of 'em are lying." Iorg's best friend in baseball, Darrell Porter, told an interviewer just months before dying in a park with cocaine in his body: "It's a funny world we live in in pro sports, and it's not very realistic. A lot of us had never done anything in our lives except play sports. Finding your purpose and goals after you leave the game can take a while."

So it was with Dane. He wanted to stay around southern Salt Lake City, where he had attended Brigham Young University, where he had settled, where he knew lots of people. But what did he offer the working world? Professional skills? Not really. So he went back to finish college at BYU. He worked toward a degree in physical education. He started coaching his sons in Little League and American Legion ball. He thought of becoming a high school coach. Then he found out how much coaches made. That ended that dream. Around the time he was graduating, though, he got a phone call. An old friend was now an executive with a lumber wholesaler called Capital Lumber Co. The company was moving into the Salt Lake market. Did Dane want to be a salesman?

It made sense. Dane had grown up in far-northern California, in lumber country. His dad had worked in lumber mills. And Dane had spent time as a teenager lifting and hauling lumber in a mill. He knew wood. He knew the language. Plus, he had been in sales before during some offseasons as a player and he seemed to have a personality suited to sales—talkative, chipper, a story-swapper.

At first, it was tough for him to get his specialty cedars and redwoods into the big retail yards. He'd walk in somewhere in the morning and the yard manager would tell him anything to get to get him to leave. But a few people recognized his name. One day he walked into Stock Building Supply in West Jordan, the highest grossing lumberyard in the state. He met Bob Pratt, one of the business managers. Pratt was a big baseball fan. "Hey, you came up in 1977, started with the Phillies, then went to the Cardinals ..." Pratt announced. It wasn't like Dane had been a baseball all-star. He had been a BYU star, an All-American, but it wasn't in football or basketball, the sports more Utah people cared about. But baseball helped break the ice for him in sales. "It got me in the door," he says.

But Dane didn't bring it up himself. That wasn't his style. He wasn't a swaggering, "I played pro ball" kind of ex-player. No, his style was a slow-talking, slow-sauntering, easygoing, good old boy kind of westerner. He was honest. He treated people right. He didn't try to rip anybody off. And he invested in relationships. One time, he told an assistant yard manager at one store about a yard manager job opening at a bigger store. The guy ended up getting the job, and through subsequent years ordered millions of dollars in lumber from Dane.

"It's definitely a relationship business," Dane says.

A decade into this job now, it's on autopilot for Dane. So much so that his golf clubs lie across the back seat of his company-provided Chevrolet Silverado pickup truck. He's the sales manager but he doesn't go into the office or handle paperwork. He just keeps up relationships with the biggest stores. Some of the time, those stores just call him up with orders to restock the wood he carries for backyard decks and porches. But he still stops by the stores, checks on inventory and hands the yard manager a slip of paper with what the store needs to reorder.

In the spring of 2004, he was having record months. As he was fond of saying: "This is awesome, man."

❈ ❈ ❈ ❈ ❈ ❈

Dane pulls the Silverado into the parking lot of a store in Orem, a south suburb of Salt Lake City. He grabs his binder of prices and a notepad to write on and walks into the back lot where the lumber is stacked on warehouse-like shelves. "See those red tags," he points at various stacks, "those are mine."

But some of those stacks are getting slim. He walks and scribbles on the notepad: 2 x 6 x 12 (two-inch by six-inch pieces that are 12-feet long); 4 x 4 x 8 pressure treated; and on and on. Then he heads into the store's back office. Just inside the door, behind a blue countertop, is six-foot, seven-inch, 300-pound Josh Grant. Dane hands him the slip of paper.

"Hey, Josh," Dane calls out.

"What's up, Dane? You're on Jeremy's [the yard manager] s-list."

Dane, smiling, raises his voice in mock anger: "What did I do now?"

"He says he was hoping you'd be here to take him to lunch today."

"Well that big baby. Where the hell is he? I'll kick him in the butt."

"You owe him lunch from buying so much Trex [a synthetic lumber for outdoor decks]."

"Good, next Monday, let's go."

"Next Monday? That's Memorial Day. You're not going to be working. You're one of those salesmen."

"That's true. So where is he?"

"He's off looking at a job site."

"Tell him I'll be back."

"What's this?" Josh asks, now noticing the slip of paper.

"It's what you need."

"Man, we need a lot."

"Eights and 10s [feet in length], that's all you need."

"I'm not sure if we're going to carry 8s and 10s."

"You carry 8s and 10s, don't give me that crap."

"They're thinking of going to 10s and 12s and 16s."

Dane lowers his voice, taking on a half-serious tone: "Bull crap."

"And if they need 8s, they'll cut 16s in half."

"They're nuts, because, you know what, you pay more for 16s and you sell enough to warrant it. Tell Jeremy, now he's on my s-list. You're carrying 8s."

"So when you coming down next?"

"Ah, let's do it a week from Monday, two weeks from today, if you'll be here then, okay? I want you to go."

"OK. You know, Dan [a competitor], he took me and Jeremy to Los Hermanos."

"Hey, you make the call. We'll go where you want to go."

"You can't afford where I want to go."

"I can afford it."

"Stuart Anderson's Black Angus."

"There we go, we're there."

After his playing days were over, Dane Iorg returned to the Salt Lake City area and went into the lumber and health products businesses. *Courtesy of Synergy Worldwide*

"Okay."

"Okay."

And finally Dane makes his way through the room and into the rest of the lumberyard office. All these guys are his "buddies," from the man behind the counter to the forklift driver, from the yard manager to the business manager. He takes them to lunch. He takes them fishing and golfing. He even takes them on trips to redwood mills.

"I'm better at this than I was at baseball," Dane explains at one point. "It's more natural for me."

As Dan Merrill, his boss at Capital Lumber, put it: "It's just his personality. Everyone thinks he's great."

And Dane's life is better now, too. He's not battling for a job every spring. He's not fretting about playing time during the year. He's not walking to the plate with his .230 average on the scoreboard and thinking he needs a hit. "Baseball, that was stress," he says. There's hardly any pressure in his life now. Sure, he's got sales goals and he's up against competition all the time. But he's developed his niche in the market and he works at keeping it, even expanding it occasionally. He's even making more money now than during his playing days.

Not that he shows it. He lives a quarter-mile from the base of the mountains, yet doesn't own a snowmobile or a four-wheeler. He could easily jet off to exotic locales with his wife, but the two of them prefer staying with the children, shuttling the 14-year-old girl, the last daughter, to her dance classes, or watching the 11-year-old boy, the youngest son, at Little League like all his brothers before him.

No, when it comes to material things, Dane is pretty emphatic. "I don't want anything. I keep telling my wife, 'I'm going to buy an old Porsche one of these days and fix it up.' But we'll see if I do."

Yeah, we'll see. After all, he's Mormon. He lives under a strict code of conduct that places moral values way above ego gratification. Plenty of pro ballplayers have been Mormons—Harmon Killebrew, Dale Murphy and Wally Joyner, to name a few, not to mention Dane's brother, Garth—and they all pretty much acted like that. So did Steve Young, perhaps the most celebrated modern Mormon athlete.

After Young signed a multimillion-dollar football contract out of college in 1984, he kept driving his father's 1965 Olds for another two years. Then he went out and bought another old clunker. In Los Angeles, he took an ocean-view apartment—and slept on a mattress on the floor. In his first years in San Francisco, he rented a room from a teammate. As Young grew older and especially after he married, that lifestyle eventually changed. Not his ego, however.

Same with Dane Iorg. Now it's late one afternoon. He's done making his lumberyard rounds. He drives up toward the mountains and pulls up to a glass-sided suburban office building. Inside is his side job, a second business. It's called Synergy Worldwide. It involves network marketing. Dane describes it as a "21st Century Amway type of thing." Members of the company team recruit others to sell an exclusive line of health supplements, weight-loss drinks and salon products, then get a share of the profits. This day, Dane settles behind the desk in a corner office he shares with another partner. In a society where even former bit-time ballplayers trumpet their major-league stats on the web sites of their post-baseball business ventures, or decorate their after-baseball offices with signed balls and framed jerseys, Dane isn't even mentioned on the company web site and his office is scarcely furnished. Just the desk, a couch and a two-door filing cabinet. No baseballs. No baseball pictures. The walls are bare.

"Don't get me wrong," he says. He's proud of what he accomplished on the field. He's just not into showing if off. That's just how he is. Even as a kid, when his baseball team won trophies, he wanted a t-shirt instead. Something useful.

Still, he can't escape baseball nowadays. Every so often he'll meet someone who pauses, thinks about the name Dane Iorg and makes the connection to a long-ago World Series. Or the name will bring a little recognition and the question will be, "Who'd you play for?"

Dane leans back in his chair in his unadorned corner office, swivels, puts his feet up on a corner of the desk and explains how he answers that question.

It's all about relationships.

He didn't build many relationships in Kansas City. He didn't come up from the minors with some of those teammates. He didn't play very long with them at all, less than two years. He didn't go out much with them. He didn't arrive early for their card games. He didn't wear a mustache like most of them, either. And he didn't have much feeling for the organization.

One glorious, historic at-bat couldn't change all that.

"If somebody asks me, 'Who'd you play for?' my first reaction is 'St. Louis Cardinals,' not anybody else, because I spent so much time there. That's where my opportunity came, with the Cardinals. They're the ones who developed me into a big-league baseball player, gave me the chance, the opportunity, and let me develop my career.

"That's where I spent my best years, my favorite years, where I developed the closest friendships and felt the most comfortable. Obviously because I was there, you know, seven and a half years.

"You know, as a player, that's a good baseball town. I really liked playing there. The fans were very respectful. They always cheered for you. They came out in droves when we were winning.

"And I will always be appreciative of being a St. Louis Cardinal."

Of course, he doesn't know that what he's saying is heresy to Royals fans. He doesn't know that it represents another case of Cardinals tradition smothering the Royals. He doesn't know that World Series heroes aren't supposed to value loyalty above glory.

CHAPTER 14

GEORGE BRETT:

"IT'S FUN TO GET INVOLVED IN THEIR LIVES"

There was George Brett, bathed in ecstasy, drenched in champagne, finally crowned a champion, with one parent by his side.

"Mom!" George shouted inside the wild Royals clubhouse after Game 7 of the 1985 World Series. "C'mon in and listen to me. I'm on a roll." Winning had opened an emotional spigot inside George and years of playoff frustration were gushing out: "A lotta people said we weren't any good on paper, and that's really great because paper never won a baseball game. What paper doesn't show you is what you saw tonight, what is in the heart and the pride and the determination to win that we had."

Ethel Brett Johnson, all dressed in royal blue, maneuvered past the geysers of bubbly, nudged through the throng of reporters and reached her youngest boy. "You might as well buy the coffin right now," Brett howled to her, "because ain't nothing you will see get any better than this."

Ethel just smiled and embraced him in a bear hug. It was the most memorable night of Brett's baseball life, and at least he could share it with his mother. Because his father was not there.

Jack Brett was back home in California. He had watched on TV, so he could fret and curse and rage on his own. He couldn't bear being at the game in person. It didn't matter that it was the most important game of his son's career. It didn't matter that his son really wanted him there.

George Brett came up big for the Royals in the '85 World Series, leading the team with a .370 batting average and making several sterling defensive plays. *Focus on Sport/Getty Images*

At times like these, George Brett couldn't understand his father. He felt unappreciated. His father wasn't always there for him.

George would make sure he did things differently when he became a father.

❋ ❋ ❋ ❋ ❋ ❋ ❋

Jack and Ethel had four boys—John, Ken, Bobby and George, all born two years apart. Jack had been a soldier in World War II, under General George Patton, and he applied a military approach to child rearing. He was a stern task master. He laid out rules and posted chores. Things had to be done a certain way. When the boys got up in the mornings, they had to make their beds, brush their teeth, wash their faces and get dressed. "If you didn't do those four things, you didn't get to eat," George remembered. "You didn't argue with him. That's the way it was."

The family settled in El Segundo, a suburb of Los Angeles along the Pacific coast, tucked between oil refineries and the L.A. airport. The homes were modest. Their yards were small. There were no fast-food restaurants in town. There was not a single movie theater. The main thing for kids to do was play sports. And the Brett boys were good. John was strong. Bobby was fast. But Ken was the star, the golden boy. Jack once said Ken looked like "the statue of David when he was growing up." As a high school pitcher, he lost three games in three varsity seasons. Casey Stengel and Yogi Berra came out to scout him. Ken was chosen in the major-league draft in 1966, and one year later he was with the Red Sox in the World Series. Jack Brett took the entire family to the series games in St. Louis. Ken got into two games—the youngest pitcher to take the mound in World Series history.

Jack Brett was sure he had a major-league star, and a potential dynasty in the making. Earlier that year, John was chosen in the major-league draft. Bobby was headed for pro ball, too.

George was just entering his teens then. He wasn't anything like his brothers. And his father let him know that constantly. George didn't have the desire to play that John did. He couldn't hit or field as well as Ken, couldn't run as fast as Bobby, didn't work as hard as John. He wasn't a model teenager like Ken, he didn't get good grades like Bobby, he wasn't strong like John, he didn't challenge himself like Ken, and he didn't read newspapers like Bobby.

"George couldn't do anything right for him," Bobby recalled once.

George was different because he was fun-loving and happy-go-lucky, not studious or serious. He hid his report cards. He avoided doing homework. He didn't seem to apply himself. And while Jack was an accountant who always dressed in a shirt and tie, with his black shoes shined, George was always in a t-shirt, shoes without socks or no shoes at all, and his hair disheveled.

What Jack saw in George was a lazy, slovenly boy who needed a good kick in the butt. So Jack gave it to him.

On Saturdays, when all four of the boys had games sometimes, Jack followed the older boys. Ethel went with George. When Jack did watch George, he was hard on the boy. If George missed a ball in the field, he'd hear about it from the stands: "You should have caught that ball," Jack would scold. One time George remembered playing shortstop and his father was announcing the game over the loudspeakers at the town's recreation ballpark. George flubbed a few balls in the field, and his dad even let him have it through the speakers: "That's another error by the shortstop."

After games like that, Jack greeted his son with icy silence, just seething. Once, after George struck out twice in a game, he endured the usual silent ride home from the game, and when they were walking up the steps to the front door, Jack got behind him and planted a swift, hard kick on George's behind. "That's for embarrassing the family," Jack told him.

George hated his father sometimes. But George's high school baseball coach, John Stevenson, once explained: "His dad was the driving force behind him, always pushing. Sometimes he may have come on a little strong, but it was always for the right reason. His dad was greatly afraid of wasted talent."

Still, Jack Brett wasn't sure George was major-league material. As a high school senior, George was already known as "Mr. Drama" for getting big hits in clutch situations, and his team won the state interscholastic federation championship. But while Ken Brett had hit .484 as a senior and Bobby had hit .462, George only reached .339 his senior year. George's parents fretted about what would become of him. In one newspaper article during George's youth, Ethel was quoted as saying: "What's George going to do? He'll probably be living with us when he's 50."

Like his brothers, though, George went into pro ball. He was selected in the second round of the major-league draft. Of course, Ken had been chosen in the first round. It took George two years to make it to the majors. Of course, it had taken Ken only one year. George made his big-league debut as a 20-year-old. Of course, Ken's had been at 19.

Even as a pro, even as a big leaguer, even as an adult, George wasn't good enough. And the comparisons always continued.

Early in George's major-league career, while he was still trying to establish himself, he called his father from the team's New York hotel after a game. Ken was pitching for the Pirates then and had played a doubleheader, getting a hit while pitching the first game and getting another hit in the second game. So Jack asked George on the phone, "Get any hits today?"

"No," George answered.

"George," his father snapped back, "your brother is a *pitcher* and he's out-hitting you."

Then Jack lit into him, screaming that George would never be as good as his brothers. George couldn't take it anymore. He hung up on his father, threw the phone against the wall, tore it out of the wall, then went around his room and slugged a mirror and threw a chair against the wall.

In 1980, George captivated America by flirting with a .400 average, a mark of baseball immortality. He kept his average there as late as September 19 before finishing at .390, five hits short. It was still the highest major-league batting average in four decades. When he came back to California after that season, however, one of the first things his father said to him when they saw each other was: "You mean to tell me you couldn't get five more hits?"

Jack Brett just didn't dole out praise. He felt a little smile, a little nod of his head, was enough to show his approval, enough to show his affection. Jack once told *The Kansas City Times* about George: "If he hit 400 homers in a row, I would not say anything to him. I would not say anything to anyone. I would just nod my head. ... My attitude is, 'He had a great game, but he was lucky.'"

Still, every day the first thing Jack Brett did in the morning was get his newspaper and check the box scores. George eventually recognized that his performance at the ballpark determined his father's mood for the day. If George had a couple of hits, his father went to work cheerful. If George went hitless or made an error, "my father's entire day would be ruined," he once remarked. That's why Jack couldn't attend George's postseason games. He'd get too wound up. Heck, Jack was listening on radio one time as the Royals played the Angels in L.A., and when George was picked off first base, Jack threw his radio against the wall, smashing it into pieces.

Only in dribs and drabs over the years did Jack give any inkling to George how proud he was of him. In the late 1980s, when Jack was about to have open-heart surgery, he turned introspective with his son about the Hall of Fame. He told George over the phone: "There's only one thing I want to do before I die, and that's to go to Cooperstown. I want to go back and see you inducted into the Hall of Fame. But you haven't made it yet. You still have a lot of things you have to accomplish in your career. Let's start now." Up to that point, Brett's injuries had kept him from reaching 500 at-bats in six of the previous eight seasons. Over his last five seasons, he would get 500 at-bats in four of them.

Finally, of course, George made it to the Hall of Fame, on the first ballot, an honor only reserved for the greatest of the greats. But by then, 1999, Jack was gone. He had died in 1992, even before George reached 3,000 hits. In his Hall of Fame acceptance speech, George reserved a special tribute for him: "Growing up, sometimes I misunderstood your tough and dominant ways, Dad, but as I've grown up I've realized what your goals were—for me and my brothers never to be content, and to be tough competitors. I think we all learned from you. Thank you."

Ultimately, George was grateful for his father's role in shaping his character and drive. As a person, George was humble and down to earth, never a braggart. As a player, George was always afraid of failure and constantly striving to avoid it. "Every game, I thought I would embarrass myself," he once said. So he showed up at the park early. He took extra batting practice. He learned to stay in shape. "You have to have some eternal drive," George once said, "and with me, it's my father."

That upbringing helped make him the ballplayer he was, but at a price—a price that he doesn't want his sons to pay now that he's a father.

✲✲✲✲✲✲✲

It's a sunny Saturday morning, one of those glorious October days in Kansas City, with the sky bright blue and the temperature in the 70s. On the grounds of a suburban school, George Brett stands along the painted grass sideline of a mini-football field. His hands are planted in the pockets of his white shorts. In front of him, seven- and eight-year-old boys are running plays and running after each other, with yellow flag belts tied around their waists, playing flag football. George's youngest son, Robin, is the tall one on defense with the unruly curly locks and sporting his father's baseball number on the back of his black jersey, No. 5.

The other team runs a sweep. Robin lopes after the ball carrier. Then there's a pass. Robin hustles in pursuit. George stands on the sidelines, hands in his pockets. Occasionally, he calls out, "Let's go, Rob." Mostly, though, he's quiet. He's not like a mother screeching at her child to run, or like some fathers who hover over their sons with instructions. No, George is attentive but low key.

This is Robin's first year playing team sports. He's not the fastest on the field, nor the slowest. But neither was George at Robin's age, so that doesn't matter. What matters is that when the game is over and Robin comes off the field, George tells him "Good game," and puts his arm around his shoulders.

George may be a father now, but he's not entirely like his father. He has a family with three sports-playing boys—Jackson, Dylan and Robin, all elementary school-aged. In the summer of 2004, all three played baseball. In the fall, two started football. And in the winter there's basketball. Most days George is a typical suburban parent shuttling his kids to and from their after-school activities. "You go to as many practices as you can with the kids. You go to all their games if you can," George says. "My dad's priorities were always on the oldest boys. That was his priority, where I split mine up. I try to be there for all three of them."

And unlike his father, being there also means serving as a coach of some sort. George is not a parent who simply drops off his kids and leaves. He stays and helps out with all the teams his sons are on. He can't be at every game or practice, between his travel as a Royals vice president and his interest in splitting time among his boys. But he notes: "If I'm in town, I'm there."

So at basketball practices, he can be heard running drills. At baseball practices, he can be found tossing batting practice. At football practices, he can be seen throwing passes in catching drills.

The other fathers are awestruck when they first see it—"My son is being coached by George Brett." But to the kids, he's just another adult. "They don't know what I did," George says. "They know I used to play baseball maybe, but when I'm sitting there trying to tell them to do something, they look at me like, 'What, are you crazy? That's not how my dad told me to do it.'" Really, though, that's just how George wants it to be.

"He doesn't want to be George Brett. He wants to be Robin's dad," says Paul Carter, Robin's football coach. "He just comes across as another dad."

"It's fun to get involved in their lives," George says. "There are so many baseball players who had kids when they were young. They didn't get to see them

George Brett is still a vice president with the Royals, but his biggest enjoyment in baseball now comes from helping coach the teams on which his three young sons play. He's a first-base coach for middle son Dylan's team, instructing runners on how to run the bases. *Courtesy of ActionPix LLC and Tyson Hofsommer*

play a game, never got to a practice, never saw anything. Here, I have the opportunity to, to be a part of their lives. And the Royals have been very understanding. Here, I have this golden opportunity to be a father."

He grew up a Brett, though, and there are subtle ways his own father rubbed off on him. He's a stickler for doing things the right way and showing respect for the games and the coaches. He's old school. He nags at kids to tuck in their shirts, to wear their baseball caps forward not backward, to run on and off the field. And he'll get on anybody—even fellow coaches.

One time, George got frustrated with a fellow base coach. George was coaching first base, the other coach was at third base, and there was a runner at second base. The third-base coach kept calling out to the boy to take a bigger lead off the base. But that's not how George had been teaching the kids. He had shown them how to take a good secondary lead, what he calls a "hop, hop" lead—start out with a smaller lead and then as the pitcher releases the ball, take two big hops forward, so your momentum is going toward third when the ball is hit or if there's a passed ball. But on this day, the third-base coach was yelling out to the runner, "Get off. Get off."

George was yelling back to the runner, "You're all right. Don't worry about it."

And the third-base coach kept yelling, "Get off. Get off."

Finally, George shouted over to his fellow coach: "Zip it. Enough. He's not getting off. Don't make him get off, okay?"

George doesn't have much patience, either, for third- or fourth-grade boys continuing to chatter when the head coach is talking, or fooling around with a buddy when they're supposed to run a football play. He gets vocal about it. At Robin's football practices, George's voice booms: "Hey, come on, get over here and pay attention. You have to pay attention." Over the years with his older boys' teams, he says, "We've got some kids that have quit probably because of me, because I was hard on them, because they screwed around. One kid screws around, it ruins it for everyone else."

Unlike his father, though, George doesn't make his boys' games a life-or-death ordeal.

He doesn't blow up over mistakes. During baseball, when one of his sons or some other boy on his team messes up, he takes the boy aside for a quiet and quick one-on-one reminder. One game, after Jackson came to bat and anxiously swung at a pitch almost over his head, George collared him after the inning was over. He put an arm on Jackson's shoulder and gently told him, "Jackson, out of all the times that you've swung at strikes, you've hit the ball pretty good. Whenever you swing at balls, you don't, you know."

He knows the kids on his teams aren't likely to wind up major leaguers—maybe not even his own sons—so he doesn't pressure them. Heck, he and his wife, Leslie, send their boys off to camp every summer, even if that means missing their baseball playoffs. George just enjoys being on the field and being with his boys. As Phil Fields, the head coach of Jackson Brett's fifth-grade baseball team, put it: "He has his head screwed on right with youth sports. They're not major-league sports. Have fun."

And have fun he does. Once he ended baseball practice among third graders with a game of leap-frog across the outfield. He'll spend a half-hour with one kid who wants hitting help, taking the boy's hands and moving them in place close to the back shoulder, and holding and shifting the boy's hips to simulate the weight transfer during a swing. During games, whenever George is coaching first base, he chats up the opponent's first baseman. One time, that player was 11-year-old Kyle Goodburn.

"What's your nickname?" George asked after seeing the name on the back of his jersey. "They call you Goody?"

When Kyle was holding a runner on first, George noticed he was standing with a foot on the base, instead of straddling it with one foot in front and one foot in back, which is the right way to receive and apply a pickoff tag. So between innings, George got around the base and demonstrated for Kyle what he should be doing. Up in the stands, Kyle's mom, Sara Goodburn, watched all this and her heart raced. She, like most everyone else growing up in Kansas City, had worshiped George as a Royals player. Now he was giving her son baseball tips. "That was neat," she said afterward. "You don't see that too often. I don't remember any other opposing coach helping my kid. You can tell, he's really good with kids."

All George wants is to be considered normal like that. But normal is not the way others see him. He's still one of the few true celebrities in Kansas City. Wherever he shows up, there's a buzz. People watch him, critique him, judge him. If he doesn't sign autographs at his restaurant, some patron thinks he's pompous. If he doesn't say hi to everyone at a celebrity tennis tournament, some spectator thinks he's unfriendly. If he raises his voice as a coach to get some kid's attention, some parent thinks he's overbearing. But strip away other people's starry-eyed standards for him, and he is a normal, engaged parent.

He attends parent-teacher conferences. He picks up kids at school as part of a carpool with other families. He shows up for recess and joins in a game of football. He sits in the audience for school musical programs. He arranges sleepovers for his boys with other parents.

He and Leslie want their boys to grow up normal, too. The boys attend public schools, not private. They're signed up for rec-league sports, not elite travel teams. They're polite and considerate, not snotty rich kids. "We just had parent-teacher conferences," George says one fall day. "You always go in expecting the worst. Usually, you can get one good one and two so-so ones. But the one thing that all the teachers told me was, my kids are very respectful. To me, that's more important than grades."

Most of all, George doesn't keep his feelings hidden from his sons, like his father did, as if love is some sort of mystery. "I think I'm more of a loving father than he was," George says. "I give kisses at night. I give kisses in the morning. Tell them I love 'em every chance I get. He never did that with us. Never. Never. Never got an 'I love you.' Never got anything."

George Brett made sure his love for his father carried on—by naming his first son, Jackson, after him. But George has also made sure to do things differently as a father.

CHAPTER 15

FRANK WHITE:

"YOU'VE ONLY GOT A FEW CHANCES IN LIFE"

I maginE.

No. 20 emerges from the dugout and strolls toward home plate to deliver his first lineup card to the umpires. The ovations begin. Fans stand in scattered waves, clapping, whistling, even hollering. "Welcome back." "Good luck." "Go Get 'em, Frank."

Frank White gives a little wave. He tries not to smile. But he can't help it. He's the hometown favorite getting a shot at turning his hometown team into a winner. He's made it back to the big leagues, back onto the field, as a manager.

He did it the only way he ever did anything in baseball, by working hard and learning. He earned this chance by taking bus rides and filing reports and hitting fungoes and teaching pivots and developing players—in the minor leagues.

Now he's where he feels he belongs. In charge of major leaguers. It's a reaffirmation of his baseball wisdom and a culmination of his post-playing baseball career. ...

If it ever comes to pass.

Because if it doesn't, Frank White will feel underappreciated in baseball. Once again.

❊ ❊ ❊ ❊ ❊ ❊

Frank White lived up to the pressure and responsibility of being the first second baseman to bat cleanup in the World Series since Jackie Robinson. *Courtesy of the Kansas City Royals/Chris Vleisides*

In the 1985 World Series, the Royals put their African-American second baseman in an almost impossible position—follow in the footsteps of the legendary Jackie Robinson. The Dodgers star had two extra-base hits and two RBIs while batting cleanup in 1956's seven-game series. Yet White came through. He even bested his idol. He led all players with four extra-base hits. He knocked in a series-high six runs. He singlehandedly put Game 3 out of reach. He had an epic at-bat in Game 7, fouling off five straight two-strike pitches, before keeping a rally alive with a hit.

And yet, Saberhagen had a baby, Biancalana outplayed a future Hall of Famer, Denkinger made a bad call, the Cardinals unraveled, Iorg delivered a historic hit, and the Royals made an improbable comeback. White's feats got lost in the mix. "That's something that should have been talked about a little more," he reflected years later. But he wasn't asked on national television shows the following week. He wasn't the subject of national newspaper profiles.

That was typical. The story of White's baseball life. Overshadowed and underrated.

White won a record-tying eight Gold Gloves. His number was retired. He was inducted into the Royals Hall of Fame. A statue of him was erected on the grounds of the stadium. All along, however, he always felt something was missing at times. Adoration. Endorsements. Basically, what he considered his proper due.

White was the first major prospect to emerge from the Royals' experimental Baseball Academy in the early 1970s. So baseball's establishment, which had laughed at the academy's philosophy of teaching fundamentals to good athletes who simply lacked baseball experience, looked upon White as some kind of circus freak. They called him the "$4 million man," referring to the team's overall investment in the academy, and "Academy Frank," suggesting he was given a roster spot not because of his talents but because of his schooling.

When the Kansas City native was given a chance to start in mid-1975, he thought he would be embraced as the hometown boy-made-good, who had grown up eating Bryant's barbeque and watching A's games from his high school stands across the street from the old Municipal Stadium. Instead, because he replaced the popular Cookie Rojas, White was serenaded with boos when he slumped at bat. "I just wanted to die," he admitted later.

As White established himself, he invariably got compared to the Yankees' Willie Randolph, who had become a starter around the same time. Randolph's strength was drawing walks. White, meanwhile, racked up Gold Gloves and was a playoff MVP in 1980. Still, because Randolph played in New York for the mighty Yankees, he was tapped for national television endorsements. White only received occasional local spots. Some aired so infrequently that he never even saw them. "It bothered me," he acknowledged at the time.

After winning his sixth Gold Glove in a row, an all-time record for second basemen, White thought maybe the baseball Hall of Fame would call for his glove, or *The Sporting News* would put him on its cover. Neither happened. "Turn on the TV, all you hear about is offense, offense, offense. The only time defense is ever mentioned is when someone makes an error," he said in the late '80s.

Always, though, such snubs only fed White's steely resolve. He used them as motivation. And over time he proved people wrong. In his first years, his dazzling defense showed the baseball establishment that he belonged in the big leagues. Eventually, his play and gentlemanly demeanor made him a fan favorite in his own right. Midway through his career, he began remaking himself as a power hitter and produced stats that dwarfed Willie Randolph's.

"You've only got a few chances in life when a special challenge is put before you," White once said.

That's how he approached things, turning slights into successes. So, after failing to receive attention for his hitting in the '85 World Series, he came out the next year and earned the Silver Slugger award as the best hitter at his position. After his string of six Gold Gloves in a row ended, he put together his best defensive seasons, statistically, and recaptured the award in his late 30s.

And that's the approach he ended up taking with his post-playing career, too.

It all began before he was ready. White felt he could still play. The Royals wanted to go with youth. So White never announced his retirement. He never got an official "day" at the ballpark while he was still in uniform. The closest he came was "Frank White Day," sponsored by an inner-city neighborhood association in late 1990. White threw out the first ball. But the Royals didn't even play him in a meaningless game. By season's end, White's offensive numbers had faded badly, but he still wanted to stick around another year. Rather than find some compromise, the team released him. That was the end of his playing career. "My last year there wasn't too happy," he remembered.

He became estranged from the Royals. He went to work for another team, the Red Sox. Then one day Kansas City called him. "They don't come to you very often," White said. So he came back. He was asked to be a first-base coach, not the more substantial third-base coach. He was asked to coach the outfielders—he, Frank White, the era's greatest second baseman. He made up his mind: he wanted to manage. The Royals offered him a job in the front office. White thought that would give him experience with player decisions and make him better managerial material. It didn't. When the Royals fired Tony Muser as manager in 2002, White declared his candidacy for the job. The team's brass, though, didn't think he had the experience. That stung. He could think of plenty of guys who lucked into major-league managerial jobs with less coaching experience and inferior credentials, like former teammate Hal McRae, or broadcasters Bob Brenly and Buck Martinez.

What could Frank White do? He thought about staying put, growing old in the front office, just continuing on with what the Royals asked of him.

Instead, he took on another "special challenge." He went to Wichita.

❄ ❄ ❄ ❄ ❄ ❄ ❄

There he is on a summer afternoon in 2004, No. 20, on the field again, as a big-league prospect.

There he is, back by second base, near the end of batting practice for the Wranglers, the Royals' AA minor-league affiliate. He's 53 now, still with thick arms and the gold chain with his nickname "Smooth" around his neck and the same mustache curving around the edges of his mouth. But there are flecks of gray in his hair and a paunch around his middle. He's got a ball in his hand. A 20-year-old infielder, Andres Blanco, stands at the bag. He's already an acrobatic gloveman who makes eye-popping plays. But there's more to fielding than that—namely, fundamentals. White tosses him the ball. Blanco practices taking the toss across the bag, pivoting his body 180 degrees and cocking his arm for a throw to first on a double play. Toss, catch and pivot. Toss, catch and pivot. Over and over and over. "Two hands," White calls out on some catches. "Push off," he calls out on some pivots. Ten minutes of this, then 10 more minutes where Blanco practices the pivot as a second baseman taking the toss from shortstop. Twenty minutes total. Every day of the summer.

"You're a teacher down here," White says later. That's what he loves most. And that's why he's willing to work out of a concrete-block office out past the outfield, in a city where the Golden Corral restaurant is the second-highest grossing one in the country, in a ballpark so sparse the players can hear teenage girls in the front row calling out who's "hot," in a league where he's only the second perennial big-league All-Star in three decades to lead a team.

Later that evening, during a game against Tulsa, a Tulsa hitter hits a routine ground ball toward second base. Ruben Gotay, another young infielder, scoots to the ball, stops, backhands it and throws to first for the out. White, standing in the dugout, turns to his two assistant coaches. White holds out his left hand like a glove. "You do that too often," he says, pretending his right hand is a ball and brushing it by his left hand, "and the ball'll take a bounce and hit off your glove." The inning ends, the next one begins, and during a lull in the game, White finds Gotay and quietly tells him, "Work a little harder to get in front of the ball. It makes things easier."

"He's my mentor," Gotay says later. "I've improved a lot since the beginning of the year."

That's ultimately what's most important at his level—player development. White chose to come here to get managerial experience. As a game manager, however, he concedes his hands are tied. He can't pinch hit for a player. He can't pinch run for a player. He's not supposed to keep a starting pitcher out past his pitch limit. He's not supposed to take out a relief pitcher before he's gotten in a full inning of work, unless the game's on the line. Basically, players are allowed to succeed or fail on their own. So White ends up being evaluated not so much on wins and losses but on how well players improve.

After every game, at home or on the road, White heads to his desk in the back of the concrete-block clubhouse out past the outfield, and he flips on his laptop computer. Then he fills out a daily game report. Not just runs and hits, but notes on quality at-bats, pitches per at-bat and hard-hit balls for each hitter. Not just innings pitched and earned runs, but number of pitches and velocity during the innings for starting pitchers. "It's not all about winning the game," he says.

And it says something about the Royals confidence in White that they've entrusted him with some of the franchise's top future hopefuls, like Blanco and Gotay and starting pitcher Denny Bautista, plus some of the Royals' struggling major leaguers like Angel Berroa and Mike MacDougal. The minor leaguers pro-

Frank White took a break from his office laptop and his reports after managing a game for the Royals' AA team, the Wichita Wranglers, during the summer of 2004. *Courtesy of author*

gressed so much that Blanco, Gotay and Bautista all played for the Royals by the end of this 2004 season, instead of moving on merely to the AAA level.

"There are plenty of players who reach the major leagues with the tools," says Shawn McGinn, the Royals' director of player development, "but they also have to have the small intangibles—the character, the work ethic, the instincts, the consistency. Those things are invaluable, and that's something Frank is getting across at the AA level."

White has given himself five years to get noticed and make it back to the big leagues as a manager. Still, at this point, during his first season guiding the Wranglers, he's not sure what kind of manager he'll be. Calm, patient and encouraging like Dick Howser? Fiery, tempestuous and volatile like Whitey Herzog? White has shown flashes of each at times.

One mid-summer game against Tulsa, the Wranglers scored five times by the fifth inning, Bautista threw seven shutout innings and the team cruised to a relatively easy 5-1 win, staying in first place temporarily during the season's second half. Yet White had noticed a few other things—a missed bunt sign, a missed steal sign, no attempt to move up a base on a long fly ball, all little things. It's something that bothers him about the game now. Today's players don't prepare as much, or play hurt, or run the bases in reckless abandon like in White's day. He tells them just about every day, "There's no substitute for preparation and hard work." So after the game, the Wichita players filed into the clubhouse and started changing out of their uniforms. Then White came in and started yelling. They weren't concentrating. They weren't hustling. "The easiest thing to do in this game is to hustle," he shouted at them.

They won the next night, with a bunt contributing to a run in a one-run game.

❊ ❊ ❊ ❊ ❊ ❊

So Frank White waits for the call.

He's hopeful. After all, when the time comes, he'll have a strong case to make. He's already handled many of the Royals' big-league players. He's taught them something. He's sped up their development. He's got managerial experience. And he's won with those players.

Still, he won't allow himself to dream about getting the top job and being in charge himself, filling out the lineup card and delivering it to home plate, with the crowd, the cheers, the personal satisfaction.

No, just work hard. Hope to get noticed. Turn a slight into a success.

He's not going to count on it, though. He knows minority managers aren't hired often. His old second-base rival, Willie Randolph, interviewed for a dozen mangerial opportunities before finally getting one. White won't wait that long. And he's not going to stoop to lobbying for a job. So already, he's readying himself for the possible disappointment, for being considered too old, for being considered too old-school, for being underappreciated again.

And if that's what happens, well, that'll just be typical of his baseball life.

CHAPTER 16

BUDDY BIANCALANA:

"I PROBABLY UNDERSTAND MORE ABOUT WHAT IT TAKES TO HIT BECAUSE I WASN'T VERY GOOD AT IT."

The instructor stands behind a screen in a long, narrow batting tunnel. He's 15 feet from home plate, tossing baseballs underhanded to an 11-year-old boy yearning to hit better.

The boy stands at the plate right-handed. Swing. *Ping* goes the aluminum bat. The ball flies into the screen.

"There you go," the instructor says softly.

Swing. *Ping*. The ball flies into the netting on the left side of the cage.

"Right hand took over," the instructor says softly.

Ping. A dribbler.

"Strong lower half," and instructor gently admonishes.

Ping. Another dribbler.

The instructor comes around from behind the screen and walks toward the boy. It's noontime on a sunny summer Wednesday in a suburb of Omaha, Nebraska. The instructor is 44 years old but looks at least a decade younger. From a distance, he even resembles Tim Robbins from the baseball movie *Bull Durham*. He's fit and trim with short-cropped dark hair, wearing a white t-shirt with the insignia of a major-league team, gray sweat shorts, ankle socks and New Balance shoes. His pupil is named Joel and he's wearing his red No. 12 jersey of the select travel team he plays on.

They're in the middle of three outdoor batting tunnels. To their left and right, a team of teenagers is taking batting practice. Coaches throw from a pitching rubber at one end to the home plate at the other end. Every few seconds, the swings in those tunnels produce loud *Pings*. Still, the instructor in the middle talks softly, confidently. "It's hands and lower body," he tells Joel while holding his right fist on top of his left fist and pushing them down and forward. Then the instructor turns and heads back behind the screen.

Swing. *Ping*. Line drive.

"There you go."

Ping. Line drive.

"That's hands and lower body."

Joel's father, Don Page, stands outside the fence behind home plate. He's the hitting coach for his son's team, but he couldn't do much with Joel. The boy was hitting around .100 several games into the season. So Page brought his boy to this instructor, possibly the only retired major league position player around Omaha. The boy has hit about .600 since.

"There's something about him, an aura about him," Page claims about this instructor. "He talks to them about having the courage to make changes. I don't know how to describe it. For some reason, he gets his message across better than anyone I've seen."

He's hardly alone in his assessment. The father of the pupil before Joel stood watching his son's instruction and proclaimed: "I've spent thousands of dollars taking Tyler to batting coaches, and I've tried teaching him myself. You'd see a little improvement and then back to the old ways. No one's been able to relate to him like he has. He's awesome."

So who is this hypnotic hitting instructor, this magician of mechanics, this Svengali of swing?

Buddy Biancalana?

Yeah, the guy who hit under .200 in each of his first three years in pro baseball. The guy who hit .188 for the Royals during the '85 season. The guy who slid out of the majors with a .205 lifetime average. The guy tagged as a "good glove, no hit" player his entire career.

Yeah. "Teaching hitting is my absolute passion," he declares.

❊ ❊ ❊ ❊ ❊ ❊

Biancalana was always defensive about that "good glove, no hit" tag. He was the Royals' first-round draft choice out of a California high school in 1978. He was a five foot 11 155-pound shortstop with good range, a better-than-average arm and quick, soft hands. Royals officials compared him to Bud Harrelson and Larry Bowa, two shortstops in the majors then who remained starters because of slick fielding and just enough hitting to get by. Biancalana had batted

Buddy Biancalana's out-of-nowhere performance in the 1985 World Series had some people thinking he was the second coming of fictional baseball star Roy Hobbs from the movie *The Natural*. So, he posed with a cutout of the movie character played by Robert Redford. *Courtesy of the Kansas City Royals*

.314 his senior year. So what if he had bunted a lot and legged out some of those hits with his speed? He thought he was a hitter.

That summer he went to the rookie league, the bottom rung of the minors. He hit .171. "I don't know who said I can't hit," he told *The Kansas City Times* after that season. "But I'll prove I can hit."

The next year he played the next rung up the minor-league ladder, Single-A ball. He hit .199. The year after that he stayed in Single-A. He hit .171. Still, the Royals promoted him to Double-A. He hit .210. That got him promoted to Triple-A. He hit .250—improving but still far from what's expected of a budding major-league hitter. "There are a lot of people who don't think I'm going to hit," he told *The Kansas City Star* that year. "I know I'm going to. ...As I grow up, my bat will get better." He'd been working out on Nautilus equipment for three years by then. He was up to 160 pounds.

The Royals' incumbent shortstops at that time—U.L. Washington and Onix Concepcion—weren't too hot with the bat, either. So the Royals called up Biancalana with other minor leaguers in the Septembers of '82 and '83. Then injuries brought him up several times in '84, and he started for much of August and September. He made some game-saving defensive plays, and at bat he enjoyed a hitting streak that brought his average up to the .250 range at one point. Then he tailed off. He ended up at .194. Going into '85, the Royals traded Washington. Biancalana was assured of a roster spot as a backup. He told *The Star* that spring: "Offensively, I've gotten to the point where I can play in the big leagues."

Well, he could play in the big leagues. Just not offensively, But this was a time in the majors when shortstops were still small and spry, and defense mattered most. Biancalana, at 160 pounds, weighed the same as Hall of Famer Luis Aparacio. Ozzie Smith was in the 150-pound range. Cal Ripken had just broken the mold as a big guy—six feet, four inches, 225 pounds. But baseball was still years away from shortstops routinely being bigger than Joe DiMaggio, like 195-pound Derek Jeter or 200-pound Miguel Tejada. All Biancalana had to do was hit a little, because he covered more ground than just about any other A.L. shortstop. He would finish '85 with the league's third-best range factor, or fielding chances per nine innings.

Alas, he couldn't even hit a little. He was starting his swing too early, leaning forward on pitches. Being off balance, he couldn't drive the ball for power, so outfielders played way in and caught many of his little looping drives that dropped in for anybody else. And Biancalana didn't go to the plate with a plan of attack, an intention of looking for a certain pitch or the ball in a certain location. "I was not a very smart hitter," he acknowledged later. By mid-July he was hitting a truly pathetic .119. His teammates kept needling him—"When are you going to contribute?" But manager Dick Howser didn't have much of an alternative. Concepcion was at .179. So, Howser kept playing Biancalana, who was better defensively.

Then in August, with his average climbing but still at .170, Biancalana's hitting became a joke. Literally. With Pete Rose nearing Ty Cobb's all-time hit record, the staff of late-night television comedian David Letterman went searching for someone they could spoof in a mock race with Rose. Letterman writer David Martin had in mind "the stereotypical light-hitting shortstop." Buddy Biancalana not only fit the statistical profile but "his name has a ring to it," Martin said at the time. So Letterman introduced the "Buddy Biancalana Hit Counter" one night. It was a lunch box-sized chart that showed Biancalana with

11 hits and needing more than 4,100 to catch Rose. Never mind that Biancalana really had 46 career hits then. The gag was funny. Except to Buddy.

Biancalana didn't need the spotlight on his hitting. But he just so happened to be in a groove. He hit a respectable .250 after the All-Star break and .259 in September. In the A.L. playoffs, he delivered a key RBI double during the Royals' comeback and batted .222. Then came the World Series, baseball's biggest stage. He batted .278 with five walks, a sterling .435 on-base percentage and the game-winning RBI in Game 5. "That series was the best baseball I played in my whole life," Biancalana remembered. He was on mentally, concentrating more. He was able to set aside his fear of failure and relax. And a little success helped him relax even more.

Of course, it helped that Cardinals pitchers always seemed to be approaching him cautiously, nibbling with their pitches, getting behind in the count, because weaker-hitting Royals pitchers batted after Biancalana and were a sure out. As Biancalana kept hitting and getting on base, Cardinals manager Whitey Herzog groused, "He looks like Baby Ruth." Fans started chanting his name as he came to bat—"Bud-dee, Bud-dee, Bud-dee." Biancalana became a folk hero.

His phone rang and rang. He was in demand. An East Coast booking agent, a guy from his old high school, wanted to represent him. Biancalana had to decide whether to capitalize on his new-found fame. He wasn't sure. Deep down, he knew he didn't deserve the attention; he was embarrassed by his hitting during the season. But his wife at the time told him, "It's kind of a once-in-a-lifetime thing." So he milked it.

He went on the Letterman show, and the comedian showed a montage of World Series highlights—Biancalana repeatedly taking ball four and drawing walks, set to Carly Simon's "The Spy Who Loved Me" song with the lyrics, "...nobody does it better." That was just the beginning. He went on the *Today* show. He rode in a Christmas parade in Florida. He lectured to IBM executives. He appeared at a charity dinner with first lady Nancy Reagan. He modeled spring fashions for *Esquire* magazine. He shot local television commercials.

And he had fun with it all. He agreed to a network TV stunt in which someone from his old high school tried to strike him out. (Biancalana hit a fly ball.) And at a dinner in his honor in his hometown of Larkspur, California, Biancalana was asked, "Who's the toughest pitcher in the American League?" In true Bob Uecker-esque fashion, he replied, "Well now, how many pitchers are there in the American League?"

He knew he still had a lot to prove. He knew the Royals were now counting on him as their starting shortstop. So whenever he could, he found a batting cage and kept practicing—even in Hawaii. Then he went to spring training in 1986. And bombed. His batting average stayed mostly under .180, even worse than the previous season. Trade rumors swirled. At the end of spring training, the Royals obtained minor-league shortstop Angel Salazar. When Salazar had last played in the majors, for half a season in 1984, he batted .155. Still, he was installed as the Royals' opening-day starter. Biancalana was a backup again. Concepcion was cut. He was so dejected that he went and got a real job in his native Puerto Rico and said, "I feel like if a guy like Buddy Biancalana can beat me out of a job at shortstop, I can't play no more."

Biancalana bided his time again. He hit a career-high .242 in '86 with a career-high 190 at-bats. Then he hit the weights harder after that season, bulking up to 180 pounds at one point. In spring training the next year, he started hitting balls off the outfield walls. "I guarantee I will hit," he declared. And he finally won the shortstop job. He was the starter on Opening Day. His name was in the lineup every day, for exactly five days. With Biancalana's batting average at .167, Salazar got the job back. By midseason, Biancalana was traded to the Houston Astros. Then he was cut, signed by another team and cut again. He spent a year back in Triple-A, hurt his back and that was it.

Out of baseball. Time to do something else.

He got his real estate license and subleased vacant store space. But he didn't like working on commission.

He invested in a video store. But it went under.

He became a player agent. But it took too long to build up the practice.

He went back into baseball, coached fielding and became a minor-league manager. But he found the pros didn't listen much to him.

All the while, he harbored a secret dream. An inner voice occasionally spoke to him: "Wouldn't it be great to teach hitting because I was such a crummy hitter?"

So during offseasons, while living in Florida, Biancalana started working with youths in batting cages. In baseball, this actually made some sense. It's a game where the best players aren't always the best teachers. The teams Ted Williams managed never hit really well. Ty Cobb and Pete Rose were mediocre managers. The best managers ended up being journeyman players, like Sparky Anderson and Tony La Russa, like Whitey Herzog and Dick Howser. The most revered and respected major-league hitting coaches of the past half-century— Charlie Lau and Walt Hriniak—were part-time players with lifetime averages under .260.

After being let go from his last managing job, Biancalana and his new wife decided to move to Omaha, where his teenage son from a previous marriage lived. Biancalana started going to youth league meetings and coming out to youth games and introducing himself and handing out fliers, which mentioned him being part of the 1985 world champion Royals. He got plenty of business. And he knew what he was doing. Teaching hitting came instinctively to him. He had studied hitting techniques all his years as a player. Plus, he had worked with so many hitting instructors, he knew what to teach and what hadn't been taught but needed to be.

Buddy, who struggled to hit in the major leagues, remains around the batting cages long after his playing days as a successful youth hitting instructor. *Courtesy of author*

"I don't feel I've been better at anything in my whole life," he says, "than teaching hitting."

* * * * * * *

So there he stands on a sunny summer day, behind a screen, tossing baseballs, conveying the secret language of hitting mechanics, like turning the hips for a "strong lower half" and keeping the upper torso steady or "quiet" until contact with the ball.

Eleven-year-old Joel gets in position at the plate. Knees slightly bent. Feet spread wider than his shoulders. Bat held in front of the back shoulder. Then Biancalana moves his arm to start a toss. Joel suddenly shifts his weight toward his back leg, extends the bat farther back and gets ready to uncoil. The toss comes in. Joel steps quickly with his front foot, then tilts his head across the plate, dips his front shoulder and swings with all his might.

Swing. *Ping.* The ball dribbles off the bat.

"Feel how violent your upper body is?" Biancalana asks.

"Yeah," the boy answers.

"Quiet things down," Biancalana tells him almost inaudibly.

Joel's father, Don Page, is still standing outside the fence behind home plate. Joel, he says, has started becoming a little standoffish with adults, not making eye contact, not paying much attention to what they're saying. But from the beginning with Biancalana, Joel connected with him. When Biancalana had something to say to him, they were eyeball to eyeball. The reason, Page insists, is Biancalana speaks softly. He doesn't use some authoritarian voice. He's respectful. And he commands the kids' attention with questions. He makes them think, and they respond to that.

"It seems," Page is saying about Biancalana, "he's at peace with himself and it's really transferred to the kids."

Swing. *Ping.* Line drive into the screen.

"Good strong lower half," Biancalana says.

Ping. Hard-hit grounder.

"There you go."

Ping. Line drive.

Biancalana stops tossing. He walks toward home plate.

"Close your eyes," he tells Joel. "Feel those last three swings."

The boy shuts his eyes, raises his hands above his head and holds the bat behind his neck.

"Notice your lower body starting first. Notice your hands accelerating."

Joel stands there a moment, visualizing. This is what, Biancalana believes, sets him apart from other hitting instructors. He calls it the mind-body connection. He instills the mental side of baseball into his lessons. It's not something he picked up as a player. It's not something he picked up from the dozen or so hitting coaches he worked with as a pro. It's something he picked up from transcendental meditation.

In the early 1990s, as he was going through a divorce, as he was getting depressed, as he was searching for something, anything to help his aching back, a friend gave him a book on meditation. Biancalana then learned more from an instructor. It was something that relaxed him, calmed the mind and unwound the body. He started meditating daily. And when he went back into baseball, he brought with him the lessons learned from meditation.

So many hitters went to the plate anxious and tense and fearful. Biancalana could talk about visualizing and deep breathing and clearing your head—many of the same things espoused by sports psychologists. He didn't push it on everyone. Some minor leaguers tried his exercises. It worked for them. Still, he knew meditation had a stigma—people sitting cross-legged, hands out with palms up, humming "Ommmmm." And baseball is notorious for being a tradition-bound industry slow to accept new techniques, whether that's statistical analysis or mental preparation. After he was fired from his last minor-league managing job, he was told some officials in the major-league organization had described him as "just ahead of his time."

So now, with kids, he touts a hitting approach "that's better than any I've seen." As one father at Biancalana's instruction session put it: "Everything is mental." Biancalana thinks he's on to something. "I don't know if that's egotistical or not," he says.

But he does know one thing: "I probably understand more about what it takes to hit," he says, "because I wasn't very good at it."

CHAPTER 17

DON DENKINGER:

"I CAN LIVE WITH MYSELF"

O ut over the rolling hills of central Iowa, beyond the one-stoplight towns, past the fields of corn and soybeans, in the middle of nowheresville to the rest of the country, Don Denkinger is in hiding, or exile, or baseball's version of the witness protection program. Or so it might seem.

But not really. Waterloo, Iowa, is just where he's always lived. He knows he can't escape from baseball infamy, even here. So he doesn't bother trying.

In his house beside a golf course, at the bottom of his basement stairs, along the walls filled with photos of his umpiring life—making a call at the plate in the 1974 World Series, working the plate for the extraordinary extra-inning pitching duel in 1991's Game 7, calling Nolan Ryan's sixth no-hitter—among all the mementos and remembrances is a poster of the moment for which he's best remembered.

It's an exaggerated depiction of the play at first base during Game 6 of the '85 World Series, its subjects portrayed with almost cartoonist features, unidentified but unmistakable. A Kansas City Royals runner is stretching his legs toward first base. A St. Louis Cardinals fielder is planted on the base, with the ball entering his outstretched glove. And behind them, the umpire already has his arms stretched wide, signaling safe before the runner has even reached the base. The poster is simply titled "The Call."

Don Denkinger's memorabilia-filled basement features autographed bats and balls, framed photos, even a poster of his blown call from the 1985 World Series. *Courtesy of author*

It's like Bill Buckner framing a picture of Mookie Wilson's World Series roller. Or Bill Clinton keeping a photo of Monica Lewinsky around the house.

Why does Denkinger keep a reminder of his infamous umpiring blunder?

"It just proves you're not always right," he says while showing off his baseball keepsakes one summer day.

Someone gave him the poster as a gift, someone who knew him, who knew his temperament, who knew how he coped with his ultimate notoriety.

"What was I going to do," Denkinger asks almost incredulously, "rip it up?"

That's what you expect he would have done. That's what you expect anyone would have done. Denkinger, however, defied expectations in how he handled his World Series mistake.

The attitude he took was particularly surprising, even laudable, considering what happened to him after that World Series.

✿✿✿✿✿✿✿

Denkinger was driving home to Iowa from Kansas City with his wife, Gayle, the day after Game 7. When he turned onto his block, he noticed police cars sitting at both ends. The officers knew him and let him go by. Denkinger turned to his wife, "What do you suppose is going on?"

He found out as soon as he stepped in the door.

The couple's three high school- and college-aged daughters had stayed there over the weekend with Gayle's parents. After the Cardinals' frustration from Game 6 spilled over into embarrassing temper tantrums during Game 7, a St. Louis radio disc jockey gave out Denkinger's home telephone number and address over the air. The phone started ringing in Denkinger's house. The girls answered it.

Ringggg. "Collect call from Joaquin Andujar."

Ringggg. "Please hold for Whitey Herzog."

Ringggg. "Tell that Denkinger he's a ------------ -----------."

Some of Denkinger's friends and colleagues had gotten through, too, to offer the family a little support and encouragement after the tumult on the field. One of Denkinger's daughters sobbed to fellow umpire Dave Phillips, "Oh Davey, they are being so mean to my Dad." And they were getting even meaner.

Ringggg. "We're going to burn your house down."

Ringggg. "You'll never see your Dad again."

Gayle's mother wasn't sure what to do. She called some family friends. They called the police.

And that was only the beginning of the nastiness. Denkinger had been a professional umpire for more than a quarter-century by then. He had worked two other World Series and five league championship series. He had never heard a peep from anybody after those. But he knew fans could be cruel sometimes. Once in the minor leagues, the air had been let out of his tires. Another time, young thugs followed him out of town. But nothing prepared him for this. The prank calls kept coming. The day he got home from the series. And the day after that. And the next.

And by then, the mail started to arrive. Hate mail. Stacks of it.

"You blew the call," one stated.

"Congratulations on changing history," another sneered.

And: "You're ------- blind."

This went on for weeks. It dragged into months. Denkinger filled a cardboard box with the letters. There were a couple hundred of them.

During the holidays, a *Sports Illustrated* reporter visited the house. Denkinger showed him the letters. *Sports Illustrated* ran a story. Then more stacks of letters started arriving—this time with a different message:

"I can't believe you were treated like that."

And: "I feel so sorry for you."

Denkinger thought it would eventually all blow over, be forgotten, become another baseball footnote. That's what typically happened with controversies during the season. But this one was taking on a life of its own, because this one had happened during the World Series.

❖ ❖ ❖ ❖ ❖ ❖ ❖

Every World Series produces a goat. Usually it's someone who doesn't hit his weight. Every so often, though, a series offers a mega-goat.

In the deciding game of the 1912 series, with his team clinging to a 1-0 lead, Fred Snodgrass of the New York Giants dropped an easy fly ball from the first batter of the ninth inning. That started a rally, the first batter eventually scored, and the Giants lost the game. When Snodgrass died in 1974, more than a half-century later, *The New York Times* headlined his obituary: "Fred Snodgrass, 86, Dead, Ballplayer Muffed 1912 Fly."

In Game 4 of 1941, with the Brooklyn Dodgers one out and one strike away from tying the series, New York Yankees slugger Tommy Henrich swung and missed at a curveball for strike three. But the ball glanced off catcher Mickey Owen's glove, and Henrich made it safely to first base on the passed ball. A Brooklyn fan, listening at home on the radio, threw a small dog off his lap and out his apartment window. The Yankees rallied and went on to win the game and take the series. As Owen walked off the field, the Brooklyn faithful hollered and threw stuff at him, and he was booed for seasons afterward.

In the seventh game of 1946, with the score tied in the eighth inning and the Cardinals' Enos Slaughter on first base, a looping single fell into left-center field. Boston Red Sox shortstop Johnny Pesky took the throw from the outfield, turned and saw Slaughter rounding third, hesitated a split second and fired home, but too late to get Slaughter. It stood up as the winning run. For years afterward, Boston sportswriters castigated Pesky for "holding the ball."

More recently, in Game 6 of the 1986 series, with the score tied in the 10th inning and the Boston Red Sox trying to win their first world championship in almost three-quarters of a century, the New York Mets' Mookie Wilson hit a dribbler down the first-base line. Boston's Bill Buckner bent down to field it and the ball skipped right past his glove. The Mets won the game and took the series, and Buckner became the poster boy for the Red Sox's infamous Curse of the Bambino, hexing the team from the time Babe Ruth was traded to the Yankees till the Red Sox finally won the World Series in 2004.

All these plays had extenuating circumstances, however, and all these men were hardly alone in deserving blame.

In 1912, Snodgrass's error only put the tying run on base; his pitcher walked what eventually was the winning run. In 1941, Owen's pitcher crossed him up, throwing a slow curve instead of a hard-curving slider, then let the next four batters reach base. In 1946, Pesky didn't have a chance to gun down Slaughter because his centerfielder was slow retrieving the ball, and none of Pesky's teammates alerted him to throw home. In 1986, Buckner's miscue only became fateful because Boston relievers blew a two-run lead in the inning and were one strike away from winning on four occasions.

Denkinger, too, was hardly the only culprit in the Cardinals' collapse. After his call, the first baseman missed a pop-up, and that batter got on base. The catcher booted a pitch, allowing the winning run to get in scoring position. And the pitcher gave up a game-winning hit.

Years afterward, some of the Cardinals players even came out and admitted they didn't think Denkinger cost the Cardinals the series, or the game. Shortstop Ozzie Smith, in his autobiography, wrote: "It wasn't Denkinger's call alone that caused us to lose that game." Pitcher Bob Forsch, in *Bob Forsch's Tales from the Cardinals Dugout*, explained: "I don't think that call at first base in Game 6 lost the game." He went on: "That call didn't even cost us a run. ... And even when we lost that game, we still could have come back in Game 7."

That's how baseball historians saw it, too. They attributed the Cardinals' fall more to their own hands than Denkinger's. Here's how Eric Enders, a former researcher at the National Baseball Hall of Fame Library, explained it in his book about the first 100 years of the World Series: "The Orta call had been blown, to be sure, but the Cardinals still managed to record only one out in the ninth inning. The way the inning played out, Kansas City might have scored at least one run even if Orta had been called out. Denkinger may have provided the gun, but it was the Cardinals alone who shot themselves in the foot."

Still, it was Denkinger who was saddled with the blame in the public's eye, just like Snodgrass, Owen, Pesky and Buckner. And like them, too, that blame dogged Denkinger for the rest of his career and even into retirement.

❋❋❋❋❋❋❋

During spring training of 1986, whenever Denkinger took the field, he heard boos. Late in one game, a vocally endowed fan yelled out, "Don't worry about it, Denkinger. You can still turn the game around." When the season started, it was the same thing, wherever he went.

The letters slowed to a trickle. But he still received them occasionally. Postcards kept coming from one disgruntled St. Louisan, Harold Kalicak. He had grown up during the Cardinals' Gashouse Gang era of the mid-1930s. He had shagged flies during Cardinals batting practice as a teenager. He had attended all the World Series the Cardinals had been in since 1946. But after Lou Brock was out at home because he failed to slide and Curt Flood slipped and missed a ball during the 1968 series, Kalicak didn't write to them. Only to Denkinger after 1985. "You blew it. Where's the apology?" Kalicak jotted on one of his postcards.

In 1987, Denkinger received another postcard. It read: "I know what you do, I know where you go, and when I point my .357 Magnum at you, it'll just blow you away." It was signed, "A Cardinal fan." That one was turned over to the FBI. "They told me they'd take care of it," Denkinger said. No more threatening letters came.

A few years later, Denkinger was chosen to work his fourth World Series. It was 1991, the first year umpires returned to the process of doling out post-season assignments based on in-season job performance. A St. Louis newspaper columnist couldn't let '85 rest. "Why would Denkinger want to reappear in the World Series, to stir up unpleasant memories?" columnist Bernie Miklasz wrote in the *Post-Dispatch.*

By then Whitey Herzog had retired. And he believed Denkinger's call might keep him out of the baseball Hall of Fame, because he won one world championship instead of two. So while no umpire had ever been blamed for a World Series loss, Herzog did his best to change that. Just about wherever he went to speak, he brought it up. At a St. Louis baseball writers dinner, he said he wished he had gone to the commissioner's box during Game 6 and asked him to overrule Denkinger. At an Arkansas State University baseball fundraiser, he told the audience, "That's one of the worst calls in history."

When baseball began inter-league play in 1997, the Cardinals and Royals met officially for the first time since '85. That set off more whining. One Cardinals fan wrote the *Post-Dispatch,* "Denkinger's blown call in Game 6 of the 1985 Series stands as the eternal yardstick to measure all crimes against the sports fans of St. Louis." Denkinger even transcended sports in that city. As St. Louisan and fellow umpire Dave Phillips explained in his autobiography: "If a sewer main breaks or there is a bad storm or anything negative happens in St. Louis, somebody will associate it with Don—it doesn't even have to be about sports." When Denkinger retired from umpiring, it set off yet another round of bellyaching in St. Louis. A story in the *Post-Dispatch* started: "Don Denkinger won't miss any more calls at first base." A radio sportscaster played the "Hallelujah Chorus" when announcing the news.

Every so often, something still drags Denkinger back into the news. In 2001, ESPN's web site ranked the "Worst Calls in Sports History." Finishing No. 1 was his blown call. A couple years after that, Cubs fan Steve Bartman reached out of the stands and deflected a catchable foul ball, then was hounded as the villain when the Cubs blew the lead that inning. So who did one baseball writer call for some perspective on what it's like to be vilified? Don Denkinger, of course.

Through the years, Denkinger's reaction to this litany of ignominy remained unwavering. "It doesn't bother me," he kept saying.

❋ ❋ ❋ ❋ ❋ ❋ ❋

For other World Series mega-goats, the constant haranguing embittered them.

Fred Snodgrass related in Lawrence Ritter's *The Glory of Their Times*: "For over half a century, I've had to live with the fact that I dropped a ball in the World Series. 'Oh yes, you're the guy who dropped that fly ball, aren't you?' And for years and years, whenever I'd be introduced to somebody, they'd start to say something and then stop, you know, afraid of hurting my feelings." Mickey Owen said decades after his gaffe, "I never stop thinking about that day." Johnny Pesky admitted once, "I was very sensitive about it." Bill Buckner, after some highly publicized run-ins with hecklers, eventually moved from Massachusetts to Idaho, to get away from it all.

And Denkinger? He vowed never to let The Call change him.

Over the years, he went on radio shows. He returned reporters' calls. He let *Sports Illustrated* and ESPN into his home. He accepted invitations to sports banquets. He never changed his telephone number. He even talked to disgruntled Cardinals fans who called his house.

He didn't hide from the attention. He didn't want it, for sure, but he had an umpire's mentality—keep an even keel, stay in control, don't let things bother you. So he handled the attention with dignity, class and aplomb.

He never yelled at hecklers or griped about how the '85 World Series was all anyone wanted to talk to him about. Even today, he feels no bitterness. He holds no grudges. He carries no hard feelings. He jokes about playing golf and being introduced by friends as "the guy who made that call in the '85 World Series."

"It's not something you run away from. Even if you try, they'll find ya," Denkinger says.

He's long made peace with his place in history. He acknowledged his mistake publicly. He felt bad about it, obviously. But he never felt he had to apologize for trying his best, and he realized he did not cost the Cardinals the series.

Major League Baseball's leadership felt the same way. Mistakes, unfortunately, were "part of the game," commissioner Peter Uebberoth said after the '85 series. Baseball did feel an injustice occurred in the series that needed correcting. It wasn't what Whitey Herzog had harped on at the time, the selection of the umpires. It was the predicament the Royals had been forced to live with—playing an entire season with a designated hitter but not in the most important series of the year. So baseball instituted a rule for the DH to be used in World Series games played in American League home parks.

Denkinger went on umpiring and went on earning more than his share of choice assignments. He worked home plate for the 1987 All-Star game. He worked a couple more league championship playoffs. He was behind the plate in the 1991 World Series for Game 7's tight, tense pitching duel—without incident. Along the way, he picked up mementos. Now they line the walls of his basement: framed photos of Denkinger making calls; stacks of baseballs signed by Hall of Famers; balls signed by both '85 World Series teams; balls signed by Tom Hanks and Bob Hope.

"What can I say, it was a great career," Denkinger says sitting in his den after showing off his collection one summer day. "If you let one little thing bother you …

"I just accept it for what it is. It's a little blip in my career that happened during a World Series and got blown out of proportion. That, basically to me, is all it is. There's not an umpire alive who's spent one year in the big leagues without having something happen that was wrong. Because that's just the way the game is.

"As far as I'm concerned, I know the kind of career I had, and that's all that really matters to me. I can live with myself."

CHAPTER 18

KANSAS CITY'S REDEMPTION, ST. LOUIS'S ANGUISH

Years after 1985, in recounting that season, *The Washington Post's* Thomas Boswell wondered: "Were these Royals the worst team ever to win the World Series? Well, let's hope so. These guys deserve to be remembered." Unfortunately, they weren't remembered.

They were hardly remembered immediately after they won. President Ronald Reagan called the Royals' victorious clubhouse after Game 7 and referred to Dan Quisenberry as "Jim." A week or so later, Bret Saberhagen went on Johnny Carson's late-night show and was introduced as "Bert." In the nearly two decades since then, it hasn't gotten any better.

In fact, the 1985 World Series has been largely forgotten around the country.

That's because baseball went on to have some even more memorable World Series.

It started with the very first series after the Royals', in 1986, with the ball rolling through Bill Buckner's legs and the Mets completing the same kind of World Series comeback the Royals had, winning after losing the first two games at home. A couple of years later, in 1988, came Kirk Gibson's strong-armed game-winning homer. A few years after that, there was another miracle team, the 1991 Twins, which went from last place to the championship, capped by Jack Morris's 10-inning shutout in the seventh game. A couple of years later, in 1993, came Joe Carter's walk-off series-winning homer. The next time the series went the distance, in 1997, the Florida Marlins rallied to tie Game 7 in the ninth inning, then won it in extra innings. A few years after that, in 2001, the Yankees tied two games with ninth-inning homers and won those games in extra innings, but Arizona came back in Game 7 with their own bottom-of-the-ninth come-back to take the series.

It's no wonder that after 2001, when Jay Greenberg of *The New York Post* listed his top 10 World Series games of all time, five had occurred since 1985.

No team, though, duplicated the Royals' main feats—coming back after falling behind 3-1 twice, or being on the brink of elimination and winning with a ninth-inning rally to force a seventh game. Still, some of the Royals' other feats became almost passé. A bottom-of-the-ninth, come-from-behind win like the Royals pulled off in Game 6 had only happened three times in the previous eight decades, but then it happened three times in the next 16 years. Heck, the World Series even saw another baby born to a pitcher who started the next game—in 1990, when the Cincinnati Reds' Tom Browning was a new father after Game 2, then went on to win Game 3.

So sportswriters recalling past World Series comebacks and heroics mostly overlooked 1985. In a book about the 100 years of Yankees baseball, author Glenn Stout wrote of Tino Martinez's ninth-inning homer off Byung-Hyun Kim in 2001's Game 4: "The game was now tied, remarkably, incredibly, improbably, 3-3, the first time in the World Series since 1947—Lavagetto versus Bevens—that a team had come back after trailing by two in the ninth."

No, actually, it had happened in Game 2 of 1985.

But that was the year New Yorkers ignored the series.

❋ ❋ ❋ ❋ ❋ ❋ ❋

The '85 series didn't drift off into oblivion for everyone. It's never been for-gotten in Missouri.

Just about every Kansas Citian who was alive in '85 can remember what they were doing during the World Series or the post-series revelries. Some can recall the final out better than their wedding night. Others who were just kids then have memories of making celebration signs at school. When 94-year-old Dolores Fields of Independence died in 2004, her obituary listed one of her life's most cherished moments as being "able to attend the 1985 World Series."

It remains the greatest sports moment in the city's history, the most surpris-ing finish and the most euphoric celebration, the pinnacle of its big-league sta-tus.

"It sticks with Kansas Citians like a full slab at Gates (barbeque)," said Kevin Kietzman, Kansas City's leading sports radio host, on 810 WHB. "The autumn of 1985 was a magical time. It was a metaphor for the city itself. The lit-tle team with the no-name pitching staff and the shortstop everyone made fun of overcame all the odds and came from behind not once but twice to win it all.

Kansas City still views itself in this image. We're not New York or even a big Midwestern city. But we'll outwork you, outhustle you and outplay you until we get it right."

Yes, the '85 World Series maintains a glow all its own to Kansas Citians, especially when it comes to St. Louis.

So much changed between the two cities after 1985. Kansas City kept rolling along like a proverbial turtle in the nation's race of progress, gaining a little here and there, reversing its decades-long population decline and renovating its Union Station, building on its telecommunications industry and building up its technology industries. Meanwhile, St. Louis slipped further from the pantheon of great cities. It nearly tumbled out of the top 50 cities in population. More people moved out of metro St. Louis than moved in during the 1990s. Even worse, in livability ratings, metro St. Louis tumbled into the mid-200s. It lagged behind just about every other large metro in job growth in new-economy tech industries. In a nutshell, St. Louis went from, at the beginning of the 20th Century, launching Charles Lindbergh on a historic airplane ride across the ocean, to at the end of the century launching Steve Fossett on a historic around-the-world balloon ride, during which he crashed.

No matter. One aspect where St. Louis far outstripped Kansas City was in sports.

Kansas City lost its NCAA and Big 12 conference headquarters. The football Chiefs flopped whenever they made the playoffs. And the Royals languished in last place for much of the late '90s and early '00s. Over in St. Louis, a domed stadium and a new arena were built. The Cardinals' Mark McGwire broke baseball's all-time single-season home run record. The football Rams won one Super Bowl and went back for another. The Cardinals' team made it back to the World Series not once, but twice. It all led Kansas City sports columnist Jason Whitlock to muse at one point: "The reality is, we're so far removed from being St. Louis's rival that we're not even on our sister city's radar anymore."

Except Kansas City always holds the trump card in the cities' rivalry. When it comes to the one and only time the two baseball teams met for all the marbles, St. Louisans can only cry, "We were robbed," or "We were the better team," as if upsets never happen in baseball. But diehard Cardinals fan Marty Prather acknowledges: "Whenever you get into a banter with a Royals fan, they hold the advantage—'We won the '85 series.' You have no comeback."

The World Series remains the one way Kansas Citians can stick it to St. Louisans after all the years St. Louisans have been sticking up their noses at Kansas City. As Kansas City journalist James J. Fisher once put it: "For Kansas Citians, the victory of the Royals over the Cardinals in the 1985 World Series was not a victory over a National League team or another Missouri team or just an exciting seven games. It was personal. It was rubbing St. Louis's nose in a substance usually found in barnyards."

And so rub it in they have, for years now. In the 2002 Missouri legislative session, during a marathon debate about funding for new sports stadiums, state senator Bill Kenney from suburban Kansas City stood up and offered an amendment that prohibited any money going to a new St. Louis stadium until Cardinals fans admitted "without reservation and in writing" that they lost the '85 series "fair and square." Kenney chuckled, then withdrew his motion.

Rubbing it in, though, has been all the more enjoyable for Kansas Citians because Cardinals partisans have never gotten over that World Series loss.

****

It started the night the Royals won. Hours before Game 7, Randy Freivogel's wife told him her water had broken. It was time to go to the hospital. So Freivogel, a St. Louis native living outside Kansas City, dutifully took his wife to the hospital. The nurses told his wife to walk, so as the game started, they made loops around the lobby, where a television was on. With each loop, Freivogel grew angrier and angrier at the Cardinals debacle. By the ninth inning, his wife was in labor. The couple knew they were having a boy and had agreed on the name Brett. But after sneaking out to see the last out, Freivogel burst in on his wife and announced, "It can't be Brett." The boy was named Ryan.

In the late 1980s, the *St. Louis Post-Dispatch* ran a tiny trivia question: Why was October 26 a significant date? The paper published the answer the next day: "Need we say more than 'Don Denkinger'?" Kansas Citian Max Brown happened to see the answer and wrote the paper, "It's just like you St. Louisans to still be crying about something that happened four years ago." This resulted in a barrage of insults from still-aggrieved Cardinals fans, like one who replied, "You'll never understand."

Around that same time, the family of teenager Tim Drone moved to Houston from St. Louis, where Drone had grown up with the Cardinals. Drone was enrolled in a private middle school. One of his new classmates became Jorge Orta Jr., son of the player who was safe on Denkinger's call. Drone and Orta played ball together, so Drone couldn't avoid him. But Drone told Orta that they could never become friends. "I could really never get over the fact that his father caused my team to lose," Drone recalled.

In the late 1990s, baseball instituted interleague play, and the Royals and Cardinals started playing annually. It was an opportunity for journalists to revisit the World Series. Had time healed all wounds for Cards fans? Not for Joe Fox, who informed *The Kansas City Star*: "We've never forgiven them." Not for Tim McNutt, whose fiancé told the *Post-Dispatch*: "He just can't handle it."

Even nowadays, Kansas Citian Chris Stathos returns home to her native St. Louis, goes with her family to their longtime Greek Orthodox church in the city, sees folks she grew up with, and while she's renewing old acquaintances, telling them she works for the Kansas City Royals, invariably someone will tell her, "You stole the '85 series."

Why? Why was the pain lasting so long? Why didn't Cardinals fans feel this way about 1968, when blunders on the base paths and in the field let victory slip away? Why didn't the fans feel this way about 1987, when a home-field advantage and bad umpiring in the final game contributed to a blown lead? Why?

Because, American cultural critic and Cardinals season ticket holder Gerald Early believed, St. Louisans took their cues from their team—losing to their cross-state little brother, throwing an ugly temper tantrum about it, then finding a villain on which to blame it all.

※ ※ ※ ※ ※ ※ ※

So it was, on the night after the Cardinals won the 2004 National League pennant, when their fans should have been preoccupied with the possibilities of the present and not on the pain of the past, Cardinals devotees got the opportunity to confront, face to face, after all these years, their 1985 villain.

He was dressed in black. But Don Denkinger, with a Whitey Herzog-like buzz cut and graying at the temples, looked considerably younger than his 68 years. He was making his first-ever appearance at a baseball memorabilia show. And he was making his first-ever public appearance in the St. Louis area. The show's organizers weren't too sure what to expect from the crowd, so they set him up at a table on the second floor, away from the rest of the show, away from onlookers, just in case. ... Denkinger wasn't too sure what to expect, either, but he figured $1,500 for a couple hours of grief couldn't be that awful.

The line waiting for him at a suburban union hall stretched down a long hallway. They came wearing assorted garb in red and bearing their scars—collectibles related to The Call. They all paid $20 or more for the chance to add his signature on items that will continue to be used to mock him. "I can't believe he has the nerve to come here," said the first person in line. That person was 12 years old, not even born when Denkinger made his mortal error.

The procession began. First up, the poster of The Call, the same one hanging in Denkinger's basement. After that, a 17 X 24 photograph of the play, Todd Worrell stretching with the ball in his glove, Orta's foot in mid-air about to land on first base, and Denkinger almost totally blocked by Orta. Next up, an 8x10 photo of the same shot, but one in which Worrell has already signed and added: "1985 World Series champs?"

"Can you write 'Safe' on it?" the photo's owner asked Denkinger.

One by one they came, some snickering politely and some barely controlling their contempt.

"Can I yell, 'You blew it?'" one man wearing a Cardinals sweatshirt whispered after passing through the line.

"You're a brave man," someone else told Denkinger.

Retired umpire—and villain to Cardinals fans—Don Denkinger came to St. Louis in the fall of 2004 for a baseball memorabilia show. Cards fans paid money and waited in long lines to get his autograph on photographs of his blown call in the 1985 World Series. *Courtesy of author*

An older gentleman approached and let it all hang out. "You're not too well thought of in St. Louis," he blared.

Denkinger kept his head down, not looking up, not responding too often, trying to lighten up the heavy air. Someone plopped a doctor's eye chart in front of him. "Oh, that's nice," Denkinger said. "You want me to sign by the 'D'?"

On and on they came, with Royals commemorative baseballs from '85, World Series ticket stubs, and a poster-sized blowup of the play whose flip side carried the message "Denkinger Lives."

"You should be in the witness protection program," a woman told Denkinger.

One man in a Cardinals t-shirt and cardinal red pants noticed the big diamond ring on Denkinger's right hand. "Hey," the man asked Denkinger, "did they give you a World Series ring, too?"

"Good thing the Cardinals won last night," someone else declared, "or (the people in line) would really be in a foul mood."

Toward the end, the show's promoter, Dave Jackson, stopped by one last time to check on the crowd. "I'm glad there wasn't any bloodshed out there," he said, only half joking.

As the Cardinals faithful gathered their novelties, snapped some pictures and turned to leave, some paused to explain their morbid fascination with Denkinger.

"That name will always be with me when I go to my grave," one man said.

"I'm very bitter still," another said.

And someone else in a Cardinals cap thought for a moment, then softly uttered a dreaded theory: "I'm afraid he's cursed us."

❈ ❈ ❈ ❈ ❈ ❈ ❈

Baseball is full of superstitions. Managers won't step on base lines. Players won't take off lucky undershirts. And teams seemingly, inexplicably, sometimes find themselves hexed.

Such was the case with the Boston Red Sox. They won five of the first 15 World Series. Then they sold their best player, Babe Ruth, to the Yankees. That launched the Yankee dynasty, and the Red Sox didn't win another World Series for decades. Baseball's literati called it "The Curse of the Bambino," in honor of Ruth's nickname. And so Johnny Pesky held the ball too long in one World Series. And the ball rolled through Bill Buckner's legs in another. Finally, the spell was broken in 2004. The Red Sox won the World Series—by sweeping the Cardinals.

So that curse is over. But maybe another curse lingers in its wake, one that's just germinating, one that hasn't dawned on the baseball populace yet.

The Curse of The Call.

The Cardinals haven't won a World Series since Don Denkinger's call. Their '87 team had the best record in the National League and were favorites in to win it all. Their 2001 team had the best record in the N.L. and lost in the first round of the playoffs. Their 2004 team had the best record in baseball by far, winning 105 games with one of the most potent and feared hitting lineups since Babe Ruth's Yankees. Still, no world titles.

The Cardinals' championship draught is now the longest since they first won one and fast approaching the franchise's worst stretch ever.

The Curse of The Call.

The Royals were the beneficiaries of Denkinger's call. Maybe it was a pact with the Devil. Through 1985, the Royals had made the post season in seven of the previous 10 years—but not once since 1985. That year marked the end of the team's run of success. Now, more time has passed since the Royals were in the World Series than the time it took the franchise to win the series.

The Curse of The Call.

It's still early in the life of a curse, just two decades so far. How long could this one last?

1985 WORLD SERIES STATISTICS

Royals Hitters

Player	G	AB	R	H	2B	3B	HR	RBI	BB	SO	AVG	OBP	SLG	SB
Steve Balboni	7	25	2	8	0	0	0	3	5	4	.320	.433	.320	0
Buddy Biancalana	7	18	2	5	0	0	0	2	5	4	.278	.435	.278	0
Bud Black	2	1	0	0	0	0	0	0	0	1	.000	.000	.000	0
George Brett	7	27	5	10	1	0	0	1	4	7	.370	.452	.407	1
Onix Concepcion	3	0	1	0	0	0	0	0	0	0	---	---	---	0
Dane Iorg	2	2	0	1	0	0	0	2	0	0	.500	.500	.500	0
Danny Jackson	2	6	0	0	0	0	0	0	0	5	.000	.000	.000	0
Lynn Jones	6	3	0	2	1	1	0	0	0	0	.667	.667	1.66	0
Charlie Leibrandt	2	4	0	0	0	0	0	0	0	2	.000	.000	.000	0
Hal McRae	3	1	0	0	0	0	0	0	1	0	.000	.667	.000	0
Darryl Motley	5	11	1	4	0	0	1	3	0	1	.364	.364	.636	0
Jorge Orta	3	3	0	1	0	0	0	0	0	0	.333	.333	.333	0
Greg Pryor	1	0	0	0	0	0	0	0	0	0	---	---	---	0
Bret Saberhagen	2	7	1	0	0	0	0	0	0	4	.000	.000	.000	0
Pat Sheridan	5	18	0	4	2	0	0	1	0	7	.222	.222	.333	0
Lonnie Smith	7	27	4	9	3	0	0	4	3	8	.333	.400	.444	2
Jim Sundberg	7	24	6	6	2	0	0	1	6	4	.250	.400	.333	0
John Wathan	2	1	0	0	0	0	0	0	0	1	.000	.000	.000	0
Frank White	7	28	4	7	3	0	1	6	3	4	.250	.323	.464	1
Willie Wilson	7	30	2	11	0	1	0	3	1	4	.367	.387	.433	3
Total	7	236	28	68	12	2	2	26	28	56	.288	.366	.381	7

Royals Pitchers

Player	G	ERA	W-L	SV	CG	IP	H	ER	BB	SO
Bret Saberhagen	2	0.50	2-0	0	2	18.0	11	1	1	10
Charlie Leibrandt	2	2.76	0-1	0	0	16.3	10	5	4	10
Danny Jackson	2	1.69	1-1	0	1	16.0	9	3	5	12
Bud Black	2	5.06	0-1	0	0	5.3	4	3	5	4
Dan Quisenberry	4	2.08	1-0	0	0	4.3	5	1	3	3
Joe Beckwith	1	0.00	0-0	0	0	2.0	1	0	0	3
Total		1.89	4-3	0	3	62.0	40	13	18	42

Cardinals Hitters

Player	G	AB	R	H	2B	3B	HR	RBI	BB	SO	AVG	OBP	SLG	SB
Joaquin Andujar	2	1	0	0	0	0	0	0	0	1	.000	.000	.000	0
Steve Braun	1	1	0	0	0	0	0	0	0	0	.000	.000	.000	0
Cesar Cedeno	5	15	1	2	1	0	0	1	2	2	.133	.235	.200	0
Jack Clark	7	25	1	6	2	0	0	4	3	9	.240	.321	.320	0
Danny Cox	2	4	0	0	0	0	0	0	0	2	.000	.000	.000	0
Ivan DeJesus	1	1	0	0	0	0	0	0	0	0	.000	.000	.000	0
Brian Harper	4	4	0	1	0	0	0	1	0	1	.250	.250	.250	0
Tom Herr	7	26	2	4	2	0	0	0	2	2	.154	.214	.231	0
Ricky Horton	3	1	0	0	0	0	0	0	0	1	.000	.000	.000	0
Mike Jorgensen	2	3	0	0	0	0	0	0	0	0	.000	.000	.000	0
Tito Landrum	7	25	3	9	2	0	1	1	0	2	.360	.360	.560	0
Tom Lawless	1	0	0	0	0	0	0	0	0	0	---	---	---	0
Willie McGee	7	27	2	7	2	0	1	2	1	3	.259	.286	.444	1
Tom Nieto	2	5	0	0	0	0	0	1	1	2	.000	.167	.000	0
Terry Pendleton	7	23	3	6	1	1	0	3	3	2	.261	.346	.391	0
Darrell Porter	5	15	0	2	0	0	0	0	2	5	.133	.235	.133	0
Ozzie Smith	7	23	1	2	0	0	0	0	4	0	.087	.222	.087	1
John Tudor	3	5	0	0	0	0	0	0	0	4	.000	.000	.000	0
Andy Van Slyke	6	11	0	1	0	0	0	0	0	5	.091	.091	.091	0
Todd Worrell	3	1	0	0	0	0	0	0	0	1	.000	.000	.000	0
Total	7	216	13	40	10	1	2	13	18	42	.185	.248	.269	2

Cardinals Pitchers

Player	G	ERA	W-L	SV	CG	IP	H	ER	BB	SO
John Tudor	3	3.00	2-1	0	1	18.0	15	6	7	14
Danny Cox	2	1.29	0-0	0	0	14.0	14	2	4	13
Ken Dayley	4	0.00	1-0	0	0	6.0	1	0	3	5
Todd Worrell	3	3.86	0-1	1	0	4.7	4	2	2	6
Bill Campbell	3	2.25	0-0	0	0	4.0	4	1	2	5
Ricky Horton	3	6.75	0-0	0	0	4.0	4	3	5	5
Joaquin Andujar	2	9.82	0-1	0	0	3.7	10	4	4	3
Jeff Lahti	3	12.27	0-0	1	0	3.7	10	5	0	2
Bob Forsch	2	12.00	0-1	0	0	3.0	6	4	1	3
Total		3.98	3-4	2	1	61.0	68	27	28	56

BIBLIOGRAPHY

Newspapers: *The Kansas City Star, The Kansas City Times, The New York Times, The Washington Post,* St. *Louis Post-Dispatch, Chicago Tribune, The Los Angeles Times, The Daily News of Los Angeles, Boston Globe, New York Post, Miami Herald, USA Today, Newsday, Asbury Park Press, The Macon Telegraph.*

Periodicals: *Sports Illustrated, The Sporting News, Time, The New Yorker, Village Voice,* ESPN's *Page 2,* the Society for American Baseball Research's *The National Pastime* and *By the Numbers.*

Books:

Adair, Robert K. *The Physics of Baseball.* New York: Harper Perennial, 1990.

Adelman, Tom. *The Long Ball: The Summer of '75 – Spaceman, Catfish, Charlie Hustle, and the Greatest World Series Ever Played.* Boston: Little Brown and Co., 2003.

Albert, Jim, and Jay Bennett. *Curve Ball: Baseball, Statistics and the Role of Chance in the Game.* New York: Copernicus Books, 2001.

Anderson, Sparky, and Dan Ewald. *Bless You Boys: Diary of the Detroit Tigers' 1984 Season.* Chicago: Contemporary Books Inc., 1984.

Armour, Mark L., and Daniel R Levitt. *Paths to Glory: How Great Baseball Teams Got That Way.* Washington D.C.: Brassey's Inc., 2003.

Birnbaum, Phil, ed. *The Best of By the Numbers: A Collection of Thought-Provoking Essays on Baseball by SABR's Statistical Analysis Committee.* Cleveland: The Society for American Baseball Research, 2003.

Boswell, Thomas. *How Life Imitates the World Series.* Garden City, N.Y.: Doubleday & Co., Inc., 1982.

Brett, George, with Steve Cameron. *George Brett: From Here to Cooperstown.* Lenexa, Kan.: Addax Publishing Group, Inc., 1999.

Buck, Jack, with Rob Rains and Bob Broeg. *Jack Buck: "That's a Winner."* Champaign, Ill.: Sagamore Publishing, 1997.

Cameron, Steve. *George Brett: Last of a Breed.* Dallas: Taylor Publishing Co., 1993.

Cantor, George. *The Tigers of '68: Baseball's Last Real Champions.* Dallas: Taylor Publishing Co., 1997.

Castle, George, and Jim Rygelski. *The I-55 Series: Cubs vs. Cardinals.* Champaign, Ill.: Sports Publishing, Inc., 1999.

Colbert, David, ed. *Baseball: The National Pastime in Art and Literature.* New York: TimeLife Books, 2001.

Engers, Eric. *100 Years of the World Series, 1903-2003.* New York: Barnes & Noble Books, 2004.

Feldmann, Doug. *Fleeter Then Birds: The 1985 St. Louis Cardinals and Small Ball's Last Hurrah.* Jefferson, N.Car.: McFarland & Company, Inc., 2002.

Fiffer, Steve. *How to Watch Baseball: A Fan's Guide to Savoring the Fine Points of the Game.* New York: Facts on File Publications, 1987.

Fitzpatrick, Frank. *You Can't Lose 'Em All: The Year the Phillies Finally Won the World Series.* Dallas, Tex.: Taylor Trade Publishing, 2001.

Forsch, Bob, with Tom Wheatley. *Bob Forsch's Tales from the Cardinals Dugout.* Champaign, Ill.: Sports Publishing L.L.C., 2003.

Garrity, John. *The George Brett Story.* New York: Coward, McCann & Geoghegan, 1981.

Gmelch, George, and J.J. Weiner. *In the Ballpark: The Working Lives of Baseball People.* Washington D.C.: Smithsonian Institution Press, 1998.

Gmelch, George. *Inside Pitch: Life in Professional Baseball.* Washington D.C.: Smithsonian Institution Press, 2001.

Golenbock, Peter. *The Spirit of St. Louis: A History of the St. Louis Cardinals and Browns.* New York: Avon Books, Inc., 2000.

Gutman, Dan. *The Way Baseball Works.* New York: Simon & Schuster, 1996.

Halberstam, David. *Summer of '49.* New York: William Morrow and Co., Inc., 1989.

Halberstam, David. *October 1964.* New York: Villard Books, 1994.

Halberstam, David. *The Teammates: A Portrait of a Friendship.* New York: Hyperion, 2003.

Hart, Stan. *Scouting Reports: The Original Reviews of Some of Baseball's Greatest Stars.* New York: Macmillan Publishing Co., 1995.

Helyar, John. *Lords of the Realm: The Real History of Baseball.* New York: Villard Books, 1994.

Hernandez, Keith, and Mike Bryan. *Pure Baseball: Pitch By Pitch for the Advanced Fan.* New York: HarperCollins Publishers Inc., 1994.

Herzog, Whitey, and Kevin Horrigan. *White Rat: A Life in Baseball.* New York: Harper & Row, 1987.

Herzog, Whitey, and Jonathan Pitts. *You're Missin' A Great Game.* New York: Simon & Schuster, 1999.

Honig, Donald. *The October Heroes: Great World Series Games Remembered By the Men Who Played Them.* Lincoln, Neb.: University of Nebraska Press, 1979.

James, Bill. *The Bill James Baseball Abstract.* Self-published, 1979-1981, and New York: Ballentine Books, 1982-1988.

James, Bill. *This Time Let's Not Eat the Bones: Bill James Without the Numbers.* New York: Villard Books, 1989.

James, Bill. *The Baseball Book.* New York: Villard Books, 1992.

James, Bill. *The Bill James Guide to Baseball Managers, from 1870 to Today.* New York: Scribner, 1997.

James, Bill. *The New Bill James Historical Baseball Abstract.* New York: The Free Press, 2001.

Kahn, Roger. *The Boys of Summer.* New York: Harper & Row, 1972.

Kahn, Roger. *The Head Game: Baseball Seen From the Pitcher's Mound.* New York: Harcourt, Inc., 2000.

Kerrane, Kevin. *Dollar Signs on the Muscle: The World of Baseball Scouting.* New York: Beaufort Books, 1984.

Launius, Roger D. *Seasons in the Sun: The Story of Big League Baseball in Missouri.* Columbia, Mo.: University of Missouri Press, 2002.

Leavy, Jane. Sandy Koufax: *A Lefty's Legacy.* New York: HarperCollins, 2002.

Levenson, Barry. *The Seventh Game: The 35 World Series That Have Gone the Distance.* New York: McGraw-Hill, 2004.

Leventhal, Josh. *The World Series: An Illustrated Encyclopedia of the Fall Classic.* New York: Black Dog & Leventhal Publishers, Inc., 2001.

Lewis, Michael. *Moneyball: The Art of Winning an Unfair Game.* New York: W.W. Norton & Co., 2003.

Matthews, Denny, and Fred White, with Matt Fulks. *Play By Play: 25 Years of Royals on Radio.* Lenexa, Kan.: Addax Publishing Group Inc., 1999.

Montgomery, Rick, and Shirl Kasper. *Kansas City: An American Story.* Kansas City, Mo.: Kansas City Star Books, 1999.

Morgan, Anne. *Prescription for Success: The Life and Values of Ewing Marion Kauffman.* Kansas City, Mo.: Andrews and McMeel, 1995.

Nagel, Paul C. *Missouri: A History.* New York: W.W. Norton & Co., Inc., 1977.

Okrent, Daniel. *Nine Innings: The Anatomy of Baseball as Seen Through the Playing of a Single Game.* New York: McGraw-Hill Book Co., 1985.

Primm, James Neal. *Lion of the Valley: St. Louis, Missouri, 1764-1980.* St. Louis: Missouri Historical Society Press, 1998.

Rains, Rob, and Alvin Reid. *Whitey's Boys: A Celebration of the '82 Cards World Championship.* Chicago: Triumph Books, 2002.

Rossi, John P. *The National Game: Baseball and American Culture.* Chicago: Ivan R. Dee, 2000.

Schneider, Russell. *The Boys of the Summer of '48.* Champaign, Ill.: Sports Publishing Inc., 1998.

Schwarz, Alan. *The Numbers Game: Baseball's Lifelong Fascination with Statistics.* New York: St. Martin's Press, 2004.

Skipper, John C. Umpires: *Classic Baseball Stories from the Men Who Made the Calls.* Jefferson, N.Car.: McFarland & Company, Inc., 1997.

Smith, Ozzie, with Rob Rains. *Wizard.* Chicago: Contemporary Books Inc., 1988.

Snyder, John. *The World Series' Most Wanted: The Top 10 Book of Championship Teams, Broken Dreams and October Oddities.* Dulles, Virg.: Brassey's Inc., 2004.

Sowell, Mike. *One Pitch Away: The Players' Stories of the 1986 League Championships and World Series.* New York: Macmillan, 1995.

Staten, Vince. *Why Is the Foul Pole Fair – Or Answers to the Baseball Questions Your Dad Hoped You Wouldn't Ask.* New York: Simon & Schuster, 2003.

The Sporting News. *Official Baseball Guide, 1986.* St. Louis: The Sporting News Publishing Co., 1986.

Thomas, G. Scott. *Leveling the Field: An Encyclopedia of Baseball's All-Time Great Performances as Revealed Through Adjusted Statistics.* New York: Black Dog & Leventhal Publishers, Inc., 2002.

Twyman, Gib. *Born to Hit: The George Brett Story.* New York: Random House, 1982.

Tygiel, Jules. *Past Time: Baseball as History.* New York: Oxford University Press, 2000.

Vanderberg, Bob. *'59: Summer of the Sox.* Champaign, Ill.: Sports Publishing Inc., 1999.

Will, George F. *Men at Work: The Craft of Baseball.* New York: Macmillan Publishing Co., 1990.

Winegardner, Mark. *Prophet of the Sandlots: Journeys With a Major League Scout.* New York: The Atlantic Monthly Press, 1990.

Wood, Bob. *Dodger Dogs to Fenway Franks: The Ultimate Guide to America's Top Baseball Parks.* New York: McGraw-Hill Book Co., 1988.

Wright, Tina, ed. *Cardinal Memories: Recollections from Baseball's Greatest Fans.* Columbia, Mo.: University of Missouri Press, 2000.

Zaret, Eli. *'84: The Last of the Great Tigers.* South Boardman, Mich.: Crofton Creek Press, 2004.

INDEX